D1546316

THE
ILLUSTRATION
HANDBOOK

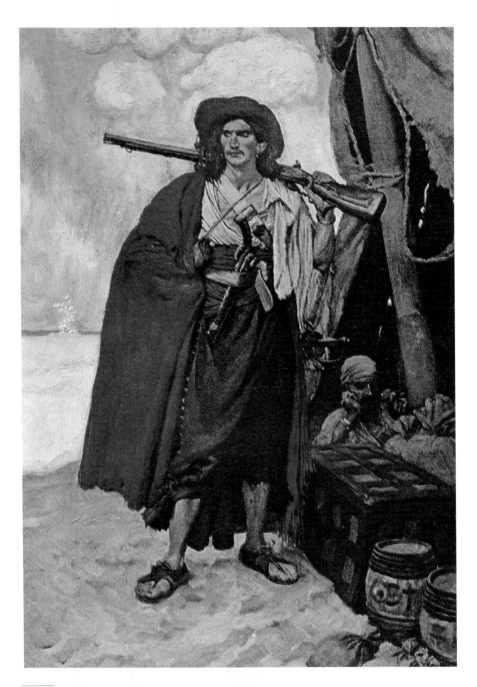

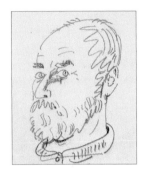

FOREWORD

ILLUSTRATION HAS LONG SUFFERED at the hands of even the most well-informed art critic. "Mere illustration"—the most common derogatory remark leveled at paintings that have sought to express or convey an idea—says it all. The cliché is both absurd and meaningless, especially today, when many artists refuse to recognize the artificial barrier between commercial and fine art. Moreover, it does not necessarily follow that an artist working to a brief is little more than a hack. Granted, some are, but the professional illustrator is the modern counterpart of the Renaissance painter, an artist who will frequently transcend the most mundane of briefs to provide the mass audience with art.

The Illustration Handbook is a hugely diverse gallery of graphic art created by the world's leading illustrators and proves my case beyond doubt. Here are assembled artists of the book and the magazine, designers of posters, reporters and satirists of the social scene, travelers, and painter-illustrators. Here too are popular artists as well as more significant artists, minor figures as well as great ones—in short, the whole spectrum of image-making that comprises the art of illustration. We are first introduced to the illustrators of the 19th century, artists active between 1850 and 1900. Their work appeared in books and magazines aimed at a buoyantly literate middle-class public to whom reading had become as much a habit as watching television is to us today. For almost an entire century these artists were at the mercy of the engraver. Until the late 1870s, Victorian printing technology was compelled to rely on wood-engraving as the sole means of reproducing an artist's design. It was a laborious process which usually obliterated the spontaneity of an original, although occasionally it could produce surprises. Only if the artist was familiar with the practice of drawing *directly* onto the woodblock with brush or pen and black ink could idiosyncrasies of style survive. Adolf Von Menzel in Germany, Charles Keene and Arthur Boyd Houghton in Britain were foremost among those who learnt from Hokusai and other masters of the *Ukiyo-e*. Guided by enlightened master engravers like the Brothers Dalziel, Joseph Swain, and William Luson Thomas, they succeeded in overcoming the daunting limitations of the medium.

As the 19th century drew to an end, photomechanical technology came to the rescue, making possible a breakthrough both in color printing and in reproduction of black-and-white originals. This was the decade of Aubrey Beardsley and Phil May, of Charles Dana Gibson and Howard Pyle, of EJ Sullivan and Paul Renouard. At this time also, the painter's contribution to illustration grew rapidly, now that it had become possible to reproduce drawings with great fidelity. One of the pleasures of looking through Parisian weeklies of the era, such as *L'Assiette au Beurre* and *Le Rire,* is in discovering editorial drawings by Juan Gris, Eugène Higgins, Frantisek Kupka, Lautrec, Jacques Villon, and Kees Van Dongen, not forgetting the dramatic input of Kathe Kollwitz, Alfred Kubin, and Jules Pascin in the pages of the Munich weekly *Simplicissimus.*

Good illustration, of course, knows no frontiers. If at one period the ball is not to be found in the court of the British or the Americans, it will be found in the court of the French or the Germans. One thinks of the revival of lithography, which led to the golden era of the poster in *belle époque* France. One thinks also of the Berlin of the 1920s and of the extraordinary satirical journalism in which a brilliant generation of editors, poets, and essayists made common cause with artists like George Grosz, Otto Dix, and John Heartfield to castigate what they felt to be an unjust system.

Indeed, the ball goes back and forth constantly. One is also reminded of American illustration of this time: the advent of superb story illustration in the *Saturday Evening Post* and *Collier's,* a reportorial tradition which lasted through World War II and into the 1960s in *Fortune, Sports Illustrated,* and *Rolling Stone.* In fact, American illustration flourishes right up to the present day in a host of new periodicals which also publish a younger generation of European illustrators, thus ensuring the cross-fertilization that is such a vital part of illustration.

William Morris maintained that illustration, though not vital to people's existence, nonetheless gave a great deal of aesthetic pleasure and was therefore a subject worthy of attention and encouragement. *The Illustration Handbook* confirms this to be true in no uncertain terms.

Paul Hogarth

INTRODUCTION

BEFORE ASSESSING THE ROLE of the illustrator within society, it is perhaps appropriate to consider first his or her position in the world of art.

For many years the notion has prevailed that, in the company of fine artists, the illustrator is something of a second-class citizen. This discrimination is predicated on the belief that the painter or sculptor is an unfettered spirit whose work gives free rein to self-expression and whose art makes statements of an intensely personal nature. Illustrators, on the other hand, are the slaves of commerce—they are invariably commissioned to produce their work, and their inspiration derives not from personal experience but from the source material with which they are provided.

Under scrutiny, this delineation quickly blurs. Some of the world's greatest art treasures were in fact commissioned, whether by the Church, the State, or by private individuals. For example, Michelangelo's paintings in the Sistine Chapel, while infused with an intensely personal vision, were nonetheless inspired by the writings of that all-time best-seller, the Bible.

The fact is that all artists, whether painters, sculptors, or illustrators, face very much the same predicament: They all work within constraints from which only the power of their imagination can free them. With the skills and materials available to them, they endeavor to create a unique interpretation of an idea, event, or observation, and it is this shared aim that validates the role of illustrator within the world of the arts.

Historically, there have been differing schools of thought on the role of illustration. At one extreme we have Eric Gill, who believed that illustration should "really illustrate, clarify and illuminate the text" and not be used for "outpourings of sensibility." At the other extreme, we find the German Expressionist illustrators, such as Lovis Corinth, whose drawings were seldom literal and who often subordinated the illustration of the text to the expression of the artist's state of mind. And quite outside this spectrum there was the Edwardian passion for gift books, which merely served as vehicles for the artists' explorations of their illustrative, imaginative, and decorative skills. However, irrespective of the style adopted and the subject matter chosen, the illustrator performs simultaneously, and sometimes unwittingly, in a secondary role—that of social historian.

Our view of history would be somewhat myopic were it not illuminated by such a wealth of illustrations for both fictional and documentary material. In Britain, artists such as John Everett Millais and Fred Walker meticulously recorded the details of Victorian life in illustrations for contemporary novels by Trollope and Thackeray. Less inadvertent were the commentaries on the state of the nation by Frank Holl and

Luke Fildes, who set out to expose the poverty of urban life, or the scathing satires of monarchy, society, and politics by Gillray, Rowlandson, and Cruickshank. Even the 1890s' passion for nostalgic and idealized depictions of country life informs us of a yearning for a pre-industrial world. In fact there is very little in the way of human behavior and feeling that has escaped the conscious investigation or unconscious recording of the illustrator.

Another role, now mostly usurped by the camera, is that of the illustrator as journalist. With the development of the newspaper in the middle of the 18th century, there was an increasing demand for the pictorial coverage of topical events. In 1854 William Simpson was sent on assignment to the Crimea, and his drawings of the war mark the arrival of the "Special Artist," now more simply known as War Artist. The conditions and dangers of battle, combined with the urgency of the public's demand for the very latest information, meant that artists rarely had time to do more than sketch the situation, dispatch the drawing, and rely on the finishing artists at home to add the details. Yet, despite the aesthetic compromises that such disconnected teamwork entailed, the artist could still capture the spirit of the occasion.

Today, in matters of reportage, the camera reigns supreme over illustration for a public which prefers to construct its own interpretation of events seen, with apparent objectivity, through the eye of a lens. However, the tradition of the artist as reporter continues, and in many countries the courtroom remains an arena of human interest to which only the illustrator, and not the photographer, has access.

Of course, the involvement of the artist in current affairs is not limited to crime and war. A sphere of activity which remains as strong today as it ever did is caricature. While politicians and royalty may shield their eyes from the flash guns of the paparazzi, there is no escaping this cruelly exaggerated, yet precise, form of cartoon drawing. The word caricature is derived from the Italian *caricare*, which means "to overload," and it was in Italy during the mid- to late 1500s that the artist Annibale Carracci discovered that if he deliberately overemphasized the characteristics of his friends, he could "grasp the perfect deformity and thus reveal the very essence of a personality." During the 18th century this art form became popular with dilettantes and amateurs who had embarked upon the Grand Tour. But by the 1900s, when there was a fascination with the belief that physiognomy revealed a near-scientific insight into personality, caricature had fallen into the hands of serious political artists, who used it to pass judgment on topical events and to lampoon the conceits of public figures.

There are few newspapers now in circulation that do not employ the talents of a caricaturist or political cartoonist. Depending on the editorial stance of the publication, these skills may be used simply to amuse the reader or to seriously ridicule and possibly damage the credibility of the individuals depicted. It is this latter faculty that leads us to consider yet another role of the illustrator – that of propagandist.

Part of the psychosis of war involves the dehumanization of the opposing forces, and to this end the art of the caricaturist can be used to supreme jingoistic effect. Since the development of newspapers and posters, there has not been a war effort or revolution that has not recruited ranks of illustrators to portray the enemy or oppressor as a gargoyle of iniquity. Some of the finest examples are to be found in the works of David Moor and Viktor Deni from the time of the Russian Revolution. Their vilification of the bourgeoisie as bloated, pig-like creatures could not have failed to focus the rage of the proletariat by reducing complex issues to simple, powerful symbols.

Although most extreme in times of conflict, the manipulative power of the illustrator has its place in peacetime, where it is used to great effect in the world of commerce and advertising. The same talents and techniques that can so successfully defame can be just as effective in the process of idealization.

Advertising agencies did not start to appear in any great number until the 1920s, but the business itself dates back to the middle of the 19th century when, for the most part, it was in the hands of the manufacturers. For the first 50 years, in the absence of photography, the principal role of the artist was simply to draw an image of the product. But as competition increased, it became necessary to create perceived differentials in virtually identical products so as to legitimize superiority claims. This sleight of hand was accomplished by the illustrator, who created an image world into which the client's product could be placed in the most flattering light. A particularly good example is the sale in the late 1890s of Millais' painting *Bubbles* to the manufacturers of Pears' Soap. In its original form this sentimental depiction of a child blowing bubbles with soapsuds would have evoked gentle feelings of innocence, the freshness of youth, beauty, protectiveness, and warmth. With the addition of the Pears' logo at the top of the image, and a bar of Pears' soap near the feet of the child, many of these emotions would have been grafted onto the product, which could then be presented to the public as a safe, pure, and wholesome way of cleansing the skin. Millais himself is said to have been outraged, but the campaign was enormously successful, and over 100 years later it is possible to trace the imagery of Pears' advertising back to Millais' work.

As well as creating a suitable emotional and aesthetic context for a product, illustration also developed many of advertising's most effective selling tools—visual hyperboles for the exaggeration of quality, the animation of company logos for branding, the exploitation of the female form, and, perhaps most important, the use of humor. The public may get tired of advertising but it never gets tired of laughing. And humour, exemplified by John Gilroy's cartoon advertisements for Guinness in the 1930s and 1940s, can engage the attention and sympathy of even the most disaffected audience.

That humor should reach advertising via the illustrator is hardly surprising, since the role of entertainer is traditional to the artist. The cartoon strip, first developed by the German artist Wilhelm Busch in the mid-19th century, is now a feature of daily life—and since the early 1840s, there has been a proliferation of magazines whose primary concern is to amuse.

Humor, however, plays little part in the last role that we should consider here, that of illustrator as teacher. This category needs to be broad enough to include the topographical work of such artists as Arthur Boyd Houghton, who visited the United States in 1870 and whose drawings helped to satisfy the craving for travel literature at that time. But it must also embrace the meticulous work of those technical illustrators who make the worlds of science, technology, and nature comprehensible to us. Their skills face increasing competition from photography, which, along with complex computer graphics and digital technology, can now offer an illustrator's control over images that originated inside a camera. For some, that challenge will once again raise the illustrator-as-artist debate with the contention that the technical illustrator is no more than a copyist whose interpretive skills are put to little use. Be that as it may, the acknowledgment of those skills is important here, as without them we would have an incomplete picture of the multifarious roles that illustration plays in our world.

In putting together this book we have tried to cover the major twists and turns in illustration's developmental path since the middle of the 19th century. We have found that for much of this journey, illustrators have paid little heed to the direction of fine art and that their progress cannot be described by a series of "isms" and schools of thought. However, many figures, such as Morris, Abbey, Pyle, and Gill have exerted a lasting influence on the course that illustration is taking, and we have tried to ensure that they are well represented. Inevitably, owing to the limitations of space and the scarcity of good material for reproduction, there are omissions, and you may find that a favorite artist has not been included. For this we apologize, while hoping that, as a source book of styles, you will still find this volume to be comprehensive and inspiring. Our lasting impression as we come to the end of compiling these images is that at every point in its history, illustration has been on the threshold of an exciting new development—and never more so than today. Technology and imagination, it would seem, know no bounds; and when one considers that illustrators can now generate original artwork on a Macintosh computer, one can only wonder as to what the future may bring.

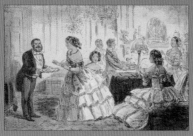

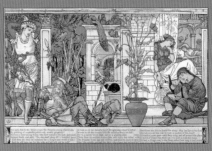

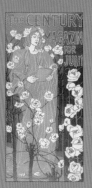

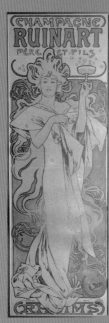

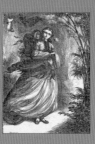

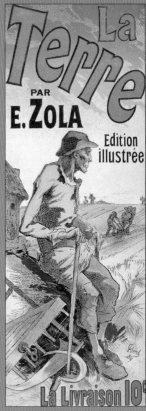

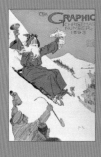

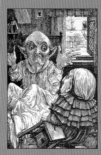

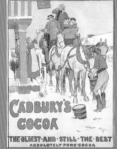

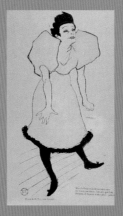

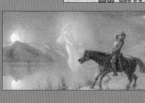

CHAPTER ONE
1850–1899

BY 1850 THE STAGE WAS SET for the dramatic entrance of the illustrator as the entertainer of the 19th century. In reaction to the bleakness of the Napoleonic war period, the previous years had seen a craving for culture spread across Europe. Literacy was increasing, and with the Victorian invention of the armchair and sofa, the first truly comfortable items of furniture, a new concept in urban recreation evolved: family get-togethers with reading material of one form or another providing the amusement. At the same time the Industrial Revolution also provided the technology for mass marketing; with the arrival of metal printing plates and chromolithography, publishers were in a position to satisfy the public's thirst for entertainment and knowledge. Their industry was transformed beyond recognition.

In mid-century France the relaxing of censorship laws, coupled with the artistic freedom afforded by the autographic litho process, encouraged a flourishing tradition of caricature. Surprisingly, in Britain it had the opposite effect: Caricaturists who had achieved prominence in such magazines as *Punch* found that the litho stone softened their work, which then lacked the spiteful line more easily achieved on copper plate.

During these years London artistic life exerted a huge influence throughout the world of illustrators. The political upheavals on the Continent had led many disaffected artists to Britain, and their influence was in part responsible for the development of social realism between 1850 and 1890. The illustrations of the lives of the poor by artists such as Luke Fildes and Frank Holl were then exported to the world at large through the distribution of such magazines as *The Graphic* and *The Illustrated London News,* which were eagerly read by artists in America and on the Continent.

As this frenzy of illustrative activity continued, various schools of thought began to emerge from the community of artists and critics. In 1848 John Everett Millais, William Holman Hunt, and Dante Gabriel Rossetti formed the Pre-Raphaelite Brotherhood in an attempt to recreate the naivety and moral realism of early Renaissance painting. With their strong literary leanings, they are credited by many with giving illustration the status of art and encouraging the practice of putting artists' names on the covers of books.

The 1860s are sometimes described as the "golden age of Victorian illustration." There was a fashion for drawings of contemporary life in the novels of Dickens, Thackeray, and Trollope, newsagents and bookstalls were appearing in every street and at every railroad station, libraries were making their first appearance, and taxes had been repealed on newspapers, making them more affordable. During this period specialist magazines were developed, and in 1860 *The Queen,* the first magazine aimed directly at women, appeared. It was such a success that other publishers soon followed suit. Magazines were enjoying similar popularity on the other side of the Atlantic, where, with the development of half-tone reproduction, the American public was eagerly reading *Harper's, Century,* and *McClure's* and enjoying the work of Charles Marion Russell and Howard Pyle.

After a brief period of decline in the 1870s, the 1880s saw a resurgence of interest and activity in book production. This was due in part to the influence of William Morris, the leading figure in the Arts and Crafts Movement as well as the private press movement, which had an impact on both European and American publishing. Morris founded the Kelmscott Press in 1891 and, with his principal illustrator Edward Burne-Jones, revived the tradition of medieval craftsmanship and the art of the woodcut. He helped to create what he referred to as the age of the "Book Beautiful."

The intensely art-conscious 1890s saw the emergence of the Aesthetic Movement, which followed the ethos of "art for art's sake" and which Morris despised. Its style of *fin de siècle* morbidity and eroticism was best captured by Aubrey Beardsley, whose drawings were particularly suited to the process reproduction of the day. The Aesthetes were championed by Oscar Wilde; although his eventual disgrace brought the movement into disrepute, the contribution of such exponents as Walter Crane, Randolph Caldecott, and Kate Greenaway was critical to the subsequent development of fantasy illustration.

But the new processes did not just revolutionize book production. In the hands of Jules Cheret (who pioneered many of the developments in chromolithographic poster printing), Toulouse-Lautrec, and Alphonse Mucha, they led to another golden age, that of the poster. This medium, which was to become so important to the advertising industry in the next century, became one of the most popular art forms, with members of the public literally tearing posters from the hoardings and taking them home.

*Born in Philadelphia, USA.
Worked in a wood engraving
studio and studied art
at evening classes at the
Pennsylvania Academy of Fine
Arts. In 1871 he moved to New
York, where the influence of
French and German black and
white art was transforming pen
drawing. He produced small
black-and-white illustrations
for Harpers and Brothers, then
illustrated some of their more
successful books, including*
Christmas Stories *by Charles
Dickens (1875),* Selections from
the Poetry of Robert Herrick
(1882), and Oliver Goldsmith's
She Stoops to Conquer *(1887).
In 1878 he settled in England
and became a prolific illustrator,
specializing in costume and
figure subjects. In contrast to
the decorative convention of the
period, his meticulous attention
to detail—which extended to
him making every effort to
achieve historical accuracy—
achieved a realism that
influenced a whole generation
of younger artists. He exhibited
his first oil painting at the Royal
Academy in 1890, and was
elected Royal Academician
in 1902.*

1, 2 *BOOK:* SHE STOOPS TO
CONQUER *by Oliver Goldsmith
DATE: c. 1887*

3, 4 *BOOK:* SCHOOL FOR
SCANDAL *by Richard Sheridan
DATE: 1885*

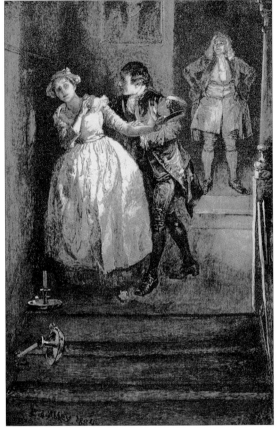

1

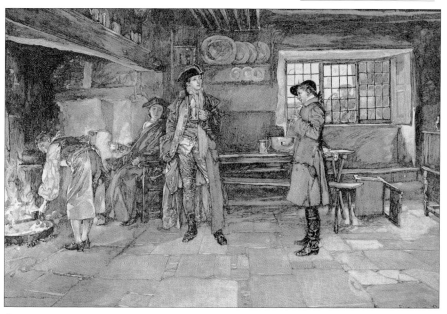

2

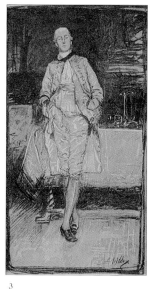

3

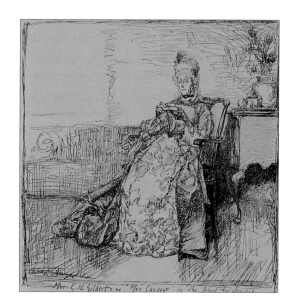

4

CHARLES HENRY BENNETT
(1829–1867)

Apparently untrained, he contributed to The Comic Times *and* Comic News *between 1855 and 1865, when he joined* Punch *magazine. He illustrated several books, including Bunyan's* Pilgrim's Progress *(1859),* Nine Lives of a Cat *(1860),* Stories Little Breeches Told *(1862), and* The Fables of Aesop *(1857). He also illustrated for a number of magazines, including* The Illustrated Times, The Cornhill Magazine, Every Boy's Magazine, *and* Punch.

1–3 *BOOK:* THE FABLES OF AESOP
DATE: 1857

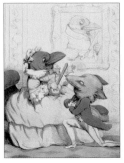

1

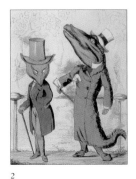

2

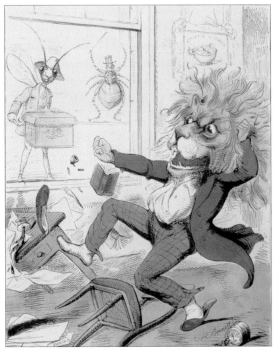

3

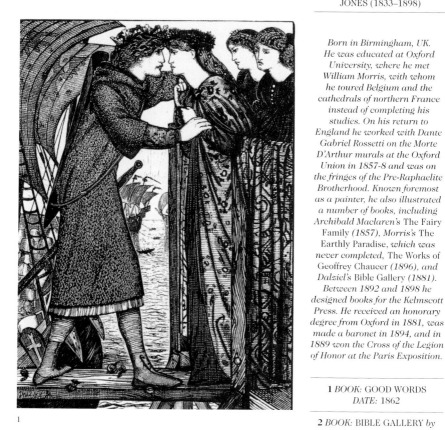

*Born in Birmingham, UK.
He was educated at Oxford
University, where he met
William Morris, with whom
he toured Belgium and the
cathedrals of northern France
instead of completing his
studies. On his return to
England he worked with Dante
Gabriel Rossetti on the Morte
D'Arthur murals at the Oxford
Union in 1857-8 and was on
the fringes of the Pre-Raphaelite
Brotherhood. Known foremost
as a painter, he also illustrated
a number of books, including
Archibald Maclaren's* The Fairy
Family *(1857), Morris's* The
Earthly Paradise, *which was
never completed,* The Works of
Geoffrey Chaucer *(1896), and
Dalziel's* Bible Gallery *(1881).
Between 1892 and 1898 he
designed books for the Kelmscott
Press. He received an honorary
degree from Oxford in 1881, was
made a baronet in 1894, and in
1889 won the Cross of the Legion
of Honor at the Paris Exposition.*

1 *BOOK:* GOOD WORDS
DATE: 1862

2 *BOOK:* BIBLE GALLERY *by
Dalziel*
DATE: 1881

3 *PAINTING:* THE DEPTHS OF
THE SEA
DATE: 1886

1

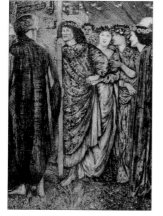

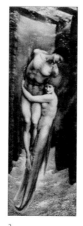

2   3

WALTER CRANE
(1845–1915)

Born in Liverpool, UK. His illustrating career began in 1863, when he was commissioned by Edmund Evans to illustrate three toy books for Warne publishers. Other books he illustrated include The House That Jack Built *(1865),* The Baby's Opera *(1877),* The Baby's Bouquet *(1878), Edmund Spenser's* The Faerie Queene *(published in 19 parts, 1894-97),* Ali Baba and the Forty Thieves *(1873), and* The Happy Prince and Other Stories *by Oscar Wilde (1888). Crane was also a painter, writer, and designer of textiles, wallpapers, and ceramics. His work was characterized by strong outlines, flat tints, and solid blacks, and was influenced by his study of early printed books, medieval illuminations, Japanese prints, and the work of the Pre-Raphaelites. He was converted to "conscious" socialism by William Morris and became a primary figure in the Arts and Crafts movement. In 1883 he joined the Socialist League and in 1884 was the first president of the Art Workers' Guild. He taught design at Manchester School of Art, was Art Director at Reading College, and was Principal of the Royal College of Art, 1898–99.*

1, 4 *BOOK:* THE BLUEBEARD
PICTURE BOOK
DATE: 1899

2 *BOOK:* ARTHURIAN LEGENDS
DATE: NOT KNOWN

3 *BOOK:* A FLOWER WEDDING
DATE: NOT KNOWN

5 *BOOK:* A ROMANCE OF THE
THREE Rs
DATE: 1886

6 *BOOK:* THE BABY'S BOUQUET
DATE: 1878

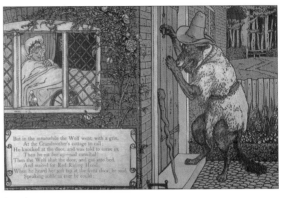

1

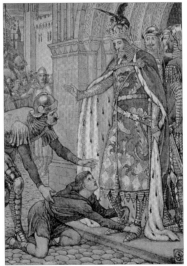

2

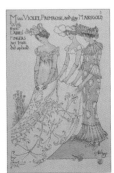

3

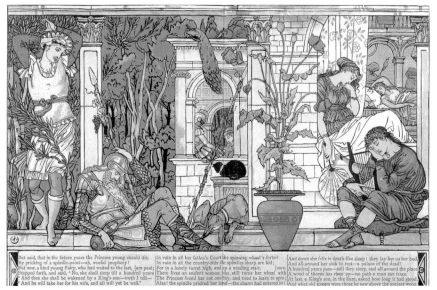

4

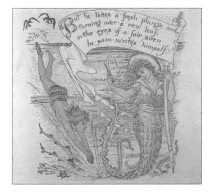

5

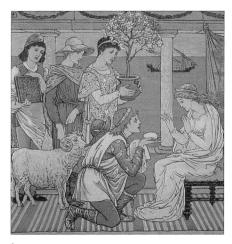

6

WILHELM BUSCH
(1832–1908)

Born in Hanover, Germany. Studied at academies in Dusseldorf, Antwerp, and Munich. In 1859, his drawings began to appear in the leading comic weekly Fliegende Blatter, *but he soon moved from work for periodicals to self-contained albums of comic-strip narratives with verses accompanying the images. In this way he was able to develop the comic-strip form more fully, and his work included social satire and cautionary tales. His best-known characters were the naughty children Max and Moritz, whose wicked pranks gave rein to Busch's talent for slapstick humor, but he was an innovative artist, producing graphic equivalents for emotional reactions and physical movement which subsequently became conventions of comic-strip art.*

1,2 *BOOK:* BUZZ ABUZZ
DATE: 1872

3 *BOOK:* MAX UND MORITZ
DATE: 1871

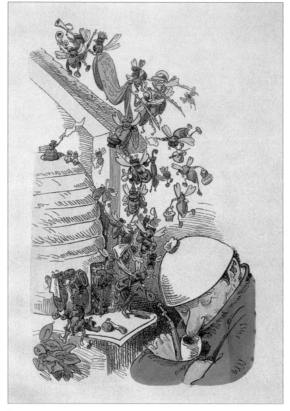

1

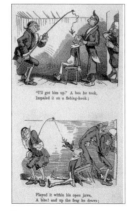

2

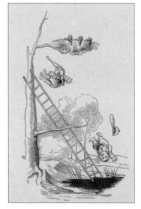

3

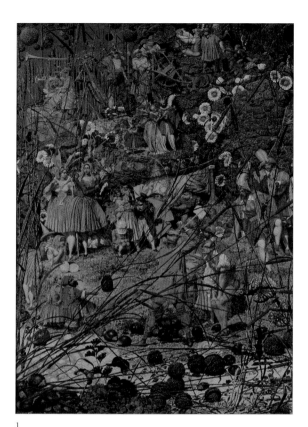

1

*Born in Kent, UK. He was
educated at William Dadson's
Academy of Art and the Royal
Academy Schools in London,
where he won the medal
for life drawing in 1840. He
contributed illustrations for* The
Book of British Ballads *(1842)
and illustrated the frontispiece
for* The Kentish Coronal *(1840).
Dadd went insane while on a
European tour with Sir Thomas
Phillips and was eventually
committed to a mental asylum
after he murdered his father in
1843. While in the asylum he
was encouraged to continue
painting and produced works of
incredible delicacy and beauty.*

1 *PAINTING:* THE FAIRY
FELLER'S MASTER STROKE
DATE: 1864

RICHARD DOYLE
(1824–1883)

*Born in London. He started
drawing from a very early
age and produced his first
book,* Home for the Holidays
*(published in 1887), when he
was only 12. His first published
work, the comic medieval
book* The Eglinton Tournament
*(1840), was a great success.
From 1843 he contributed
regularly to* Punch, *and in
January 1844 designed its sixth
cover, a procession of figures
based on Titian's "Bacchus
and Ariadne" which remained
unchanged until 1954. He
eventually resigned from the
magazine in protest against its
anti-Catholic views and for the
rest of his career concentrated
on illustrating books. His own*
Manners and Customs of Ye
Englishe *(1849) and* Bird's Eye
Views of Society *(1864) made
him a household name. He also
illustrated* The Fairy Ring *by
the Brothers Grimm (1845),
Mark Lemon's* The Enchanted
Doll *(1849), Ruskin's* The King
of the Golden River *(1851),
and his masterpiece, William
Allingham's* In Fairyland *(1870),
the illustrations for which were
put to a new story in 1884,*
The Princess Nobody *by
Andrew Lang.*

1 *PAINTING:* THE KNIGHT AND
THE SPECTRE
DATE: NOT KNOWN

2 *BOOK:* THE PRINCESS
NOBODY *by A D Lang*
DATE: 1884

3, 4 *BOOK:* IN FAIRYLAND *by*
William Allingham
DATE: 1870

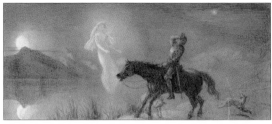

1

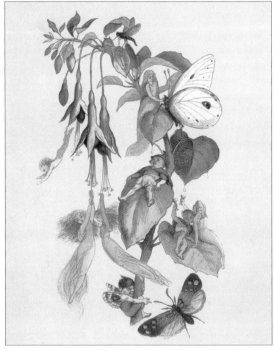

2

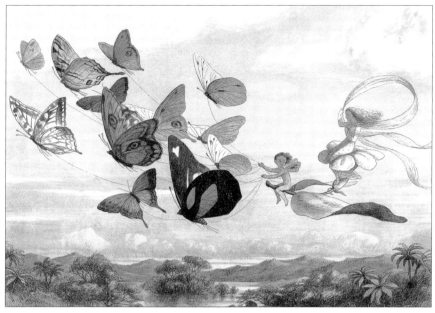

3

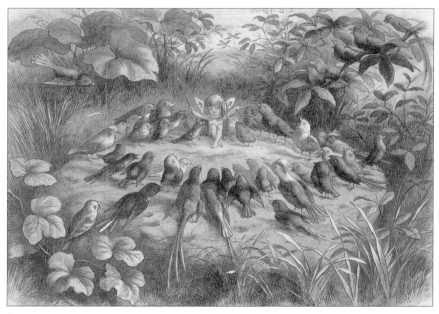

4

Born in Liverpool, UK. Studied
at Warrington School of Art
and the South Kensington and
Royal Academy Schools in
London. He was renowned as
a black-and-white artist in the
social realist vein, producing
powerful images of the poor and
the destitute. Fildes' drawing of
Charles Dickens' study entitled
"The Empty Chair," done the
day after the author's death,
was published in The Graphic
and was the inspiration for van
Gogh's painting "The Yellow
Chair." Fildes' illustrations also
appeared in Sunday Magazine,
The Cornhill Magazine, and
The Gentleman's Magazine.
He illustrated a number of
books, including Thackeray's
Catherine (1894) and Dickens'
Edwin Drood (1869). He decided
to concentrate on painting
after 1872 and became a
major portrait painter of the
Edwardian era. He was elected
to the Royal Academy in 1887
and was knighted in 1906.

1 *MAGAZINE:* SUNDAY
MAGAZINE *DATE: 1866*

2 *MAGAZINE:* SUNDAY
MAGAZINE *DATE: 1868*

3 *MAGAZINE:* SUNDAY
MAGAZINE *DATE: 1868*

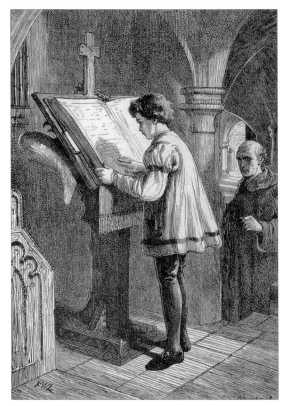

1

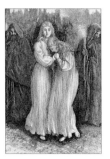

2

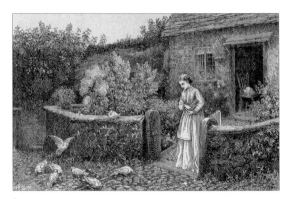

3

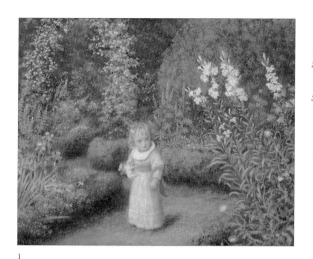

1

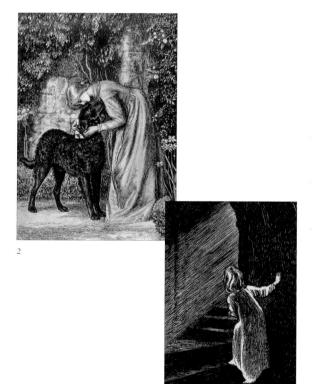

2

3

Born in London. He entered the Government School of Design at Somerset House at the unusually young age of 14, and at 15 enrolled at the Royal Academy Schools, where he won the silver medal for antique drawing two years later. In 1851 he first came into contact with the Pre-Raphaelite Brotherhood and was subsequently involved in the painting of the Oxford Union murals with Dante Gabriel Rossetti and others. He also painted a number of famous pictures, including Home from the Sea *and* The Long Engagement. *Hughes is best known for his black-and-white work and for his insistence on integrating his illustrations into the design of the book as a whole. His most notable period as an illustrator was his association with the writer George MacDonald on books such as* At the Back of the North Wind *(1871),* The Princess and the Goblin *(1872), and* Phantasies *(1905). He also illustrated for magazines such as* The Graphic *and* Good Words for the Young.

1 *PAINTING:* ALICE IN WONDERLAND
DATE: NOT KNOWN

2,3 *MAGAZINE:* GOOD WORDS FOR THE YOUNG
DATE: 1871

PAUL GUSTAVE CHRISTOPHE DORÉ (1832–1883)

Born in Strasbourg, France. He learned lithography while still at school in Bourg-en-Bresse. At the age of 11 his family moved to Paris, where eventually he was placed under contract to Charles Philippon's Journal Pour Rire, *contributing a weekly page. He had his first lithographs published at the age of 13 and by the age of 22 he was already famous for his illustrated* Rabelais. *There followed a series of classic titles, including Dante's* Divine Comedy *(1861), Coleridge's* Rime of the Ancient Mariner *(1865), Tennyson's* The Story of King Arthur and Queen Guinevere *(1868), and Milton's* Paradise Lost *(1866). He also produced his own book of caricatures,* Two Hundred Sketches, Humorous and Grotesque *(1867). His work appeared in many publications, including* The Illustrated London News *and* The Illustrated Times.

1-4 *BOOK:* VISION OF HELL
by Dante
DATE: 1860

5 *BOOK:* GARGANTUAET PANTAGRUEL *by François Rabelais*
DATE: NOT KNOWN

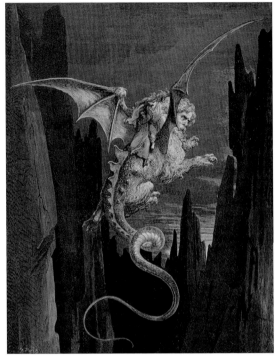

1

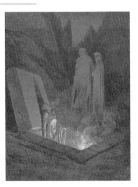

2

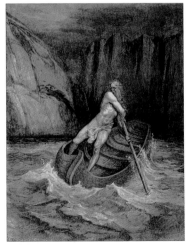

3

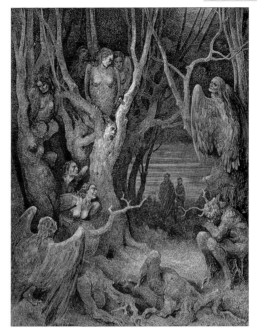

4

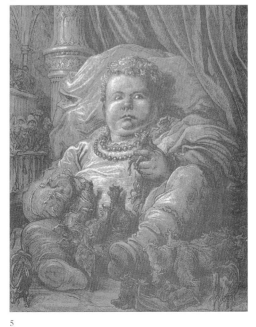

5

JOHN LEECH
(1817–1864)

Born in London. Studied
medicine at St Bartholomew's
Hospital before deciding to
become an artist. He soon
made his name as a black-and-
white artist and illustrated
for a number of periodicals,
including The Sporting Review,
Illustrated London Magazine,
New Monthly Magazine, and
The London Magazine. In 1840
he joined the staff of Bentley's
Miscellany, and in 1841 he
found a platform for his own
brand of pictorial satire in
the newly established journal
Punch. But he was best known
for his caricatures depicting
Victorian middle-class life,
epitomized in the characters
of Tom Noddy and Mr. Briggs.
Books illustrated include
Etchings and Sketchings (1835),
The Ingoldsby Legends (1840),
Jack the Giant Killer (1843), and
Uncle Tom's Cabin (1852).

1 BOOK: ASK MAMMA by
R S Surtees
DATE: 1858

2 MAGAZINE: PUNCH
DATE UNKNOWN

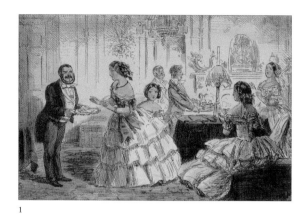

1

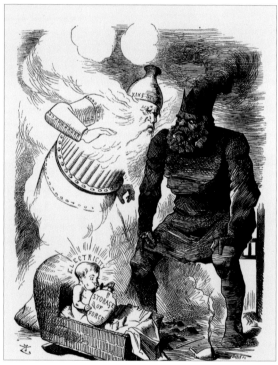

2

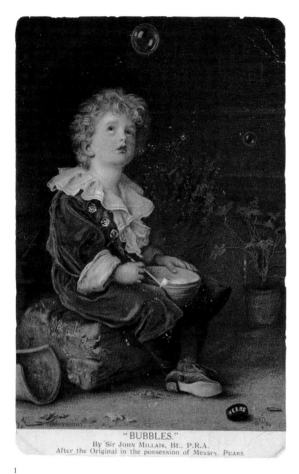

"BUBBLES."
By Sir JOHN MILLAIS, Bt., P.R.A.
After the Original in the possession of Messrs. PEARS.

1

*Born in Southampton, UK.
Studied at the Royal Academy
Schools. In 1848 he founded
the Pre-Raphaelite Brotherhood
with Dante Gabriel Rossetti and
Holman Hunt. He was much
admired for his brilliant black-
and-white illustrations, which,
like those of the American
Edwin Austin Abbey, show an
incredible attention to detail
and a concern for realism,
both visual and moral. He
illustrated the novels of Anthony
Trollope, which were serialized
in* The Cornhill Magazine
in 1860, and contributed to
Punch *and the Pre-Raphaelite
magazine* The Germ. *His best
period is considered to have
ended by 1863, when he was
elected Royal Academician, by
which time he had given up
illustrating in favor of painting
portraits and landscapes. In
1885 he was made a baronet
and in 1896 became President
of the Royal Academy, which he
remained until his death from
throat cancer six months later.*

1 *ADVERTISEMENT:* "PEARS
SOAP" *(based on the original
painting* "Bubbles")
DATE: 1896

2, 3 *BOOK:* THE DALZIEL
BIBLE
DATE: 1864

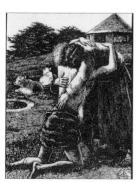

2

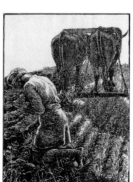

3

GEORGE DU MAURIER
(1834–1896)

English but born in Paris, the son of a frustrated opera singer. He moved to London as a child and showed an early talent for drawing. In 1851 he studied chemistry at University College London, but left in 1856 to study art in Paris, where he met James McNeill Whistler and E J Poynter. From 1857 to 1860 he studied in Antwerp under De Keyser and Van Lerius, but the loss of an eye forced him to abandon his plans to become a painter and he returned to London to pursue a career as a black-and-white artist. From 1860 he became a regular contributor to Punch *with his caricatures poking fun at the Victorian bourgeoisie. He was the greatest social satirist of the period and the accuracy of his ink drawings provides a complete chronicle of Victorian life. He also illustrated for* Harpers, The Graphic, The Illustrated Times, *and* The Cornhill magazine, *and in middle age he wrote and illustrated three novels,* Peter Ibbetson *(1891),* Trilby *(1894), and* The Martian *(1896).*

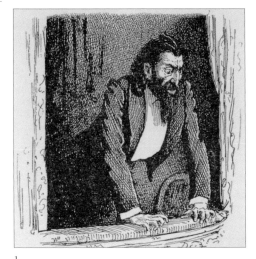

1

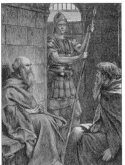

2

1 *BOOK:* TRILBY *by George Du Maurier*
DATE: 1894

2 *BOOK:* OUR LIFE
DATE: 1865

3 *MAGAZINE:* CORNHILL MAGAZINE
DATE: 1863

4 *BOOK:* GOOD WORDS
DATE: 1861

5 *BOOK:* PICTURES OF ENGLISH LITERATURE
DATE: 1870

6 *MAGAZINE:* PUNCH
DATE: c. 1860

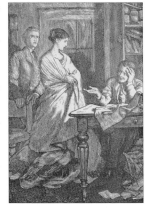

3

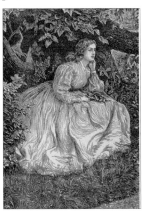

4

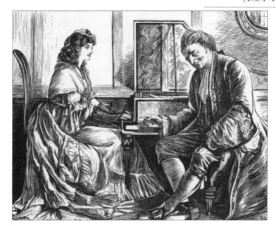

5

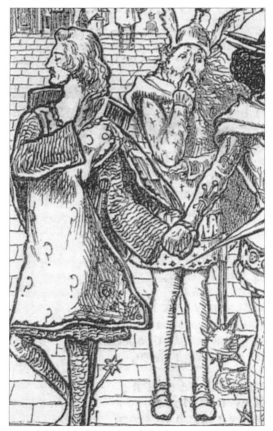

6

*Born in London. His unmarried
sister Ann taught him to
paint and by the age of 15
he was already setting his
drawings of birds. He made
his name with his superb
hand-colored illustrations of
parrots, published in 1832 as*
The Family of Psittacidae, or
Parrots. *From 1832 to 1836
Lear was employed by the Earl
of Derby to draw his collection
of rare birds and animals for
a book, the privately printed*
Knowsley Menagerie *(1856).
For the amusement of the earl's
children, he composed and
illustrated humorous limericks
in a deliberately childish but
wonderfully expressive style.
These were published in 1846
as* A Book of Nonsense, *the
popularity of which remained
confined to upper-class
households until a revised
version of the book published
by Routledge-Warne in 1861
became a best-seller. His most
famous rhymes,* Hey Diddle
Diddle *and* The Owl and the
Pussycat, *from* Nonsense Songs,
Stories, Botany and Alphabets
*(1871), are perennial favorites,
probably more popular today
than ever. His last book,*
Laughable Lyrics, *was published
in 1871.*

1, 2 *BOOK:* THE LEAR
ALPHABET *by Edward Lear*
DATE: 1871

3, 4 *BOOK:* A BOOK OF
NONSENSE *by Edward Lear*
DATE: 1846

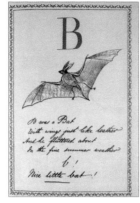

1

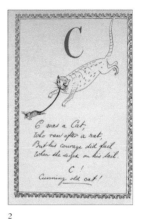

2

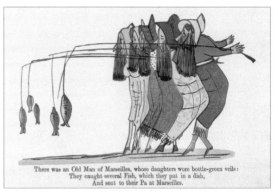

There was an Old Man of Marseilles, whose daughters wore bottle-green veils:
They caught several Fish, which they put in a dish,
And sent to their Pa at Marseilles.

3

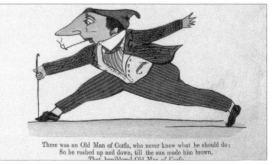

There was an Old Man of Corfu, who never knew what he should do;
So he rushed up and down, till the sun made him brown,
That bewildered Old Man of Corfu.

4

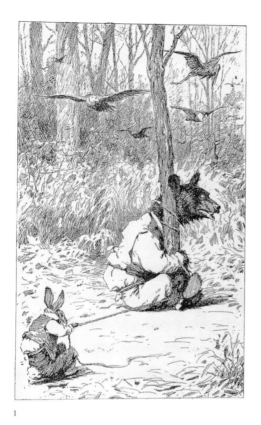

1

Born in Philadelphia, USA. At the age of 23 his first illustrated book, Out of the Hurly Burly, *sold over a million copies and launched his career. Frost was loved by Americans for his warm and humorous portrayal of animals and people. He was a master draftsman and his drawings captured the mood and detail of rural American life. He had a remarkable sense of color values, yet he was color-blind and his wife or sons had to label the colors of his palette for him. He illustrated the novels of Mark Twain, in which he created the enduring images of Tom Sawyer and Huckleberry Finn, but he is best known for his illustrations for Joel Chandler Harris' Uncle Remus and Brer Rabbit stories. In 1876 he joined the staff of Harper's and was cartoonist on the New York Daily Graphic for 20 years.*

1, 2 *BOOK:* UNCLE REMUS *by J Chandler Harris*
DATE: 1893

3, 4 *BOOK:* A TANGLED TALE *by Lewis Carroll*
DATE: 1886

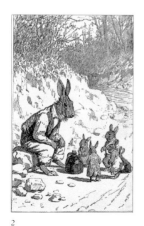

2

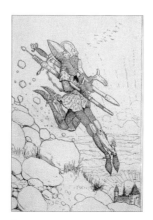

3

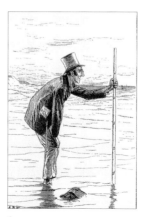

4

ARTHUR BOYD HOUGHTON
(1836–1875)

Born in Kotagiri, Madras. Educated in England at Leigh's Academy and the Royal Academy Schools, where he came under the influence of the Pre-Raphaelite Brotherhood and developed an interest in Japanese prints—the effects of which are particularly evident in his illustrations for Dalziel's Arabian Nights *(1864). In 1869* The Graphic *magazine sent him on a journalistic assignment to the USA to draw the Americans and their way of life. The results are among his best work. His illustrated books include* Longfellow's Poems *(1867) and* Dalziel's *Bible Gallery (1880), and he contributed to* The Argosy, Every Boy's Magazine, The Sunday Magazine, The Graphic, *and* The Broadway.

1, 2 *BOOK:* ARABIAN NIGHTS
DATE: 1864

3 *MAGAZINE:* THE SUNDAY
MAGAZINE
DATE: 1867

4 *MAGAZINE:* THE SUNDAY
MAGAZINE
DATE: 1867

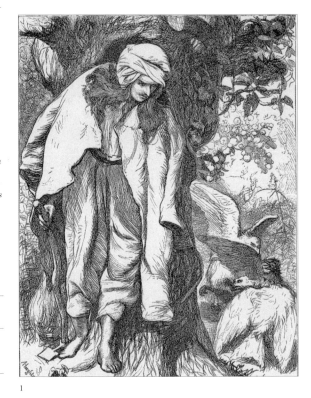

1

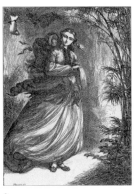

2

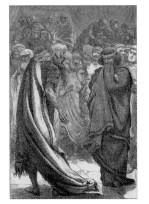

3

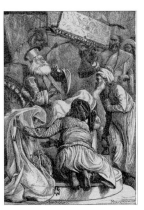

4

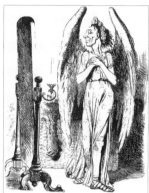

1

2

Born in London. In spite of
being accidentally blinded
in one eye during a fencing
match with his father, he was a
superb draughtsman and was
essentially self-taught, having
studied only briefly at the Royal
Academy Schools and the
Clipstone Street Life Academy.
His illustrations to Aesop's
Fables (1848) brought him to the
attention of Punch magazine,
then at its most radical. He
replaced Doyle as a full-time
member of staff in 1851, and his
pencil drawings over the next 50
years summed up the essence of
Victorian society. He illustrated
a number of books, but is best
known for his illustrations to the
first edition of Lewis Carroll's
Alice in Wonderland (1865).
This was a difficult commission
because Carroll, disappointed
at having his own illustrations
for the book rejected by the
publisher, consequently wanted
complete artistic control over
Tenniel, which led to a great
many arguments. Because of
these difficulties, and in spite of
the fact that Alice in Wonderland
achieved international acclaim
on publication, Tenniel initially
refused to illustrate the
subsequent Alice Through the
Looking Glass. He finally gave
in, however, and it came out in
1871, when it was an instant
success. He was knighted in
1893 and retired from Punch
magazine at the age of 80.

1 *MAGAZINE:* PUNCH
DATE: 1853

2 *MAGAZINE:* PUNCH
DATE: 1853

3 *BOOK:* ALICE THROUGH
THE LOOKING GLASS *by Lewis
Carroll*
DATE: 1871

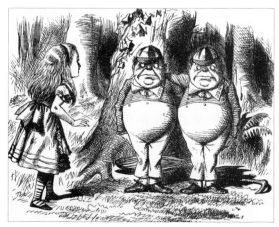

3

*Born in Slough, UK. Studied
animal anatomy at the South
Kensington School of Art and
animal painting under Frank W
Calderon. Aldin's activities as a
huntsman enabled him to draw
the funny side of English country
life, and his comic hunting
scenes, olde-worlde inns, and
dog portraits, drawn in a jovial
style, were immensely popular.
He was particularly well
known for his series of* Puppy
Dog *books (1904–14), which
were favorites with children.
His books included Hodder
and Stoughton's* Christmas Eve
*(1910), which owes much to the
influence of Caldecott, and Anna
Sewell's* Black Beauty *(1912).
He contributed to numerous
periodicals during the 1890s,
including* The English Illustrated
Magazine, Lady's Pictorial, Boy's
Own Paper, *and* Illustrated
Sporting and Dramatic News.

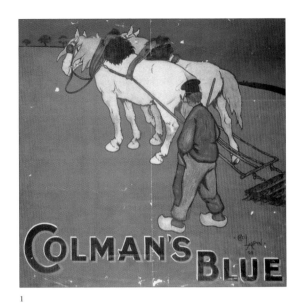

1

1 *ADVERTISEMENT:* COLMAN'S
BLUE
DATE: 1898

2 *ADVERTISEMENT:* COLMAN'S
STARCH
DATE: c. 1898

3 *ADVERTISEMENT:* CADBURY'S
COCOA
DATE: c. 1899

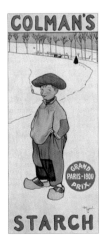

2

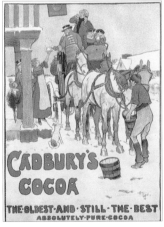

3

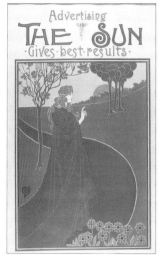

1

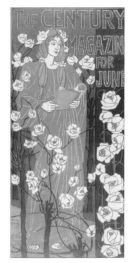

2

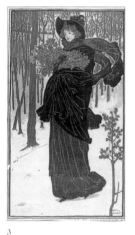

3

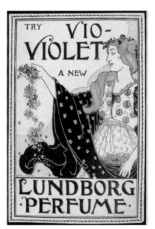

4

*Born in Staffordshire, UK.
Studied art in London and
Paris, where meeting with
Grasset proved a strong
influence towards a career in
poster design. He then emigrated
to the USA, where he settled in
Brooklyn. His work included
portraits, posters, lithographs,
ceramics, watercolour, and
line illustrations. His clients
included* The New York Sun,
Scribner's *and* The Century.
*Rhead's style owed much to Art
Nouveau, but he was criticized
for weak drawing, sometimes
masked by over-elaboration
of decorative elements. He
collaborated with his brothers
George and Frederick,
individually and as a team, on
book illustrations—*The Pilgrim's
Progress *(1898),* Tennyson's
Idylls of the King *(1898), and*
Robinson Crusoe *(1900). He
illustrated children's stories for*
Harper's Bazaar *and his own
book as author and illustrator,*
Bold Robin Hood and his Outlaw
Band, *was published in 1923.*

1 *ADVERTISEMENT: "THE SUN
MAGAZINE"
DATE:* 1894

2 *MAGAZINE COVER:* THE
CENTURY
DATE. c. 1895

3 *MAGAZINE COVER:*
SCRIBNER'S
DATE: c. 1895

4 *ADVERTISEMENT:
"LUNDBORG PERFUME"
DATE.* c. 1895

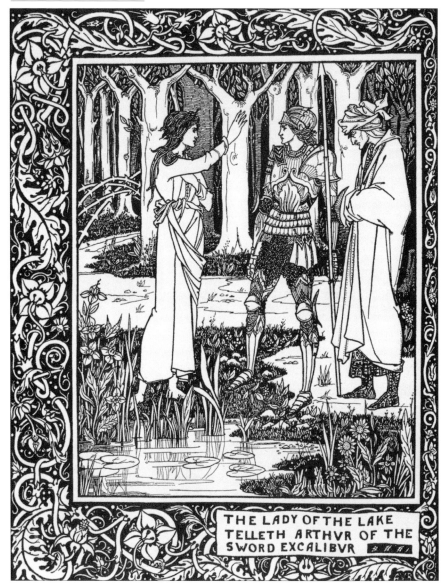

THE LADY OF THE LAKE
TELLETH ARTHVR OF THE
SWORD EXCALIBVR

1

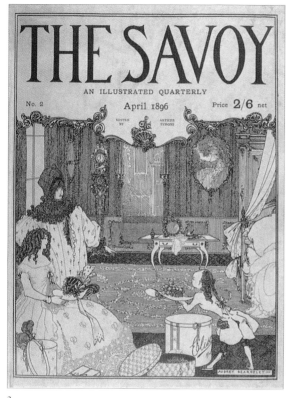

2

Born in Brighton, UK. His family circumstances precluded any formal art training, though he had shown a talent for drawing and caricature while at school. While he was working as a clerk in London, the artist Edward Burne-Jones encouraged him to attend evening classes at Westminster School of Art. In 1892 he visited Paris, where he was inspired by the posters of Toulouse-Lautrec and the current interest in Japanese prints. His first commission was from Messrs Dent, who asked him to illustrate their new edition of Malory's Le Morte d'Arthur (1893). He then became Art Editor of The Yellow Book quarterly (1894–96) and illustrator for The Savoy (1896–98). Books illustrated include Pope's The Rape of the Lock (1896), The Lysistrata of Aristophanes (1896), Oscar Wilde's Salomé (1894), and A Book of Fifty Drawings by Aubrey Beardsley (1897). He developed his own very personal version of the Art Nouveau style, featuring highly stylized forms, sinuous curves, and the use of areas of heavy decoration set against areas of white space. His fascination with the decadence of the fin-de-siècle period was reflected in the sinister eroticism of his images, which shocked the public at the time. The acknowledged genius of black-and-white art, he influenced many subsequent artists. He died of tuberculosis at 25.

1 BOOK: LE MORTE D'ARTHUR
by Malory
DATE: 1893

2 MAGAZINE COVER: THE
SAVOY
DATE: 1896

3, 4 BOOK: SALOME
by Oscar Wilde
DATE: 1894

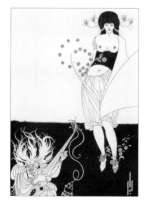

3

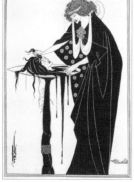

4

RANDOLPH CALDECOTT
(1846–1886)

Born in Chester, UK. After leaving school he worked as a bank clerk while studying in the evenings at Manchester School of Art. There he met Thomas Armstrong, who showed Caldecott's work to the editor of London Society *magazine, who then published his first drawings in 1871. Caldecott's unfussy style, using strong outlines and flat areas of color, was perfectly suited to children's book illustration, and he was employed by the engraver Edmund Evans to take over the illustration of Routledge's* Shilling Toybooks *when his friend Walter Crane left after a quarrel about royalties. Caldecott had a particular love for the era that preceded the Industrial Revolution and his idealization of life in the country captured the heart of the general public. Books illustrated include Washington Irving's* Old Christmas *(1875),* The Diverting History of John Gilpin, The House That Jack Built *(both 1878), and* Three Jovial Huntsmen Sing a Song of Sixpence *(1880). He also illustrated for* Punch, Boy's Own Paper, *and* The Graphic.

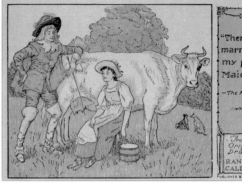
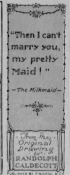

1

1 *NURSERY POSTER*
DATE: 1884

2, 3 *BOOK:* RANDOLPH CALDECOTT'S COLLECTION OF PICTURES AND SONGS
DATE: 1880

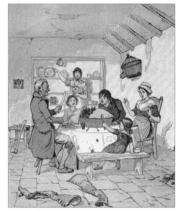

2

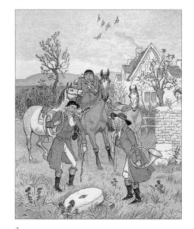

3

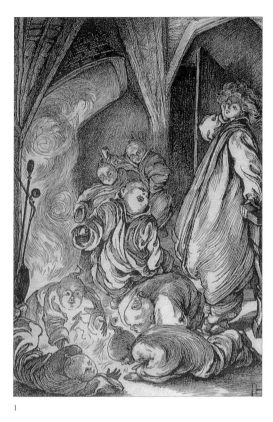

1

LAURENCE HOUSMAN
(1865–1959)

Born in Bromsgrove, UK. Studied at Lambeth School of Art and the Royal College of Art. He began work as a book illustrator, but when his eyesight began to fail he turned to writing adult books, plays, and fairy stories, which he illustrated himself. He published a great deal on feminism, socialism, and pacifism. His bold use of black-and-white shows the influence of Aubrey Beardsley, but he was also influenced by the social realism of Dante Gabriel Rossetti and others of the Pre-Raphaelite Brotherhood. Books illustrated include his own The Blue Moon *(1904), Christina Rossetti's* Goblin Market *(1893), and Shelley's* The Sensitive Plant *(1898).*

1–4 *BOOK:* THE FIELD OF CLOVER
DATE: 1898

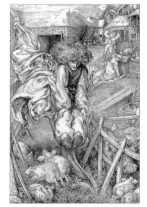

2

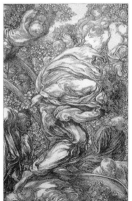

3

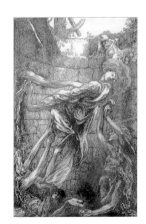

4

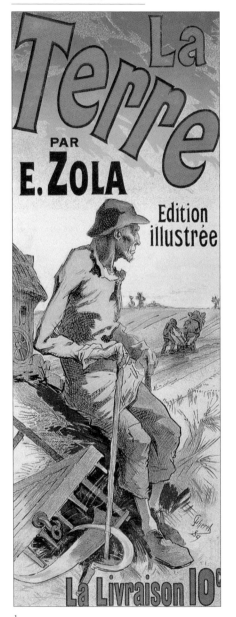

1

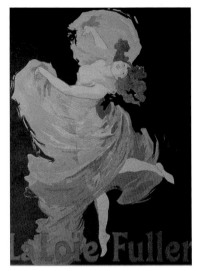

2

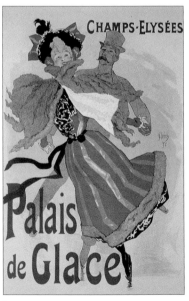

3

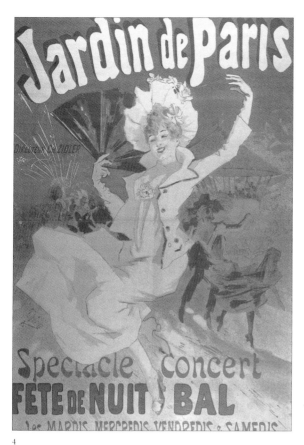

4

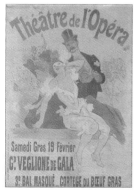

5

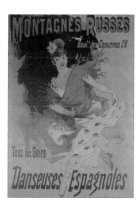

6

JULES CHÉRET
(1836–1932)

Born in Paris. After working as a lithographer he moved to London in 1859, to study the new techniques of printing in color lithography being developed there, and earned his living designing book covers for Cramer Publishing and posters for the opera, circus, and music hall. He also met and became the protégé of the perfumer Eugène Rimmel. In 1866 Rimmel provided the financial backing for Chéret to set up his own lithographic printing studio in Paris, from where he produced the first French posters printed in colour. His pioneering work in the development of chromolithography enabled the mass production of posters and contributed to the development of the advertising poster as an artistic medium. His own posters capture the joie de vivre of the cabarets, music and dance halls, operas, and theaters of Paris. He designed posters for the American dancer Loïe Fuller for her début at the Folies-Bergère, and his many images of lively dancing girls were popularly known as "Cherettes."

1 *PUBLICITY POSTER: "LATERRE BY EMILE ZOLA" DATE: 1889*

2 *POSTER: "LOÏE FULLER" DATE: 1893*

3 *POSTER: "PALAIS DE GLACE" DATE: 1896*

4 *POSTER: "JARDIN DE PARIS" DATE: 1890*

5 *POSTER: "THEATRE DEL'OPERA" DATE: c. 1896*

6 *POSTER: "DANSEUSES ESPAGNOLES" DATE: c. 1896*

KATE GREENAWAY
(1846–1901)

Born in London. Studied at Heatherley's and the Slade School of Art, and began her career illustrating greeting cards. In 1877 she met the printer Edmund Evans, for whom she wrote and illustrated Under the Window *(1878). This was a great success and was followed by, among others,* The Birthday Book *(1880),* The Marigold Garden *(1885), and* The Pied Piper of Hamelin *(1888). She was encouraged in her career by John Ruskin, whom she befriended in 1882 and who, along with Gauguin and the public at large, was a great admirer of her simple style and nostalgic view of childhood.*

1 *PAINTING*
DATE: c. 1899

2 *BOOK:* MOTHER GOOSE
DATE: 1881

3 *FRONTISPIECE:* THE
MARIGOLD GARDEN
by Kate Greenaway
DATE: 1885

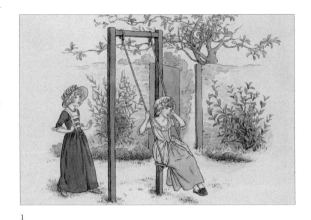

1

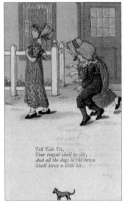

2

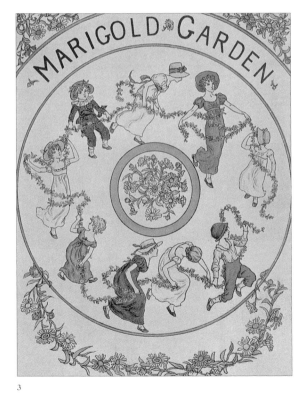

3

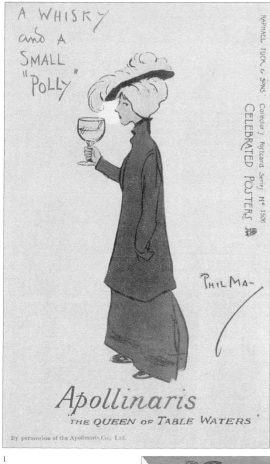

Born in Leeds, UK. He left
school at 13 and became an
assistant scene painter at the
Leeds Grand Theatre, where he
sold his drawings of the actors
and actresses for a shilling
each. At 14 he started drawing
for the Yorkshire Post and at
16 moved to London, where
he contributed to St Stephen's
Review. He then emigrated to
Australia and worked for three
years on the Sydney Bulletin.
Returning penniless to London,
he started the highly successful
"Parson and Painter" series
for St Stephen's Review, which
was published as a series of
annuals from 1891 to 1904. He
also drew for many periodicals,
including The Graphic, The
Daily Graphic, and The Sketch.
In 1895 he joined the staff of
Punch, where he remained until
his death. Sometimes referred
to as the "grandfather of British
illustration," he was regarded
by many as the most important
and influential black-and-white
artist of his generation. He lived
a bohemian life and died of
cirrhosis of the liver and TB at
the age of 39.

1 ADVERTISEMENT:
"APOLLINARIS TABLE WATER"
DATE: c. 1899

2 MAGAZINE: THE GRAPHIC
DATE: 1893

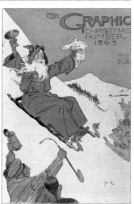

2

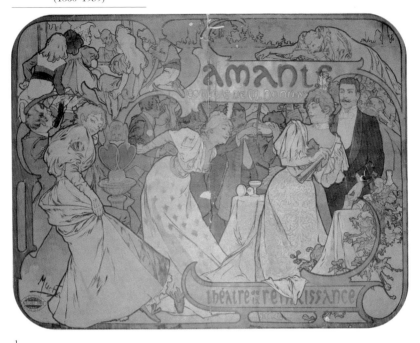

1

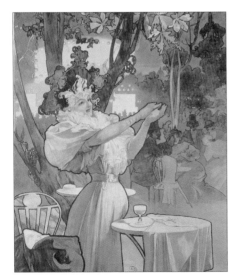

2

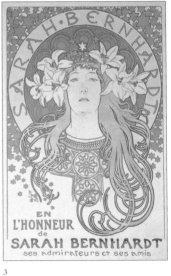

3

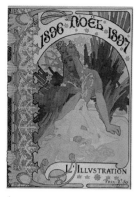

4

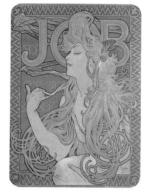

5

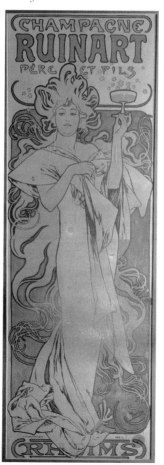

6

Born in Czechoslovakia, now the Czech Republic. Count Karl Khuen Belasi commissioned him to paint a series of murals for his country home, and subsequently financed Mucha's studies at the Munich Academy. The Count's suicide in 1889 was a financial blow to Mucha, and he turned to illustrating books and journals to make a living. His rise to fame as a leading Art Nouveau designer began with a commission in 1894 to design a poster for Sarah Bernhardt in her leading role in Gismonda.

The poster so delighted Bernhardt that she gave Mucha a six-year contract to design posters, stage sets, costumes, jewelry, and programs for her productions. During his career Mucha designed many posters and decorative panels, typically featuring maidens in flowing robes surrounded by formalized decorative symbols. Between 1904 and 1912 he taught in New York and Chicago, where his work appeared in The New York Daily News *and* The Century *magazine.*

1 *POSTER: "LES AMANTS"*
DATE: 1895

2 *POSTER: "AU CAFÉ-CONCERT"*
DATE: 1900

3 *POSTER: "SARAH BERNHARDT"*
DATE: c. 1900

4 *MAGAZINE COVER: L'ILLUSTRATION*
DATE: 1896

5 *ADVERTISEMENT: "JOB"*
DATE: c. 1890

6 *ADVERTISEMENT: "RUINART CHAMPAGNE"*
DATE: c. 1890

*Born in Albi, France. His
early talent for drawing was
encouraged by his uncle and
two family friends, the sporting
painters René Princeteau
and John Lewis Brown. After
studying art under Florentin
Léon Bonnat and at the school
of Fernand Cormon (where
he met Vincent van Gogh), he
was given an allowance in
1885 to set up his own studio
in the Montmartre district
of Paris. There he produced
his brilliant series of posters,
paintings, and drawings
depicting popular singers,
dancers, and scenes of Parisian
nightlife. Lautrec admired the
work of Degas and Gauguin,
and the current fashion for
Japanese art inspired his daring
layouts, bold outlines, and solid
blocks of color. In addition
to his posters, he produced
over 300 lithographs. He also
contributed to Courrier Français
and other Paris newspapers
and illustrated Jules Renard's
Histoires Naturelles (1899).*

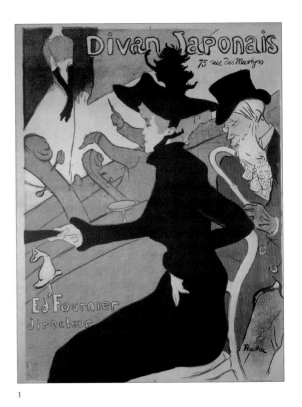

1

1 *POSTER: "DIVAN JAPONAIS"*
DATE: 1892

2 *POSTER: "MAY BELFORT"*
DATE: 1895

3 *POSTER: "LAGOULUE"*
DATE: 1892

4 *MAGAZINE:* LERIRE
DATE: 1895

5 *MAGAZINE:* LERIRE
DATE: 1896

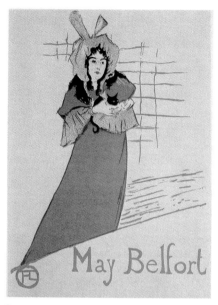

2

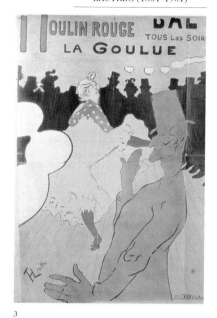

3

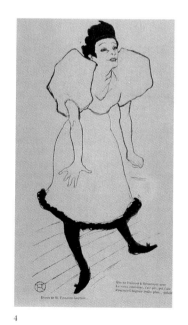

4

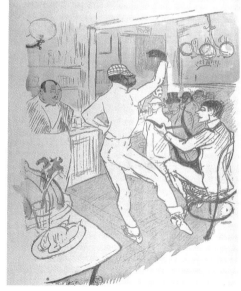

5

Born in London. He was apprenticed to an engraver and subsequently opened a studio of his own and attended St. Martin's Lane School. Using the name "Phiz," he illustrated most of the novels of Dickens, including Pickwick Papers *(1836)*, Little Dorrit *(1857)*, and Nicholas Nickleby *(1839)*. He contributed to various magazines, including New Sporting Magazine, London Magazine, The Illustrated Times, Punch, *and* The Illustrated London Magazine.

1 *BOOK:* LITTLE DORRIT *by*
Charles Dickens
DATE: 1857

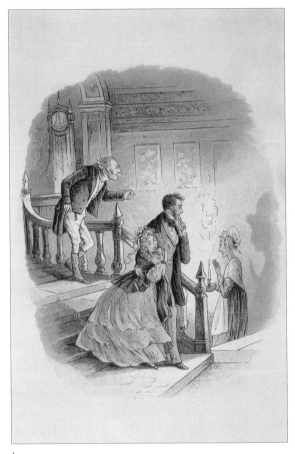

1

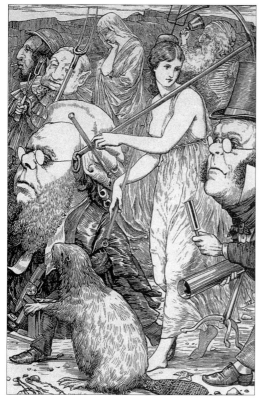

1

Born in London. Studied at Leigh's Academy and the Royal Academy Schools. His interest in the Pre-Raphaelite Brotherhood led to him befriending Holman Hunt and Burne-Jones, who had a major influence on his work. He is best known as a stained glass artist, but achieved fame as an illustrator for his illustrations for Lewis Carroll's The Hunting of the Snark *(1876).*

1–4 *BOOK:* THE HUNTING OF THE SNARK *by Lewis Carroll*
DATE: 1876

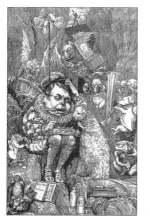

2

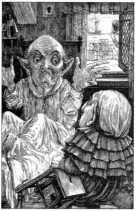

3

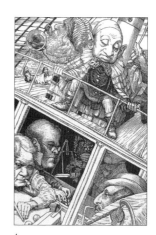

4

PIERRE BONNARD
(1867–1947)

Born in Paris. Studied painting at the Académie Julien in Paris in the late 1880s. With fellow students, including Maurice Denis and Edouard Vuillard, he founded the Nabis, a group of artists with a shared interest in the graphic and decorative arts. In 1891 Bonnard's first commercial poster, France-Champagne, was published. Thereafter, posters, prints, and book illustrations constituted a major part of his work for a number of years. His graphic oeuvre includes a set of lithographs entitled Aspects of the Life of Paris and illustrations for, among other works, Jules Renard's Histoires Naturelles (1904) and Octave Mirbeau's La 628 E 8 (1908), an account of an automobile trip through Europe. Subsequently Bonnard returned to the preoccupations of pure painting and is best known for the work of his later years: interior scenes suffused with color and light.

1 EXHIBITION POSTER: "THE PRINT AND THE POSTER"
DATE: 1897

2 POSTER: "SALON DESCENT"
DATE: 1896

3 ADVERTISEMENT: "LE FIGARO"
DATE: c. 1899

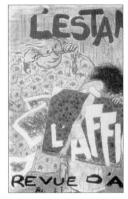

1

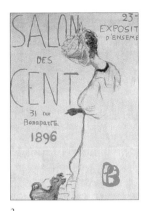

2

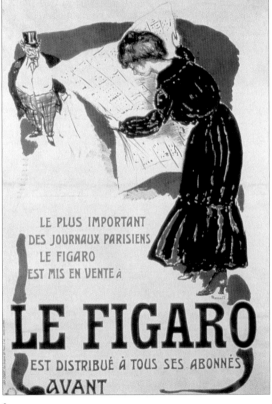

3

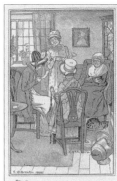

"The enjoyment of Elinor's company"
Chapter XLIX

1

"You are extremely kind" replied Miss Bates.
Chapter XXI

2

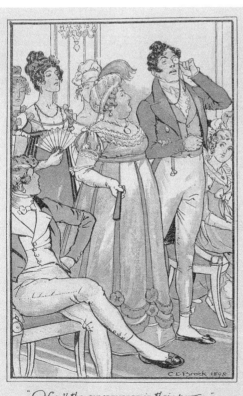

"Of all the consequence in their power"
Chapter XX

3

CHARLES EDMUND BROCK
(1870–1938)

*Born in Cambridge, UK.
Educated at Cambridge School
and in the studio of the sculptor
Henry Wiles. He shared a studio
with his younger brother, Henry
Matthew, and their work was
very similar, although Charles'
use of line was more tentative.
They were equally successful
and during their careers
illustrated most of the classics,
conjuring up images of "the
good old days" in the manner
of Hugh Thomson. Charles
began illustrating in 1891. His
first major commission was
for Thomas Hood's* Humorous
Poems *(1893), which was very
popular and led to his most
successful book, Swift's*
Gulliver's Travels *(1894).*

1 *BOOK:* SENSE AND
SENSIBILITY *by Jane Austen*
DATE: 1898

2 *BOOK:* PERSUASION
by Jane Austen
DATE: 1898

3 *BOOK:* EMMA *by Jane Austen*
DATE: 1898

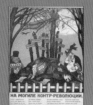

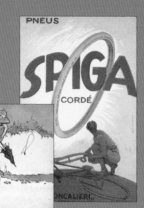

PNEUS

SPIGA

CORDÉ

NCALIERI.

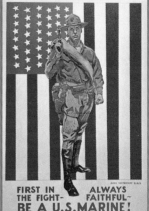

FIRST IN
THE FIGHT-

ALWAYS
FAITHFUL~

BE A U.S. MARINE!

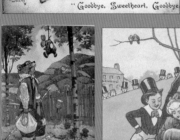

"Goodbye, Sweetheart, Goodbye."

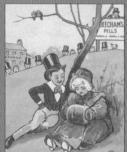

BEECHAM'S
PILLS

AM'S
LLS

"EYES FRONT"

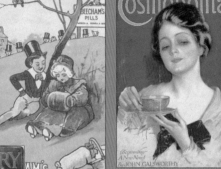

Cosmopolitan

Beginning
A New Novel
By JOHN GALSWORTHY

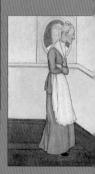

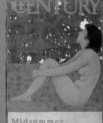

CENTURY

Midsummer
Holiday Number.
August.

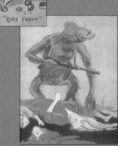

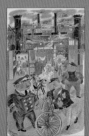

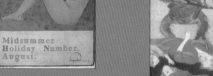

PULLS like—SHELL!

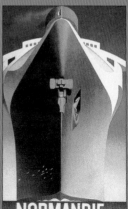

NORMANDIE

Cⁱᵉ Gᵉ TRANSATLANTIQUE

CHAPTER TWO
1900–1939

AFTER THE DECADENCE OF THE FIN DE SIÈCLE, Britain entered the 20th century with a fascination for the decorative arts, which found the perfect medium in the Edwardian gift book.

Many of these were children's stories, but the Net Book Agreement in 1900 had put an end to the booksellers' price war, and the increased cost of these volumes ensured that many, if not most of them, were for adult entertainment and not destined to suffer the clumsy attentions of boisterous children. Besides which, the subject matter was not of primary importance, as the overriding concern was with the decorative possibilities of the book as a whole and not with a close interpretation of the text. The influence of Art Nouveau and Japanese art was extremely marked throughout this period, and the legacy of Aubrey Beardsley, who died in 1898 at the tragically young age of 25, continued to inspire. Beardsley's works were perfectly suited to the line-block process, and there are those who believe he had no peers and that his style died with him. However, in the first decades of the 20th century, one can see his inspiration at work in the drawings of such artists as Alastair, Kay Nielson, Harry Clarke, Edmund Dulac, and, to a lesser extent, Arthur Rackham, whose sepia-toned drawings have become definitive of the period. While Britain and Europe were in the grip of Art Nouveau, America was enjoying its own "golden age of illustration." In the 1890s Howard Pyle had injected a new lease of life into an otherwise dull period of children's illustration with his all-action, black-and-white drawings of adventure on the high seas. His pirate stories were immensely popular, and his prolific output was made possible by his habit of dictating the narrative to his secretary while working on the artwork at his easel.

However, Pyle's fame now rests more on the color illustrations he did for magazines such as *Harper's* and on the extent of his influence as a teacher, a role that has earned him the title "the father of American illustration." He set up his own school at Chadd's Ford, Pennsylvania, where his star pupils were N C Wyeth, who produced a classic edition of *Treasure Island,* and Frank Schoonover, who inherited Pyle's Pre-Raphaelite obsession with authenticity as well as his love of the Wild West. But the influence of the Pyle school extended way beyond his pupils, and artists like Fred Remington traveled extensively to record the lives of trappers, cowboys, and outbackers with a truthful and not romantic eye.

Of course, at that time America was also producing prominent artists who were outside Pyle's sphere of influence, two examples being Maxfield Parrish and Charles Dana Gibson.

Parrish worked mainly for the major American magazines: *Harpers, Colliers, The Century,* and *Life.* But the experimental nature of his work is beautifully captured in his illustrations for Kenneth Graham's *The Golden Age,* in which, using photographs as reference material, he recreated a child's view of the world by drawing it from a low eye level.

Charles Dana Gibson specialized in pen drawings of fashionable young women and his "Gibson Girls" made him famous and extremely rich. In 1904 *Collier's Weekly* offered him a four-year contract worth $100,000 (about £500,000 in today's terms). When you consider the staggering size of such a fee, it is hardly surprising that magazines attracted the cream of American illustrative talent.

Throughout this period, while Europe dominated the field of book production, American publishers favored the magazine. From an investor's point of view they were a safer bet, as sales could be predicted from fairly stable circulation figures, and the United States had superior technology that could withstand the constant pressure of deadlines while maintaining high standards of color reproduction.

Gibson's eminence in this milieu is interesting, as it limited his interest to a particular subject matter. In the first decades of the 20th century, on both sides of the Atlantic, this sort of specialization became increasingly commonplace among illustrators. One only has to think of Louis Wain's cats, George Studdy's dogs, Cecil Aldin's horses, Bateman's outraged generals, J A Shepherd's animals clothed in human attire, or Mabel Lucie Attwell's rosy-cheeked children to wonder whether this limiting of vision was a condition of the artist's imagination or the force of commerce sustaining a winning formula.

Certainly times were hard for most illustrators, and the arrival of poster and print advertising was a welcome opportunity for diversification. The economic depression after World War I led to a decline in the illustrated book market, but the 1920s and 1930s, particularly in Europe, saw dramatic developments in advertising art.

In Britain, Jack Beddington, the publicity manager of Shell, instigated some of the most famous advertising of all time and became an influential patron of the arts by commissioning the likes of Graham Sutherland, E McKnight Kauffer, and Tom Purvis. On the Continent, advertising posters reached dizzying aesthetic heights in the work of the Futurist-inspired A M Cassandre.

This need for artists to find new outlets and media for their talents had been encouraged by the two world wars. Propaganda to support the war efforts had been in heavy demand and some artists, such as James Montgomery Flagg in America, had become famous because of it. At the same time these conflicts encouraged the development of political and social satire, and illustration was broadly used to strengthen the voice of protest.

By the beginning of the 1940s the diversification of illustration had led the artist into every realm of human activity.

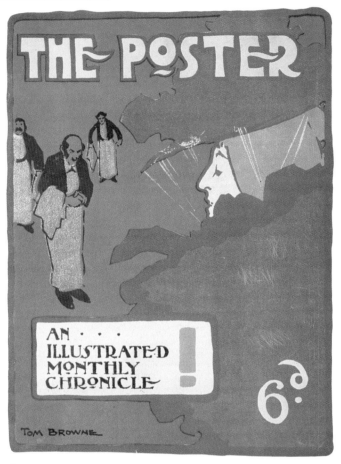

1

2

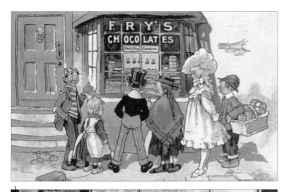

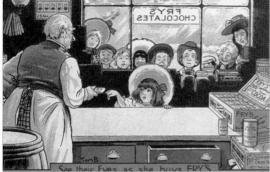

TOM BROWNE
(1872–1910)

Born in Nottingham, UK. He left school at 11 to work as an errand boy for a local milliner and in 1886 was apprenticed to a firm of lithographic printers for no pay. After a year he was earning one shilling a week. At 17, he became interested in cartoons and sent drawings to the editor of Scraps *comic, which earned him 30 shillings.*

At 19 he moved to London, where he invented the popular "Weary Willie" and "Tired Tim" comic characters and went on to work for the weekly illustrated papers and Punch. *He was a member of the Royal Society of British Artists and founder-member of the London Sketch Club. From 1904 he also enjoyed some success in the USA with a series of comic characters called "Boston Types." He contributed to numerous magazines, including* Cycling, The Wheel, *and* Cycle Magazine *and designed posters for Raleigh bicycles. He is most famous for his advertising poster for Johnnie Walker Whisky.*

1 *MAGAZINE:* THE POSTER
DATE: c. 1900

2 *ADVERTISEMENT:* "FRY'S CHOCOLATE"
DATE: c. 1905

3, 4 *ADVERTISEMENT:* "FRY'S CHOCOLATE"
DATE: c. 1900

5 *ADVERTISEMENT:* "BEECHAM'S PILLS"
DATE: c. 1905

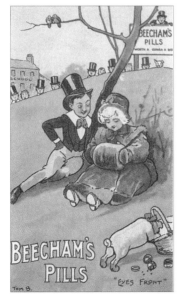

*Born in London. She was
entirely self-taught as a water
colorist and displayed a natural
gift for drawing animals
from a very early age. Her
first book,* The Tale of Peter
Rabbit, *was turned down by
several publishers, including
her subsequent publishers
Frederick Warne and Co., before
she published it at her own
expense in 1901. She published*
The Tailor of Gloucester *the
following year. Frederick Warne
then published revised versions
with illustrations in color and
followed them with* The Tale of
Benjamin Bunny *(1904) and*
The Tale of Tom Kitten *(1907).
Nineteen books in the Peter
Rabbit series were to follow.
Beatrix Potter's little books,
with their delicate watercolor
vignettes and small blocks
of text have become part of
English nursery folklore. Her
animals, though endowed with
human attributes and dressed
in clothes, are nevertheless
real because they are sharply
observed from nature. She
cited the Pre-Raphaelites and
Randolph Caldecott as major
influences, and admired Mrs
Blackburn's bird and animal
illustrations as well as Thomas
Bewick's woodcuts.*

1, 2 *BOOK:* THE TALE OF
PETER RABBIT
DATE: 1901

3, 5 *BOOK:* THE TAILOR OF
GLOUCESTER
DATE: 1902

4 *BOOK:* THE TALE OF TOM
KITTEN
DATE: 1907

6 *BOOK:* THE TALE OF
BENJAMIN BUNNY
DATE: 1904

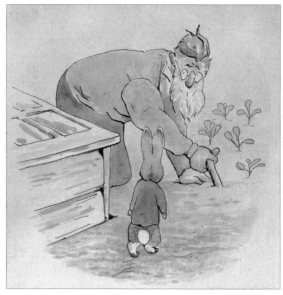

1

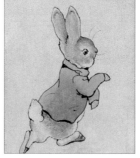

2

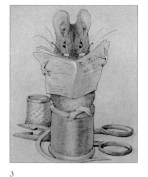

3

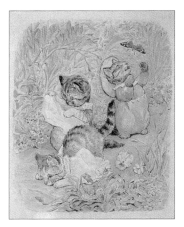

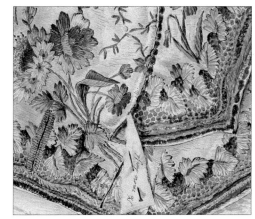

4   5

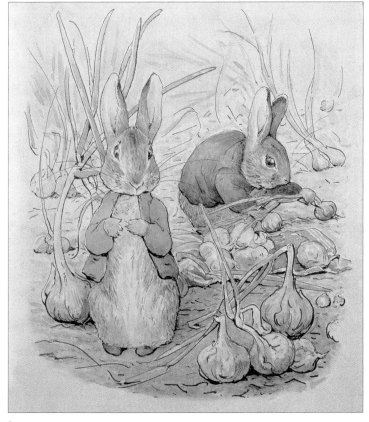

6

CHARLES DANA GIBSON
(1867–1944)

*Born in Massachusetts, USA.
Studied at the Art Students
League in New York and at
the Académie Julien in Paris.
Gibson quickly became an
international figure, famous
for his drawings chronicling
American high society, and
created a beautiful type of all-
American girl known as "the
Gibson Girl." He sold his first
drawing to Life magazine when
he was 19, beginning a lifelong
association which culminated
in his becoming its owner and
editor after World War I. An
early admirer of Abbey, Frost,
and Pyle, he later developed
a special liking for the British
illustrators Charles Keene,
George du Maurier, and Phil
May. He was President of the
Society of Illustrators during
World War I.*

1, 2 *BOOK:* AMERICANS *by
Charles Dana Gibson
DATE: 1901*

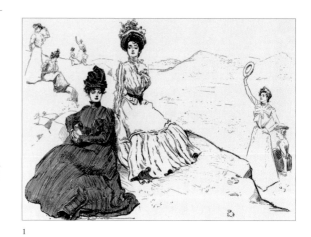

1

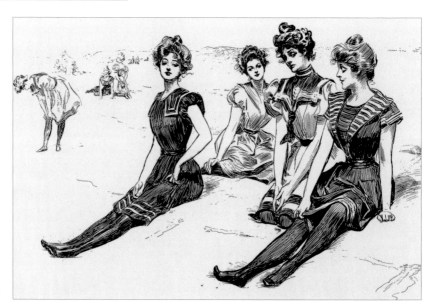

2

DEAN CORNWELL
(1892–1960)

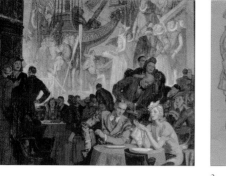

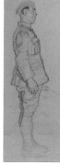

1

2

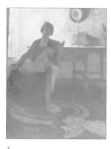

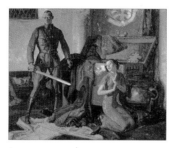

3

4

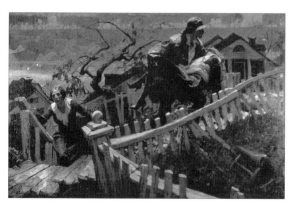

5

Cornwell was a student of Harvey Dunn, through whom he inherited much of the teaching of Howard Pyle, and he also studied under the muralist Frank Brangwyn. Although obviously an exponent of the Pyle school Cornwell's style was more elaboratively decorative. He worked in oils and was painstaking in his approach to the subject, making many preliminary sketches, and throughout the 1920s his beautiful illustrations of swashbuckling romantic costume dramas dominated such magazines as Redbook *and* Cosmopolitan.
However, it was Norman Rockwell's belief that Cornwell's best work was a series on the life of Christ, for Good Housekeeping, *which he painted after a trip to the Middle East. His murals are no less impressive than his illustrations, the most notable being those for the Los Angeles Public Library, the Lincoln Memorial in California, and the Tennessee State Office Building. He taught illustration at the Art Students League in New York, where he created the "Cornwell School," and had a profound influence on such artists as Harry Beckhoff Dan Content, Rico Tomaso, Robert Benney, and Frank Reilly. From 1922 to 1926 he was President of the Society of Illustrators and was elected to its Hall of Fame in 1959.*

1 *MAGAZINE:* COSMOPOLITAN
DATE: 1923

2. *DRAWING:* WWI DOUGHBOY
DATE: c. 1918

3 *MAGAZINE:* COSMOPOLITAN
DATE: c. 1918

4 *PAINTING*
DATE: 1938

5 *MAGAZINE:* COSMOPOLITAN
DATE: 1923

Born in London. Edward and his twin brother Charles Maurice started drawing in early childhood and though neither had received any formal training, both exhibited at the Royal Academy from the age of 14. They collaborated on several books, including Pictures from Birdland *(1899) and Kipling's* The Jungle Book *(1903), until Charles Maurice committed suicide in 1908 at the age of 25. Alone, Edward illustrated* The Fables of Aesop *(1909), Fabre's* Book of Insects *(1921), and* The Arabian Nights (Tales From One Thousand and One Nights) *(1924), which shows the strong influence of Japanese prints and Eastern miniature painting. He specialized in drawing animals and plants, often placed in fantastical settings.*

1, 2 *BOOK:* THE JUNGLE BOOK
by Rudyard Kipling
DATE: 1903

3 *BOOK:* HOURS OF GLADNESS
by M Maeterlinck
DATE: 1912

4, 5 *BOOK:* OUR LITTLE
NEIGHBORS, ANIMALS OF THE
FARM AND WOOD
DATE: 1921

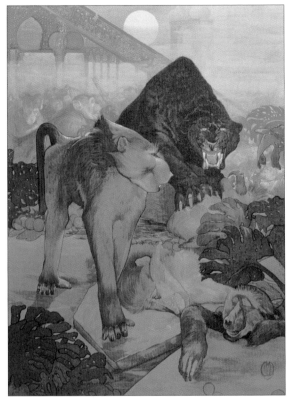

1

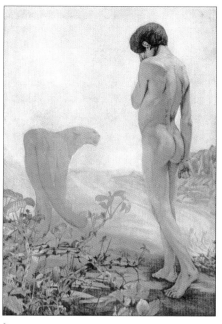

2

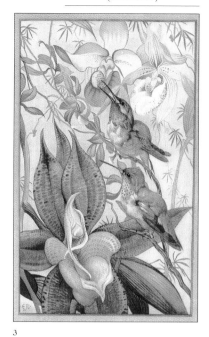

3

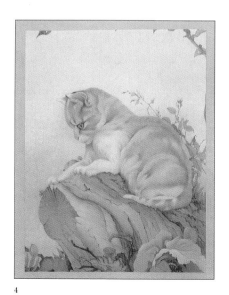

4

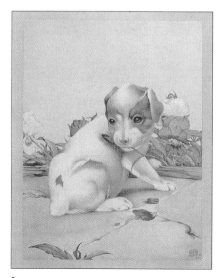

5

Born in Missouri, USA. Russell's childhood interest in drawing cowboys and Indians was to shape his life. He left school at 16 and worked as a cowboy, then as a fur-trapper. In 1888 he spent six months living with the Blackfoot Indians and learned to communicate with them in sign language. As an artist he was entirely self-taught. His wife Nancy encouraged him to become a full-time illustrator, handling his finances and organizing his commissions.

His work appeared in many magazines, including Recreation, Western Field, Sports Afield, *and* Outing, *and he later contributed to* Scribner's, McClures, *and* The Saturday Evening Post. *A contemporary of Fred Remington, his beautifully colored paintings captured the spirit of the life he depicted and showed a remarkable understanding of animal anatomy. He was elected posthumously to the Illustrators' Hall of Fame in 1985.*

1 *PAINTING:* COWBOYS
ROPING A STEER
DATE: c. 1900

2 *PAINTING:* COWBOYS
ROPING A STEER
DATE: 1904

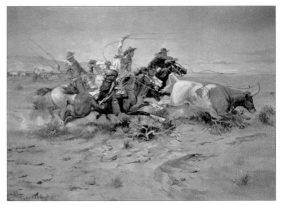

1

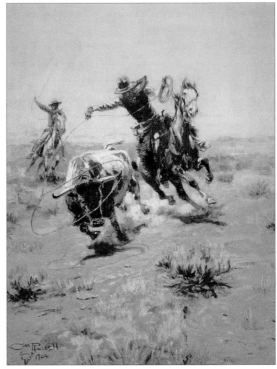

2

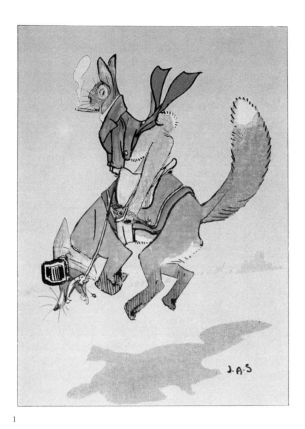

1

Born in London. He had no
formal training, but learned
his art while working for
the magazine Moonshine,
developing a particular talent
for drawing birds and animals
in pen and ink, which became
his specialty. Although comic
and usually clothed in human
attire, his creatures are
nevertheless entirely plausible
characters, his illustrations
for Uncle Remus (1901)
being excellent examples. He
had a long association with
Punch magazine from 1893
and drew for several other
magazines, including The
Sporting and Dramatic News
and Cassell's Family Magazine.
His caricatures for The Strand
Magazine, known as "Zig-Zags,"
proved so popular that they
were subsequently published as
a book, Zig-Zag Fables, in 1897.
Other books include The Three
Jovial Puppies (1907) and The
Life of a Foxhound (1910).

1–3 BOOK: UNCLE REMUS
by J Chandler Harris
DATE: 1901

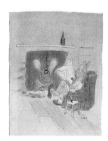

2

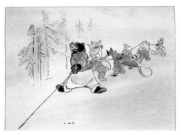

3

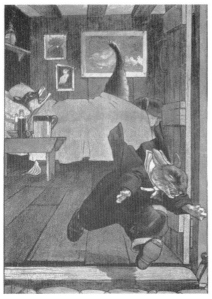

1

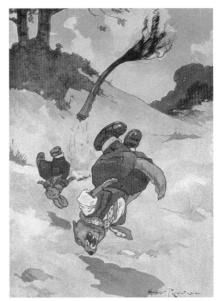

2

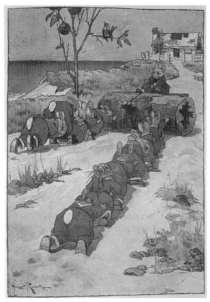

3

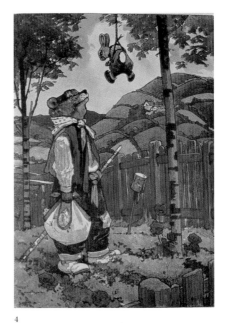

4

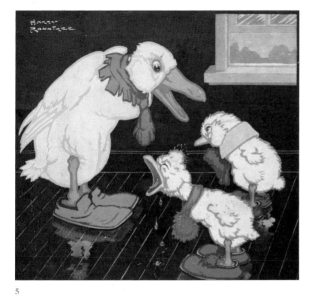

5

Born in Auckland, New Zealand, the son of a banker. He worked as a lithographer before moving to London in 1901. His humorous drawings of animals and children were commissioned by Little Folks, The Humorist, Playtime, and Punch. He became one of the most successful children's illustrators of his day and in 1914 was President of the London Sketch Club. Books illustrated include Alice in Wonderland (1908), Alice Through the Looking Glass (1928), and The Magic Wand (1908). Among his own works were Birds, Beasts and Fishes (1929) and Rabbit Rhymes (1934). He also illustrated for magazines such as The Sketch, The Graphic, and The Strand Magazine.

1–4 BOOK: UNCLE REMUS
by J Chandler Harris
DATE: 1906

5 ORIGINAL PRINT
DATE: NOT KNOWN

6, 7 BOOK: AESOP'S FABLES
DATE: 1924

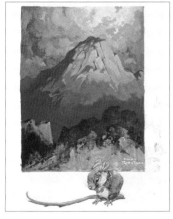

6

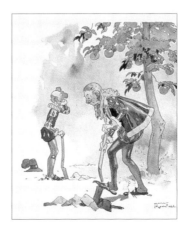

7

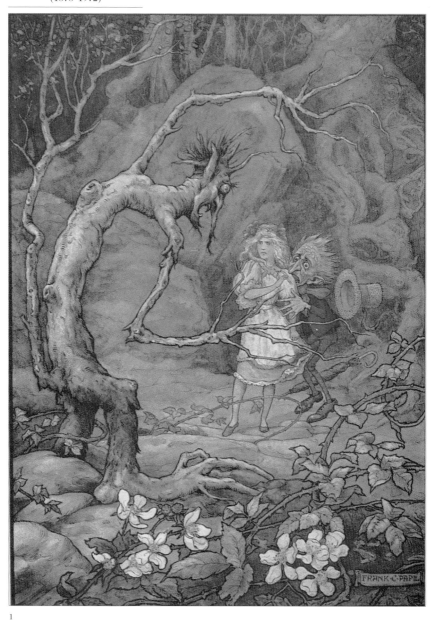

1

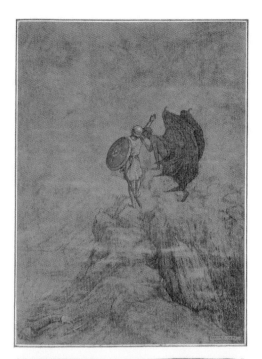

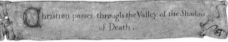

Christian passes through the Valley of the Shadow of Death.

Little biographical detail is known about this artist, but he was a prolific illustrator with an expert understanding of the various reproduction media. His finely drawn line work appeared in The Children of the Dawn (1908), The Book of Psalms (1912), and The Story Without an End (1912). He illustrated classics from The Pilgrim's Progress (1910) to Tales from the Arabian Nights (1934) and also contemporary novels, and contributed to The Boy's Herald, Cassell's Magazine, and The Pall Mall Magazine. His illustrations to six works by Anatole France, produced in the 1920s, are regarded as among his finest and he became something of a cult figure during that period. His wife, Agnes Stringer, collaborated with him on some projects, providing the color work to his drawings.

1 BOOK: THE PEDLAR AND HIS DOG by Mary C Rowsell DATE: 1922

2–5 BOOK: THE PILGRIM'S PROGRESS by John Bunyan DATE: c. 1909

2

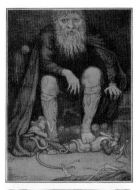

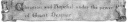

Here came to him a Hand with some of the leaves of the tree of life.

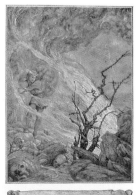

Christian on his way to Begaltys house.

3

4

5

LOUIS WAIN
(1860–1939)

Born in London. Attended the West London School of Art, 1877–80, and taught there during the following two years. Encouraged by his wife, Emily, he sold his first drawing of a cat (based on his own, Peter) to The Illustrated London News *in 1884. His first book,* Madam Tabby's Establishment *(1886), made him a household name as "the man who drew cats," and in 1890 he was made President of the National Cat Club, devising their coat of arms and motto. From 1890, Wain invented a world of "humanized" cats sporting top hats and monocles, playing tennis, and drinking tea. The public loved them, and Wain was approached to illustrate countless books, articles, and picture postcards. In 1907 he went to New York, where he drew a cat strip cartoon for* New York American. *In 1917 he produced an animated film,* Pussyfoot, *with the pioneer film-maker H F Wood. The first Louis Wain Annual appeared in 1901 and annuals appeared regularly until 1921, when the public appetite for Wain's drawings diminished. Diagnosed as schizophrenic at the age of 63, he spent his last years at the Royal Bethlem Hospital in south London.*

1 *CATS TEA PARTY*
(unpublished)
DATE: c. 1910

2 *THE CHAIRMAN*
(unpublished)
DATE: c. 1910

3 *POSTCARD*
DATE: NOT KNOWN

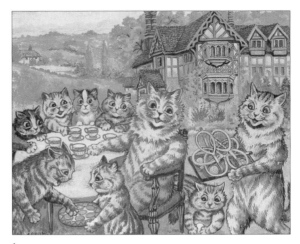

1

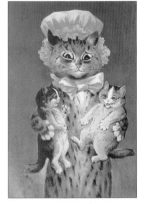

2

3

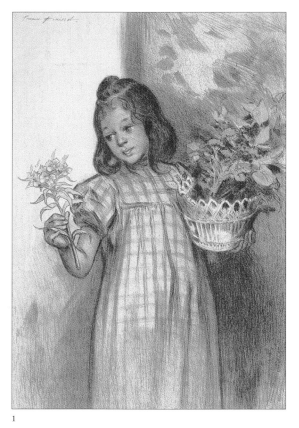

1

Born in Mossac, France. Brother of the artist Felix François Bouisset, he was a painter, engraver, and illustrator. His style was very much of the Art Nouveau period, and he is best remembered for his paintings of children and for his posters, most notably those for Meunier chocolate and Job papers. His work also appeared in the publications Le Capitan (1883) and L'Estampe Moderne (1899) and his illustrated books include Lajournée de Bébé (1885) and Les Bébés d'Alsace de Lorraine (1886). He died in Paris at the age of 66.

1 LABOUQUETIÉRE
(unpublished)
DATE: c. 1900

2 POSTER: "LONDON COUNTRY & WESTMINSTER BANK (PARIS) LTD"
DATE: 1919

3 ADVERTISEMENT: "CHOCOLAT DE L'UNION"
DATE: c. 1900

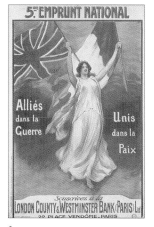

2

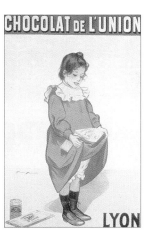

3

Born in Delaware, USA, and educated at the Art Students League in New York. Pyle is often referred to as "the father of American illustration" because of the enormous influence both of his work and his teaching. He taught at the Drexel Institute in Philadelphia and then at the Art Students League in New York before setting up his own art schools at Chadd's Ford, Pennsylvania, and Wilmington, Delaware, where no fees were charged. Some of his star pupils included N C Wyeth, Frank Schoonover, and Jessie Wilcox Smith. Books illustrated include The Merry Adventures of Robin Hood *(1883), a series of books which he also wrote retelling the legends of King Arthur, and* Book of Pirates *(1902). He also contributed to a number of magazines, including* Harper's.

1–3 *BOOK:* HOWARD PYLE'S
BOOK OF PIRATES
DATE: 1902

4 *MAGAZINE:* HARPER'S
MONTHLY
DATE: 1911

5 *MAGAZINE:* HARPER'S
MONTHLY
DATE: 1906

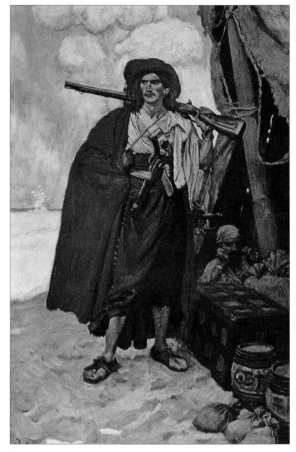

1

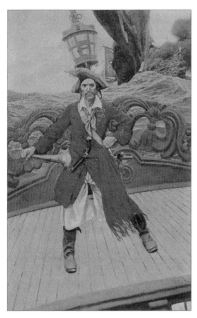

2

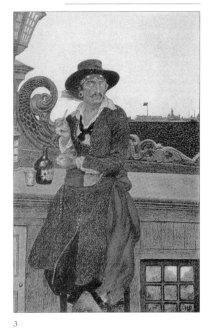

3

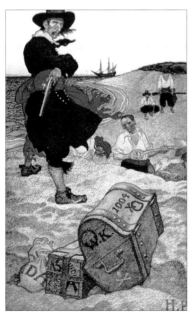

4

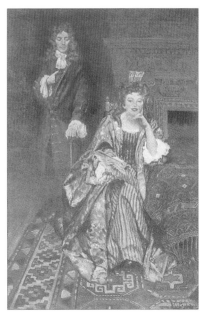

5

EL LISSITZKY
(1890–1941)

Born in Smolensk, Russia. Studied in Germany and took up book illustration on his return to Russia in 1912. He illustrated seven children's books, including The Kid *(1917), which revealed the influence of Marc Chagall,* Ukrainian Fairy Tales *(1919), and* The Four Billygoats *(1924). In 1919 he entered what he termed his "Proun" period, the name he gave to his abstract style and which was an acronym meaning "Project for the Establishment of the New Art." In 1920 he produced* Of Two Squares, *an abstract play book for children that showed a red square attacking and defeating a black square. In 1921 he returned to Germany, where he was deeply impressed by the Dadaists and Expressionists, and in 1925 wrote* The Isms of Art *with Hans Arp. Throughout his career he was a highly influential political artist, famous for his posters and his geometric use of typography. He designed the first flag of the Central Committee of the Communist Party of the Soviet Union and between 1932 and 1937 created a series of montages called "Building the USSR," which bring to mind the work of John Heartfield.*

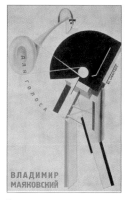

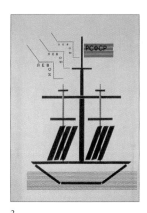

1   2

1, 2 *BOOK:* DLIA GOLOSA
(published in Russia)
DATE: 1923

3 *BOOK:* SOLNTSE NA IZLETE.
VTORAIA KNIGA STIKHOV
(published in Russia)
DATE: 1916

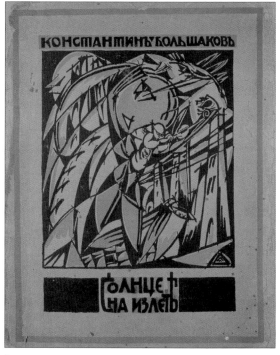

3

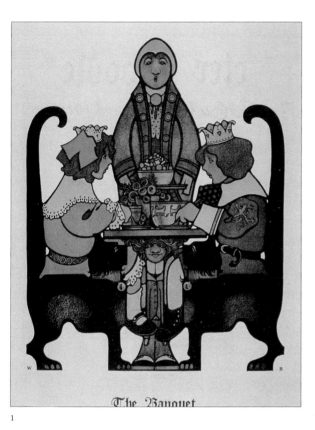

The Banquet

1

Born in Boston, USA. He started work at the age of 12 on a Michigan newspaper and in 1895 illustrated his first book, Fringilla by R D Blackmore, which clearly shows the influence of Beardsley and Art Nouveau. In the same year he founded his own Wayside Press Company in Springfield, Massachusetts, and developed his interest in typography and book design. He wrote, illustrated, and produced Peter Poodle: Toy Maker to the King (1906) and Launcelot and the Ladies (1927). He was also a talented poster designer and was art director of Collier's, Metropolitan, and The Century magazines.

1 BOOK: PETER POODLE: TOY MAKER TO THE KING
DATE: 1906

2 POSTER
DATE: c. 1920

3 BOOK JACKET: THE CHAP BOOK by Will Bradley
DATE: NOT KNOWN

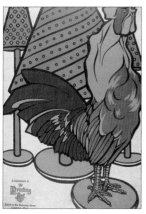

2

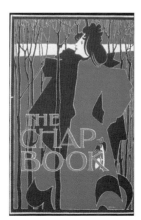

3

LUDWIG HOHLWEIN
(1874–1949)

Born in Wiesbaden, Germany. Trained as an architect and practiced until 1906, with a special interest in exhibition design. He was self-taught as an artist, but his first poster design, a sporting guns advertisement, won him immediate recognition. His personal interest in hunting, field sports, and animal life was frequently reflected in the style and content of his commercial work. Whether for tailoring or perfumes, tobacco or confectionery, or the circus, his posters show his confident handling of form, color, and pattern, assembled into bold and inventive imagery. In a poster for Grathwohl cigarettes (1921), the product is represented only by a tiny red glow at the mouth of a silhouetted figure; frequently figures appear as outlined shapes filled with solid blocks of color and pattern. In later work, high tonal contrasts and a network of interlocking shapes provide modeling of three-dimensional forms. His style is unmistakable and was powerfully adapted to propagandist posters in both world wars.

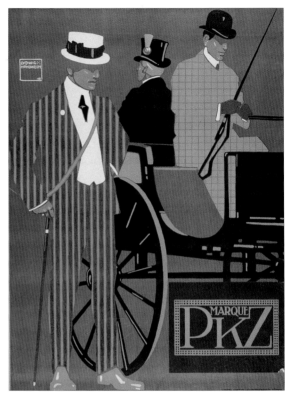

1

1 *ADVERTISEMENT: "PKZ"*
DATE: 1908

2 *ADVERTISEMENT: "MACHOLL COGNAC"*
DATE: c. 1910

3 *ADVERTISEMENT: "RIQUETTA"*
DATE: c. 1910

4 *WWI POSTER: "THE LUDENDORFF FUND FOR THE WAR WOUNDED"*
DATE: 1917

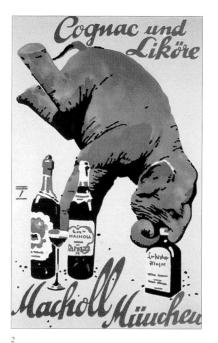

2

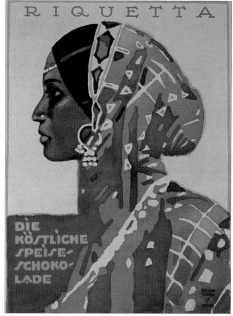

3

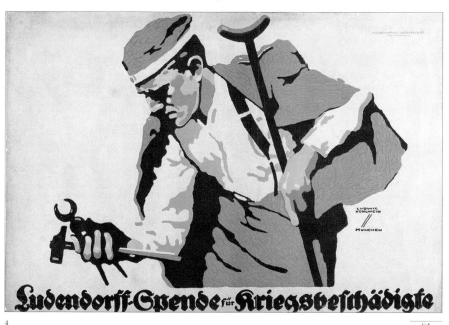

4

EDMUND DULAC
(1882–1953)

Born in Toulouse, France. He took evening classes in art while studying law at Toulouse University and won a scholarship to the Académie Julien in Paris, but left after three weeks to concentrate on his career as an illustrator. He was an Anglophile from childhood (his nickname at school was "l'Anglais") and settled in London in 1905. By the time he became a naturalized British subject in 1912, he was established as one of the leading artists in his field. During World War I he designed charity stamps and later Jubilee and Coronation stamps and was commissioned by Charles de Gaulle to design posters, bank notes, and postage stamps. He was a friend of WB Yeats, many of whose works he illustrated, and collaborated with him on a production of At the Hawk's Well, *composing the music and designing the costumes, sets, and make-up. Books illustrated include* Stories of the Arabian Nights, *retold by Laurence Housman (1907), Shakespeare's* The Tempest *(1908),* Stories from Hans Christian Andersen *(1911), and the novels of the Brontë sisters in ten volumes (1905). Dulac's brilliant use of flat color owes a great deal to the influence of Japanese prints and his passionate interest in Persian miniatures.*

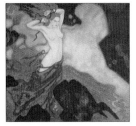

1

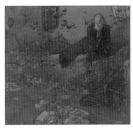

2

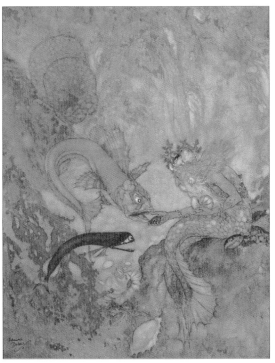

3

1 *BOOK:* KING ALBERT
DATE: 1914

2 *PAINTING:* THE ENTOMOLOGIST
DATE: 1909

3 *BOOK:* THE MERMAID KING *by Hans Christian Andersen*
DATE: 1911

4 *CARICATURE:* SIR EDWARD PENISONROSS
DATE: 1915

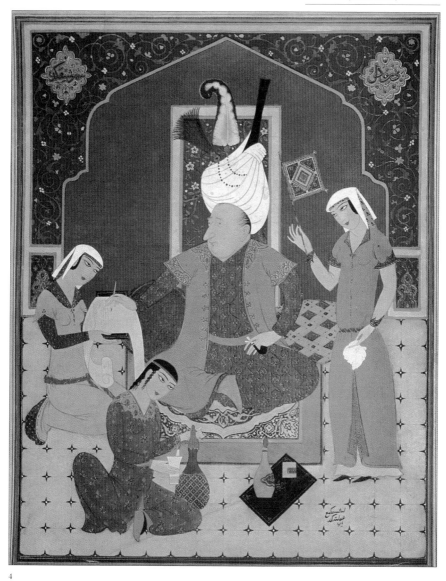

4

HENRY MATTHEW BROCK
(1875–1960)

Born in Cambridge, UK, younger brother of Charles Edmund Brock. Studied at Cambridge School of Art. He illustrated for numerous periodicals, including The Graphic, Punch, *and* The Sketch. *Books illustrated include Walter Scott's* Ivanhoe *(1900), Defoe's* Robinson Crusoe *(1904), Hans Andersen's* Fairy Tales and Stories *(1905), Dent's* The Novels of Jane Austen, *and R L Stevenson's* Treasure Island *(1928). He also designed posters for the D'Oyly Carte during the 1920s. Brock worked almost entirely in pen and ink. His flair for drama and action, and his fluent and vigorous line, made him popular as an illustrator of boys' stories. He was described by the illustrator A E Bestall as "probably the last of the era of perfectionists."*

1–3 *BOOK:* THE BOOK OF FAIRY TALES
DATE: 1914

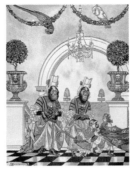

1

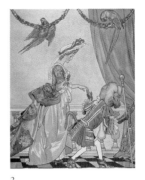

2

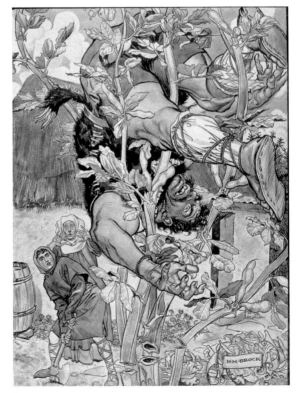

3

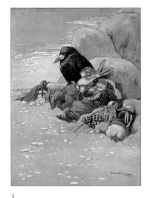

1

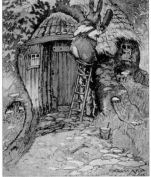

2

Born in Bradford, UK. Studied at Bradford School of Art and the Royal College of Art, London. He began work as a portrait painter but went on to a successful career as an illustrator of children's books. He contributed illustrations to children's stories in The Graphic, and book titles include Tales for Tiny Tots and The Rock-a-Bye Stories (1919), The Woodland Series (1919), Famous Animal Tales (1935), and The Brambledown Tales (1946). His work was published in the USA, Canada, and Australia as well as in the UK.

1 BOOK: THE TREASURE SEEKERS by E Nesbit
DATE: 1917

2 BOOK: THE HOUSE THAT JACK BUILT (traditional rhyme)
DATE: 1920

3 POSTER: "LONDON UNITED TRAMWAYS"
DATE: 1915

4 POSTER: "LONDON UNITED TRAMWAYS"
DATE: 1915

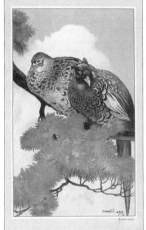

3

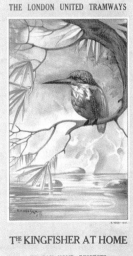

4

ROBERT ANNING BELL
(1863–1933)

Born in London. Trained at Westminster School of Art and the Royal Academy Schools. He also studied under Sir George Frampton in England and Morot in Paris. Books illustrated include Jack the Giant Killer and Beauty and the Beast *and* The Sleeping Beauty and Dick Whittington *(both published in 1894),* Poems *by John Keats (1897),* Shelley's Poems *(1902),* Shakespeare's *The* Tempest *(1901), and his most successful book,* A Midsummer Night's Dream *(1895). He also contributed to* The Yellow Book *quarterly. Bell's work was firmly rooted in the Arts and Crafts tradition, often featuring long, angular figures without shading contained within decorative borders. As well as being an illustrator, he was a sculptor and designer of stained glass and mosaics. (Examples of his mosaics may be seen at the Houses of Parliament and at Westminster Cathedral.) He taught at Liverpool Municipal College, the Glasgow School of Art, and the Royal College of Art and became a member of the Royal Academy in 1922.*

1 *BOOK:* DAILY CHRONICLE
PORTFOLIO
DATE: 1911

2 *BOOK PLATE*
DATE: 1910

3 *BOOK:* PALGRAVE'S GOLDEN
TREASURY
DATE: c. 1914

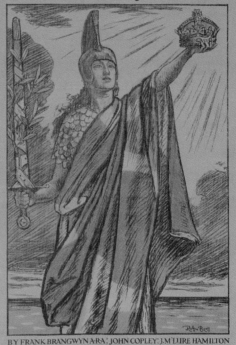

1

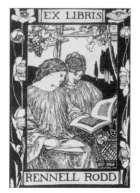

2

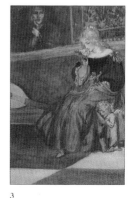

3

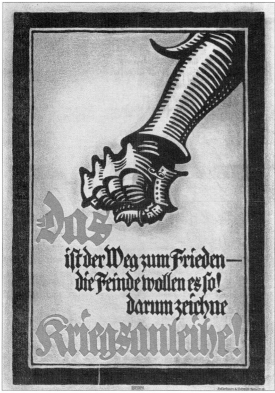

1

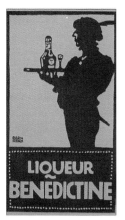

2

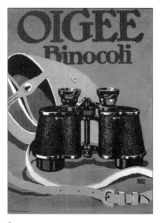

3

*Born in Stuttgart, Germany.
Mainly self taught, in 1905 he
won a competition sponsored
by the Berlin Chamber of
Commerce with a poster for
Priester matches, an image
which set the hallmark of his
style—descriptively economical
shapes, bold colors, and the
strong presence of the brand
name—later applied to posters
for Stiller shoes, Manoli
cigarettes, Osram lamps
and Adler typewriters. This
concentration on the advertised
product, eliminating all other
elements that might distract,
became known as sachplakat
(object-poster). During World
War I, Bernhard's expertise was
applied to war propaganda
posters. In 1920 he became the
first Professor of Poster Design
at the (then) Royal Academy in
Berlin, and with Dr Hans Sachs
he established the magazine
Das Plakat. In 1923 he moved
to the USA, where he became
a founding member of the New
York design firm Contempora,
Inc. with Rockwell Kent
and others. His design skills
were applied to trademarks,
packaging emblems, and
printers' ornaments, and he
is well known for type design,
with 36 typefaces to his credit,
including Bernhard-Antigua
and Fraktur.*

1 *WWI POSTER: "WAR LOAN"
DATE: 1917*

2 *ADVERTISEMENT:
"BENEDICTINE LIQUEUR"
DATE: 1921*

3 *ADVERTISEMENT: "OIGEE
BINOCULARS"
DATE: 1912*

EMIL CARDINAUX
(1877–1937)

Born in Berne, Switzerland. He begun drawing as a child and by the age of 18 he had already illustrated The Legend of William Tell. *He studied art under Paul Volmars at Berne University and in 1898 studied under Franz Stuck at the Munich Art Academy. He traveled and lived in various parts of Europe and from 1903–04 worked as an artist in France and Italy. His versatile technique enabled him to succeed as a caricaturist, illustrator, and poster designer.*

1 *TRAVEL POSTER: "ZERMATT"*
DATE: 1908

2 *TRAVEL POSTER: "DAVOS"*
DATE: 1918

3 *TRAVEL POSTER:*
LOTSCHBERG
DATE: c. 1916

4 *POSTER: "SWISS COUNTY EXHIBITION, BERNE"*
DATE: 1914

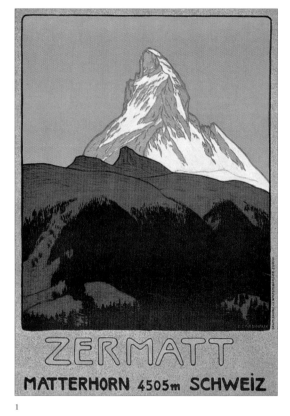

1

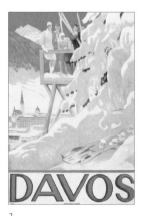

2

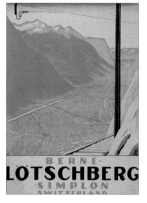

3

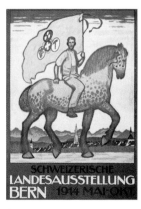

4

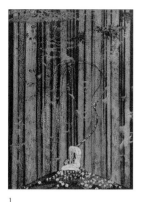

1

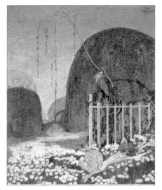

2

Born in Copenhagen, Denmark. He spent his childhood surrounded by artists, writers, and musicians, among them Ibsen and Grieg. His early talent for drawing was encouraged by his parents and at the age of 17 he was sent to the Académie Julien in Paris, where he came under the influence of Art Nouveau, Japanese art, and the work of Aubrey Beardsley. His first commission was for In Powder and Crinoline (1913), which was later published as Twelve Dancing Princesses in the USA. He also illustrated One Thousand and One Nights (1918–22), East of the Sun and West of the Moon (1914), and Hans Andersen's Fairy Tales (1924). Nielsen was a brilliant colorist whose intensely decorative style came under a number of influences, including Beardsley, Alastair, Vernon Hill, Middle Eastern art, and the sculptural effects of the incipient Art Deco. After exhibiting in New York in 1917 he emigrated to the USA in 1922, moving to Hollywood in 1939, where he designed for a number of film companies, including Walt Disney.

1 BOOK: THE KING ALBERT BOOK
DATE: 1914

2, 3 BOOK: IN POWDER AND CRINOLINE
DATE: 1913

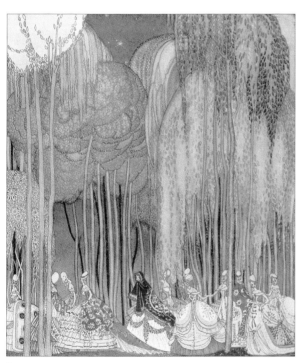

3

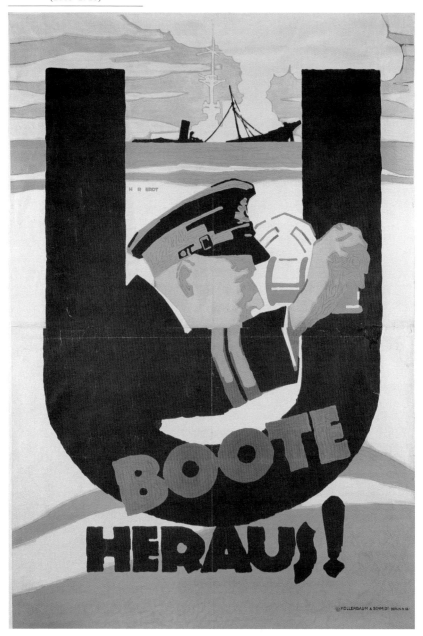

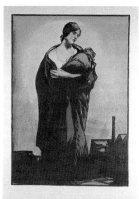

MOTHERS-VOTE LABOUR

1

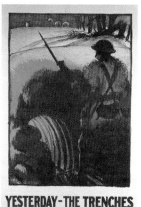

YESTERDAY-THE TRENCHES

2

HANS RUDI ERDT
(1883–1918)

Born in South Bavaria. After leaving grammar school he studied at the Industrial Art College in Munich, where he was the protégé of his professor, Maximilian von Dasio. In 1905 he moved to Berlin and became a commercial poster artist. His style tended toward two-dimensional caricatures and his early work shows the influence of Ludwig Hohlwein, whereas in his later drawings one can see his admiration for the compositions and technique of Lucian Bernhard.

1 *POSTER*
DATE: 1917

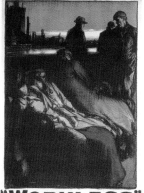

"WORKLESS"

3

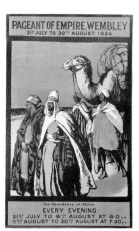

4

GERALD SPENCER PRYSE
(1882–1956)
Born in Ashton, UK. He studied art in London and Paris, became a member of the International Society, and exhibited at Venice from 1907. He lived in Morocco from 1950 until his death. His illustrations appeared in Punch, The Strand Magazine, *and* The Graphic.

1 *POSTER*
DATE: c. 1919

2 *POSTER*
DATE: c. 1919

3 *POSTER*
DATE: c. 1919

4 *POSTER*
DATE: 1924

Born in London. Attended
evening classes at Lambeth
School of Art while working as
a clerk. By 1891 he was selling
illustrations to The Pall Mall
Gazette, Scraps, and Illustrated
Bits, and in 1892 he joined the
staff of The Westminster Budget
Magazine. Rackham was one of
the foremost Edwardian book
illustrators, specializing in tales
with a mystical, magical, or
legendary theme. Until 1905 he
was highly regarded as a line
illustrator, but the introduction
of color printing in the early
1900s enabled him also to use
the subtle tints and muted tones
for which he is now so widely
known. He was influenced by
Doyle, Houghton, and Beardsley,
as well as the prints of Dürer
and Altdorfer. He illustrated over
50 books, including The Fairy
Tales of the Brothers Grimm
(1900), Rip Van Winkle (1905),
Alice in Wonderland (1907),
The Arthur Rackham Fairy Book
(1933), Christina Rossetti's
Goblin Market (1933), Edgar
Allan Poe's Tales of Mystery and
Imagination (1935), and Kenneth
Grahame's The Wind in the
Willows (1940).

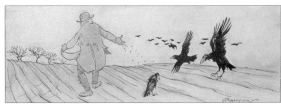

1

1 ORIGINAL DESIGN: THE
HOUSE THAT JACK BUILT
(traditional rhyme)
DATE: 1913

2 BOOK: PEER GYNT
by Henrik Ibsen
DATE: 1936

3 SOURCE: NOT KNOWN
DATE: NOT KNOWN

4 BOOK: THE NIGHT BEFORE
CHRISTMAS by C C Moore
DATE: 1931

5 BOOK: PETER PAN IN
KENSINGTON GARDENS
by J M Barrie
DATE: 1906

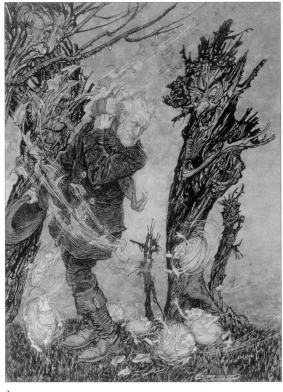

2

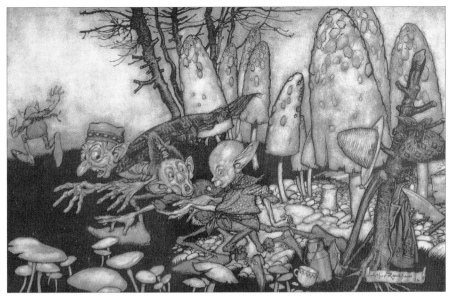

3

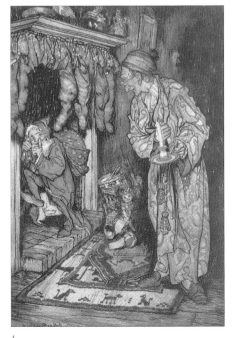

4

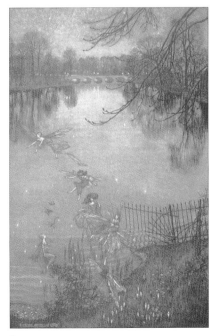

5

FRED REMINGTON
(1861–1909)

Born in New York State. He was educated for a short while at Yale University before going west to work as a cowboy, where he began drawing images of the disappearing Wild West. The early drawings which he sent to Harpers magazine were published only after being redrawn by staff artists, but his work improved and he eventually joined the magazine staff himself. Books illustrated include Ranch Life and the Hunting Trail *(1888) by his friend Theodore Roosevelt, and Longfellow's* The Song of Hiawatha *(1891).*

1 *PAINTING:* STAMPEDED BY LIGHTNING
DATE: 1908

2 *PAINTING:* SMOKE SIGNALS
DATE: 1905

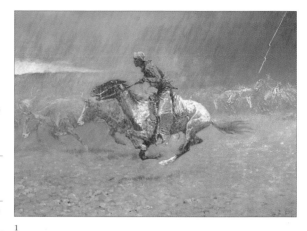

1

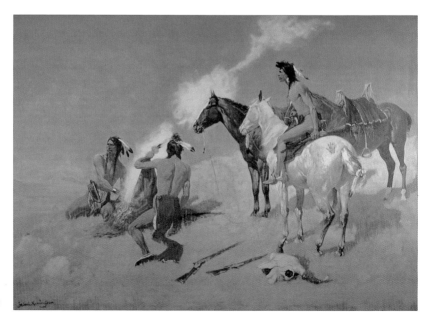

2

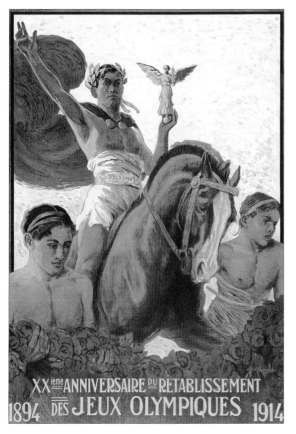

*Born in Neuenburg,
Switzerland. Studied fine art
at the art school in La Chaux-
de-Fonds under Georges Aubert
and at the Académie Julien in
Paris. He began his career as an
illustrator for various Parisian
publishing companies, and from
1906 he illustrated books and
worked for the Geneva Tribune
newspaper. His favorite
themes were circus and racing
horses, which he both painted
and sculpted. His brilliant
use of color and typography
ensured his success as a
poster artist, and his work for
various clients covered a broad
range of subjects.*

1 *POSTER: "20th ANNIVERSARY
OF THE REVIVAL OF THE
OLYMPIC GAMES"
DATE: 1914*

2 *TRAVEL POSTER: "WINTER
SPORTS, FRANCE"
DATE: 1905*

3 *TRAVEL POSTER:
"NEUCHATEL, SWITZERLAND"
DATE: 1914*

1

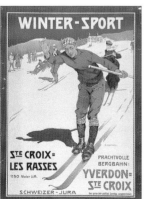

2

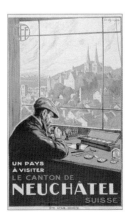

3

Born in Londonderry, Northern Ireland. He began work at the age of 17 designing Christmas cards for Messrs Marcus Ward in Belfast. He moved to London in 1883 and became a regular contributor to The English Illustrated *magazine. Thomson was a great admirer of E A Abbey, whose influence can be seen in his excellent black-and-white drawings, which perfectly captured the period details of the stories he illustrated. From the mid-1880s, his work graced the pages of novels by authors such as Goldsmith, Jane Austen, Sheridan, and Mrs Gaskell. His first major success was* Tristram's Coaching Days and Coaching Ways *(1888), followed in 1891 by the even more successful* Vicar of Wakefield *by Oliver Goldsmith. Other books illustrated included Goldsmith's* She Stoops to Conquer *(1912), J M Barrie's* Quality Street *(1913), and several Shakespeare plays. He also illustrated for most of the major magazines, including* Black & White, The Pall Mall Budget, *and* The Graphic. *A pioneer of the new photomechanical process in the early 1900s, Thomson did his best work between 1900 and 1915 and was enormously influential on a whole generation of younger artists.*

---

1 *BOOK:* QUALITY STREET *by J M Barrie*
DATE: 1913

---

2 *BOOK:* EMMA *by Jane Austen*
DATE: c. 1900

---

3 *BOOK:* THE MERRY WIVES OF WINDSOR *by William Shakespeare*
DATE: 1910

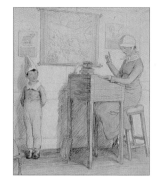

1

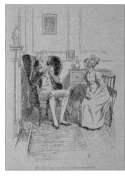

2

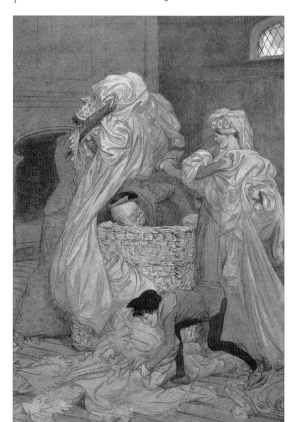

3

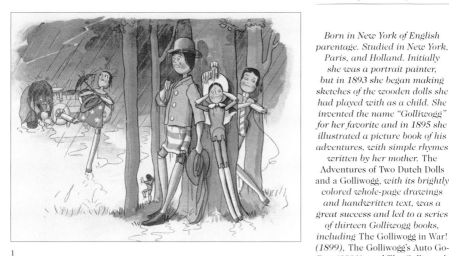

1

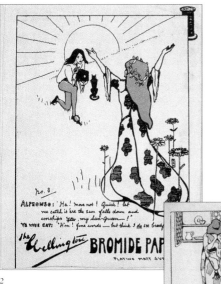

2

3

Born in New York of English parentage. Studied in New York, Paris, and Holland. Initially she was a portrait painter, but in 1893 she began making sketches of the wooden dolls she had played with as a child. She invented the name "Golliwogg" for her favorite and in 1895 she illustrated a picture book of his adventures, with simple rhymes written by her mother. The Adventures of Two Dutch Dolls and a Golliwogg, *with its brightly colored whole-page drawings and handwritten text, was a great success and led to a series of thirteen Golliwogg books, including* The Golliwogg in War! *(1899),* The Golliwogg's Auto Go-Cart *(1901), and* The Golliwogg's Fox Hunt *(1905). The original manuscripts and the doll itself were auctioned for charity and are now kept at Chequers, the country home of British Prime Ministers.*

1 *BOOK:* THE GOLLIWOGG'S
AUTO GO-CART
DATE: 1901

2 *ADVERTISEMENT:*
"WELLINGTON BROMIDE"
PAPERS
DATE: c. 1910

3 *ADVERTISEMENT:*
"WELLINGTON CELLULOID
FILM"
DATE: c. 1910

(Baroness H van Tuyllvan Serooskerken.) Born in Rotterdam, Holland. Her parents were patrons of the arts and on the advice of the French illustrator Maurice Boutet de Monvel (by whose work she was deeply influenced), she was educated at the Rotterdam Academy. Her first British book, Our Old Nursery Rhymes, *was published in 1911 and over the next two decades her delicate pastel illustrations of children became increasingly popular. Her work appeared in* Old Dutch Nursery Rhymes *(1917), A A Milne's* A Gallery of Children *(1925), and RL Stevenson's* A Child's Garden of Verses *(1926). Her interest in a child's world extended beyond illustration, as she also designed children's tableware.*

1–3 *BOOK:* OUR OLD NURSERY RHYMES
DATE: 1911

1 ORANGES AND LEMONS

2 HERE WE GO ROUND THE MULBERRY BUSH

3 HICKORY DICKORY DOCK

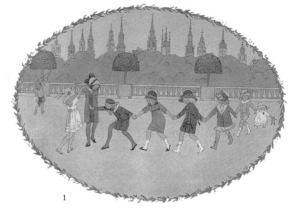

1

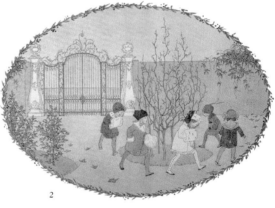

2

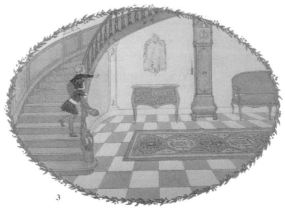

3

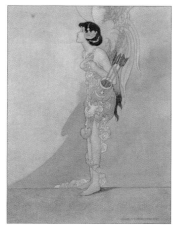

1   2

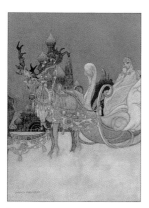

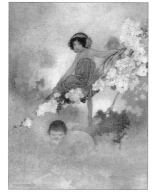

3   4

*Born in London, the brother
of William Heath Robinson.
He won a scholarship to the
Royal Academy Schools but
was financially unable to take
it up. Instead he worked as an
apprentice printer during the
day and attended art classes
in the evenings. In 1895 his
illustrations were printed in* The
Studio *magazine, which led to
him being invited to illustrate R
Stevenson's* A Child's Garden of
Verse *(1895). He subsequently
illustrated well over a hundred
books, mostly for children,
including Lewis Carroll's* Alice's
Adventures in Wonderland
(1907), The Big Book of Fairy
Tales *(1911), and Oscar Wilde's*
The Happy Prince and Other
Stories *(1913). He illustrated for
magazines including* Black &
White, The Graphic, The Queen,
and The Yellow Book. *Robinson
painted delicate and sensitive
watercolors, and his black-and-
white illustrations, reflecting the
influence of Beardsley, Dürer,
and Walter Crane, made him as
famous in his day as Beardsley
had been in his.*

1 *BOOK:* THE SENSITIVE
PLANT *by Percy Shelley*
DATE: 1911

2–4 *BOOK:* THE HAPPY PRINCE
AND OTHER STORIES *by
Oscar Wilde*
DATE: 1913

*Born in Philadelphia, USA.
He worked as a clerk while
taking evening classes at
the Pennsylvania School of
Industrial Art until he was
expelled for leading a student
rebellion in 1879. He attended
the Pennsylvania Academy of
Fine Arts, but left in 1880 to
become a freelance illustrator
and writer. He married
Elizabeth Robins, the authoress,
and they settled in England in
1884. There the Pennells wrote
a biography of their friend the
artist James McNeill Whistler
and also brought the young
illustrator Aubrey Beardsley to
public attention with an article
on his work in the first edition
of* The Studio *magazine. Pennell
lectured in illustration at the
Slade School of Art and the
Royal College of Art and won
many awards, including gold
medals at the Paris and Dresden
Expositions. His illustrations
appeared in magazines such as*
The Yellow Book, The Graphic,
The English Illustrated, *and* Pall
Mall. *Books illustrated include*
The Jew at Home *(1892) and
Henry James's* A Little Tour
in France *(1900), as well as
numerous travel books written
by his wife.*

1 *WW I POSTER: "BUY LIBERTY
BONDS"*
DATE: 1917

2 *ENGRAVING*
DATE: 1909

3 *ENGRAVING*
DATE: 1911

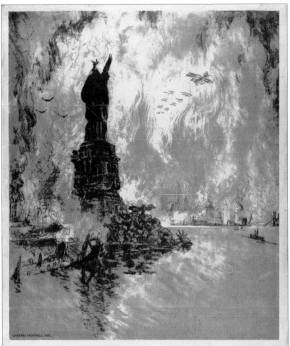

1

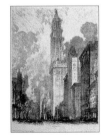

2

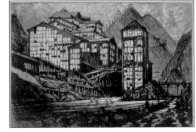

3

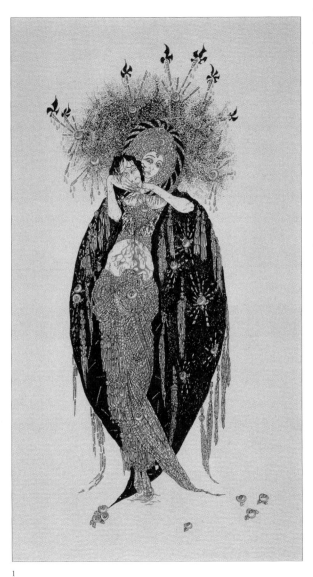

Real name: Baron Hans Henning
Voight. Born in Karlsruhe,
Germany. Self-taught as an
artist, he was also a dancer,
mime artist, pianist, and writer.
His career as a graphic artist
was launched in 1914 when
John Lane published Forty-
Three Drawings by Alastair.
He also illustrated Oscar
Wilde's The Sphinx (1920),
Edgar Allan Poe's The Fall of
the House of Usher (1928),
Choderlos de Laclos's Les
Liaisons Dangereuses (1929),
and his own Fifty Drawings by
Alastair (1925). Like Beardsley,
whom he greatly admired,
Alastair's illustrations combined
decorative elegance with a
fascination for the perverse and
the sinister. His drawings, in
black and white and sometimes
colored ink, were compositions
inspired by novels, poems,
plays, or figures of legend
or history. He exhibited at
the Weyhe Gallery in New York
in 1925.

1 BOOK: THE SPHINX
by Oscar Wilde
DATE: 1920

1

FRANK EARLE SCHOONOVER
(1877–1972)

Born in Oxford, New Jersey, USA. Studied under Howard Pyle at the Drexel Institute and then at Pyle's school at Chadd's Ford, Pennsylvania. He studied hard, and the influence of Pyle as mentor is evident in his painterly style and his choice of subject matter. Both men had a love of the colonial past and the Wild West, and Schoonover subscribed to Pyle's view that an illustrator must be closely involved with the subject of his work. To this end he traveled widely and in difficult circumstances to record the lives of cowboys, Indians, and Eskimos. His work appeared in Arctic Stowaways *(1917),* Ivanhoe *(1922), J W Schultz's* Quested of the Desert *(1925), M P Smith's* Boy Captives of Old Deerfield *(1929), and V M Collier's* Roland the Warrior *(1934), among others.*

1 *PAINTING:* BELLEAU WOOD
DATE: 1918

2 *ADVERTISEMENT: "COLT'S FIREARMS"*
DATE: 1925

3 *BOOK:* JOAN OF ARC
DATE: 1920

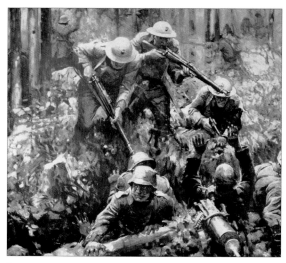

1

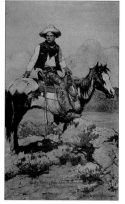

2

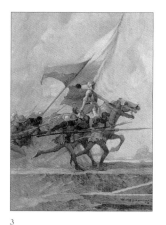

3

JESSIE MARION KING
(1876–1949)

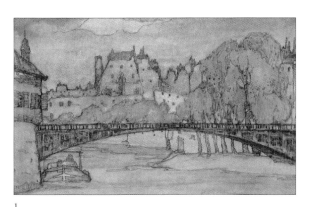

1

*Born in Scotland. Studied
at Glasgow School of Art,
where she later taught, and
at the Royal College of Art in
London. An early member of the
"Glasgow School" with Charles
Rennie Mackintosh, she was
very much a part of the Art
Nouveau movement. Her style is
often attributed to the influence
of Aubrey Beardsley, but the
delicacy of her line and color
was the product of her own
imaginative world, populated
as it was by her real belief in
fairies. In 1902 she won a gold
medal for her drawings at the
Turin International Exhibition
of Modern Decorative Art.
Her illustrated books include
William Morris's* The Defence
of Queen Guinevere and Other
Poems *(1906), Milton's* Comus
(1906), and Oscar Wilde's A
House of Pomegranates *(1915),
after which there was a
noticeable strengthening in her
use of both line and color. She
also illustrated for a number
of magazines, including* The
Studio.

1 *BOOK:* PONTS DE PARIS
DATE: 1912

2 *BOOK:* THE STUDIO
DATE: 1919

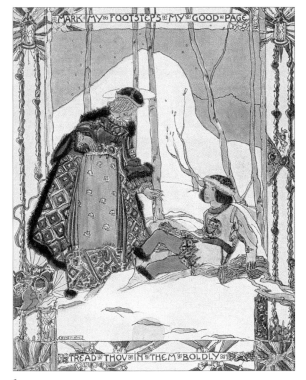

MARK MY FOOTSTEPS MY GOOD PAGE

TREAD THOU IN THEM BOLDLY

2

*Born in Philadelphia, USA.
Studied at the Pennsylvania
Academy of Fine Art under
Thomas Eakins and at the
Drexel Institute under Howard
Pyle. Abandoning her original
plans to be a kindergarten
teacher, she concentrated
instead on a career as an
illustrator. She became very
successful, especially with
her portrayals of mothers and
babies and children at work and
at play, and she also illustrated
a number of books, including
Robert Louis Stevenson's* A
Child's Garden of Verses *(1905),
Charles Kingsley's* The Water
Babies *(1911), Johanna Spyri's*
Heidi *(1922), a U.S. edition
of* Alice in Wonderland, *and
Louisa M Alcott's* Little Women
*(1915). She worked for a
number of advertising clients
and contributed to* Ladies' Home
Journal, Collier's, Harper's,
Scribner's, *and* The Century.
*From 1918 to 1932 her pictures
of adorable, beautifully dressed
children appeared monthly on
the covers of* Good Housekeeping
magazine.

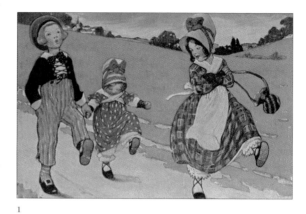

1

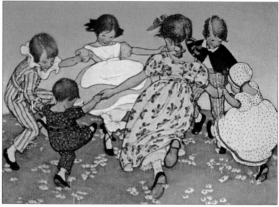

2

1–3 *BOOK:* MOTHER GOOSE
DATE: 1914

4 *BOOK:* THE WATER BABIES
by Charles Kingsley
DATE: 1911

5 *BOOK:* THE EVERYDAY FAIRY
BOOK
DATE: 1917

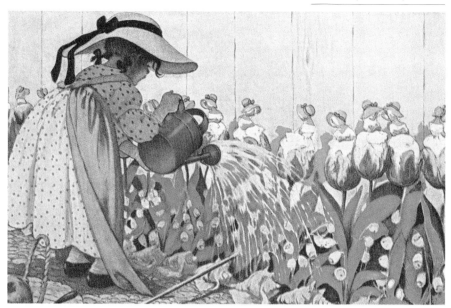

3

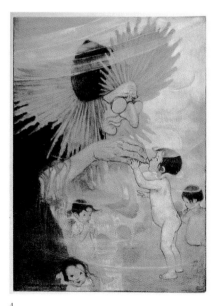

4

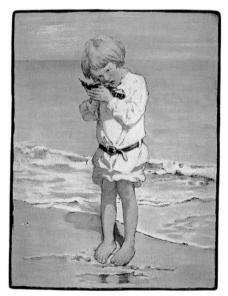

5

*Born in Edinburgh, Scotland.
Trained at Heatherley's
Art School in London and
subsequently joined the staff
of* The Illustrated London
News, *where he remained
until 1907. Books illustrated
include* The Song of Solomon
(1909), The Imitation of Christ
(1908), Joseph Conrad's The
Duel *(1905), Chaucer's* The
Canterbury Tales *(1913), and
Malory's* Le Morte D'Arthur
*(1911). Magazine clients
included* Tatler, The English
Illustrated Magazine, Black
& White, The Idler, *and* The
Sketch. *From the 1920s, Flint
made his name as a technically
brilliant water colorist,
specializing in scenes featuring
sensual semi-nude nymphets
in idealized landscapes. These,
and his color illustrations for
lavishly produced gift books
published by the Medici Society,
were enthusiastically acclaimed
by the public. He was elected
Royal Academician in 1933 and
was knighted in 1947.*

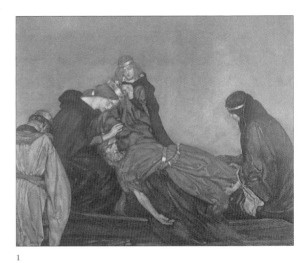

1

1 *BOOK:* LE MORTE D'ARTHUR
by Thomas Malory
DATE: 1911

2 *BOOK:* THE HEROES *by
Charles Kingsley*
DATE: 1912

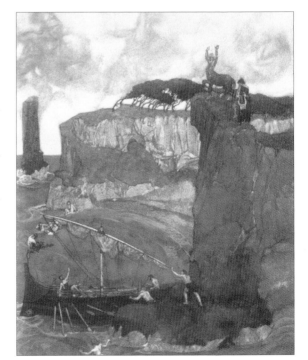

2

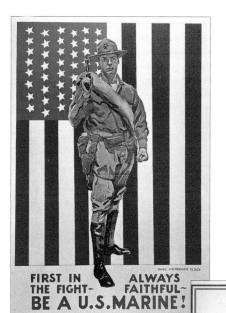

1

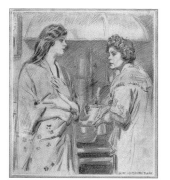

2

Born in New York. He started drawing as a child and by the age of 14 was already financially independent of his family through selling his drawings. At 14 he sold his first illustration to Life *magazine, and subsequently became a member of its staff. At 16 he studied at the Art Students League in New York and at 20 he spent a year in England where he illustrated his first book,* Yankee Girls Abroad. *His magazine clients included* Judge, Life, Good Housekeeping, Cosmopolitan, Liberty, *and* Harper's Weekly. *From 1903 he drew portraits of the Hollywood stars for* Photoplay *magazine, and these were later collated in a book called* Celebrities *(1951). Other books include* City People *(1909) and* The Adventures of Kitty Cobb *(1912). Flagg designed 46 posters for the war effort during World War I, including the "I Want You" image for* Leslie's Weekly. *During World War II, his "Uncle Sam" posters re-emerged and could be found outside recruiting stations across America.*

1 *POSTER:* "U.S. MARINES"
DATE: c. 1914

2 *POSTER:* "U.S. ARMY"
DATE: c. 1914

3 *MAGAZINE:* COSMOPOLITAN
DATE: 1918

4 *MAGAZINE:* COSMOPOLITAN
DATE: 1918

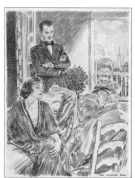

3

4

Illustrator, graphic designer, and poster designer. His work tended to rely on strong, simple imagery and flat colors, and was perfectly suited to the style that emerged from the development of the London Underground and LNER railway posters in the 1930s. In 1926 he wrote and illustrated a book, Training in Commercial Art, which covered every aspect of the subject. In his instructions on the subject of travel posters he reveals the underlying principles of his own work: "It is not easy to render trees, grasslands, water etc. in broad, flat treatment. Make careful studies of the different formations and shapes of trees, shrubs etc. Whenever possible avoid putting in clouds. Clear skies indicate fine weather and clear atmosphere." His work was prolific and he was a champion of the belief that the aesthetic statements of commercial art were as important and as valid as those found in fine art.

1 ADVERTISEMENT: "SHELL"
DATE: 1926

2 POSTER: "LNER"
DATE: 1920

3 POSTER: "LNER"
DATE: 1924

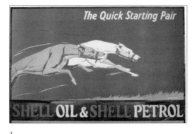

1

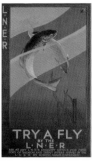

2

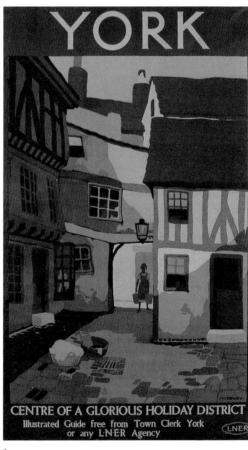

3

MAXWELL ARMFIELD
(1882–1972)

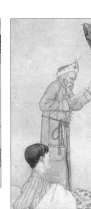

1

Born in Ringwood, UK. Studied at Birmingham School of Art and in France and Italy. He lived in the USA between 1915 and 1922 and lectured on design and stage decoration at the universities of Columbia, California, and New Mexico—he also published a number of books on technique. He was also a painter, etcher, poet, composer, and writer. Books illustrated included his own The Hanging Garden *(1914), Andersen's* The Ugly Duckling and Other Tales *(1913), Armfield's* Animal Book *(1922), and Shakespeare's* The Winter's Tale. *Armfield was a leading member of the Tempera Society, and his decorative works, executed with care and refinement, were influenced by early Renaissance painting.*

1, 2 *BOOK:* ARMFIELD'S
ANIMAL BOOK
DATE: 1922

3, 4 *BOOK:* HANS ANDERSEN'S
TALES
DATE: 1910

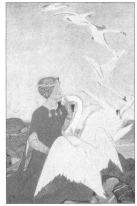

2

3

4

LEONETTO CAPIELLO
(1875–1942)

Born at Livorno, Italy. After studies in his native town he settled in Paris to work as a poster artist and illustrator. He published a book of caricatures (1896) and contributed to Le Rive, Le Journal, Le Figaro, and Le Gaulois. His theater and advertising posters—such as "Folies-Betgère" (1900), "Cinzano" (1910), and "Le P'tit Jeune Homme" (for the play Polaire, 1910) show his mastery of line and rhythm, and he held to the importance of these elements, believing color to be a secondary factor in the success of a design. In reducing the graphic elaboration that had been a feature of earlier poster work, Capiello moved towards the modern interpretation of the poster as an instantly attractive and memorable image.

1 ADVERTISEMENT: *"REVEL UMBRELLAS"*
DATE: 1922

2 ADVERTISEMENT: *"THERMOGENE"*
DATE: 1909

3 ADVERTISEMENT: *"CAMPARI CORDIAL"*
DATE: 1921

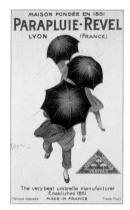

1

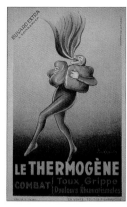

2

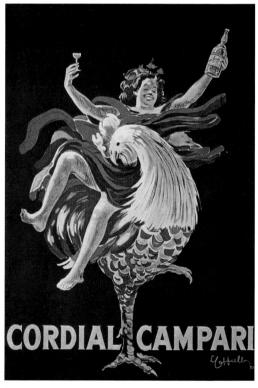

3

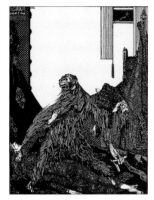

1   2

Born in Dublin, Ireland, the son of a stained-glass artist. Studied at Dublin Metropolitan School of Art, where he won a traveling scholarship in 1914 to study early stained glass in the Ile-de-France. Clarke was one of the most successful followers of Beardsley, his imagery encompassing a powerful blend of horror, drama, and humor. He is remembered today both for the beauty of his illustrations for the fairy tales of Hans Andersen and Charles Perrault and for the power and invention of his horror-fantasy style, which has influenced many fantasy and science fiction artists since. His illustrations for Edgar Allan Poe's Tales of Mystery and Imagination *(1919) and Goethe's* Faust *(1925) moved an art critic writing in* The Studio *in 1923 to write: "Never before have these marvellous tales been visually interpreted with such flesh-creeping, brain-taunting illusions of horror, terror and the unspeakable." Clarke was also a talented designer of stained glass and won the only gold medals awarded for stained glass at the Kensington Exhibitions in 1911, 1912, and 1913. He died of tuberculosis at the age of 42.*

1 *BOOK:* THE YEARS AT THE SPRING
DATE: 1920

2, 3 *BOOK:* TALES OF MYSTERY AND IMAGINATION *by Edgar Allan Poe*
DATE: 1919

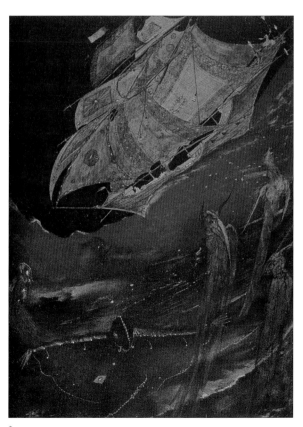

3

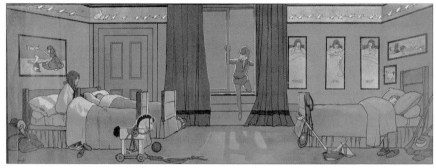

1

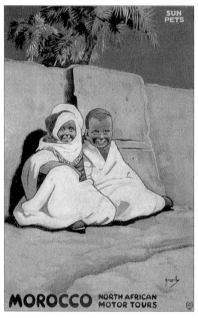

2

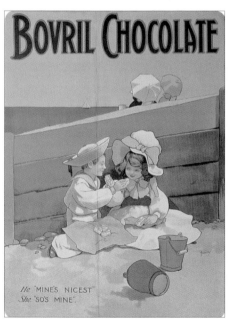

3

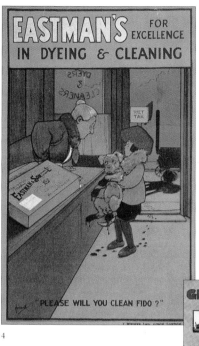

"PLEASE WILL YOU CLEAN FIDO ?"

4

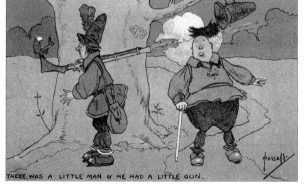

REALIZING THE FAMOUS PICTURE

5

THERE WAS A LITTLE MAN & HE HAD A LITTLE GUN.

6

JOHN HASSALL
(1868–1948)

Born in Walmer, UK, and educated in Devon and Heidelberg, Germany. After a brief spell as a farmer in Manitoba, Canada, he took up art, and had drawings accepted by The Graphic *and* Punch. *After studying art in Antwerp and Paris, he returned to England in 1895, where he became a successful cartoonist and advertising artist, designing some of the most effective posters of his day, including the well-known "Skegness Is So Bracing" (1908). He was granted a civil pension by George VI for his services to poster art. Hassall began illustrating children's books in the late 1890s, using the bold outlines and flat color washes that characterized his posters. He also illustrated* John Hassall's New Picture Book *(1908),* Keep Smiling *(1916), and* Ye Berlyn Tapestrie *(1916), and he contributed to* The Daily Sketch, Illustrated Bits, The Graphic, The Idler, *and* The West End Review.

1 POSTER: "THE ARRIVAL OF PETER PAN"
DATE: c. 1920

2 TRAVEL POSTER: "NORTH AFRICAN MOTOR TOURS"
DATE: c. 1922

3 ADVERTISEMENT: "BOVRIL CHOCOLATE"
DATE: c. 1920

4 ADVERTISEMENT: "EASTMAN'S CLEANING"
DATE: c. 1900

5 ADVERTISEMENT: "HMV GRAMOPHONES"
DATE: c. 1915

6 BOOK: NURSERY RHYMES ILLUSTRATED
DATE: c. 1910

Born in Zurich, Switzerland. Apprenticed to a lithographer, then went on to study at the Konigliche Akademie in Munich and also in Paris and London. In 1920 he worked on stage designs for productions in Berlin and Zurich, and in the same year began to teach lithography and life drawing at the School of Arts and Crafts in Zurich. His commercial work in the 1920s typically included "super-real" lithography images advertising clothing products—coats, hats, shoes—but he also produced highly graphic information posters constructed of geometric shapes and typography. During the 1930s he developed a looser, almost painterly style. His career demonstrated a range of design interests, from illustration and advertising design to stage design and mural painting.

1 *ADVERTISEMENT: "PKZ"*
DATE: 1922

2 *ADVERTISEMENT: "FACO*
FLOOR COVERINGS"
DATE: c. 1919

3 *ADVERTISEMENT:*
"DOSENBACH'S SHOE
MARKET"
DATE: c. 1919

4 *ADVERTISEMENT: "WECK"*
DATE: c. 1919

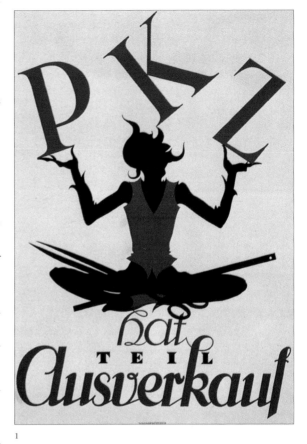

1

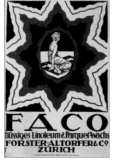

2

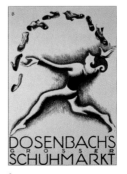

3

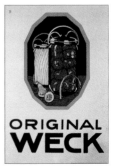

4

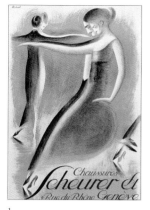

1

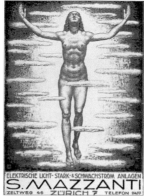

2

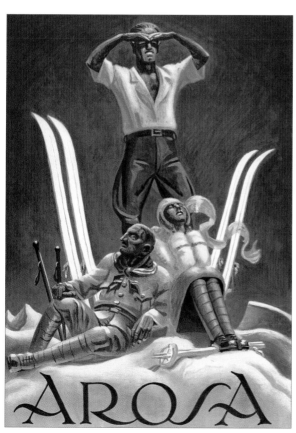

3

Born in Zurich. During his lifetime Bickel worked as an illustrator, painter, sculptor, and graphic artist. From 1900 to 1904 he was an apprentice lithographer, and then spent four years in a Zurich advertising agency while taking evening classes at the School of Arts and Crafts, where he studied under E Stiefel. In 1908 he started his own advertising agency and continued his studies until he moved to Italy in 1912. He spent a year there and was strongly influenced by the works of Michelangelo and Leonardo da Vinci. On his return to Switzerland he made his first attempts at sculpture and from 1914 to 1917 concentrated on portraiture, etching, and landscape painting. From 1917 until his death he was primarily a commercial artist, designing and illustrating stamps, posters, and murals.

1 *ADVERTISEMENT: "SCHEURER SHOES" DATE: 1920*

2 *ADVERTISEMENT: "MAZZANTI LIGHTING" DATE: 1915*

3 *TRAVEL POSTER: "AROSA" DATE: 1927*

JEAN DE BOSSCHERE
(1878–1953)

Born in Uccle, Belgium. Studied
at the Beaux Arts d'Anvers.
After working in Paris, Brussels,
London, and Italy, he finally
settled at Fontainebleau,
near Paris, in 1929. His work
was wide-ranging as writer,
illustrator, designer, printer,
and book collector. His first
book as author and illustrator
was Béale-Gyne (1909); his
own books included The City
Curious (1920) and Job le
Pauvre (1923), and Gulliver's
Travels (1920) and Don Quixote
(1922) were among the classic
titles that he illustrated.
He also contributed to The
Little Review, The Monthly
Chapbook, The New Coterie,
and Reveille. In his Beardsley-
esque images, with solid blacks
set against rhythmic lines, the
characterization sometimes has
a hint of the surreal.

1, 2 BOOK: THE POEMS OF
OSCAR WILDE
DATE: 1927

3, 4 BOOK: THE CITY CURIOUS
DATE: 1920

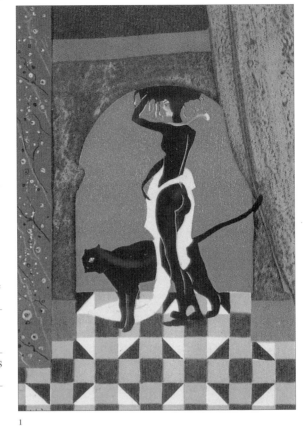

1

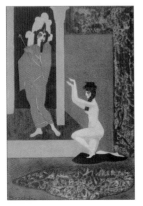

2

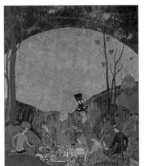

3

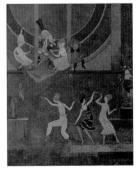

4

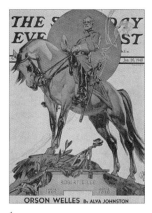

1

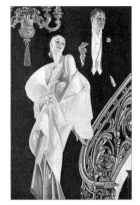

2

*Born in Montabour, Germany.
In 1882 he moved with his
parents to Chicago, USA and
at age 16 was apprenticed
to an engraving company, at
the same time taking evening
classes at the Chicago Art
Institute. In 1896 he won first
prize in* The Century *magazine's
competition to illustrate one of
their covers (Maxfield Parrish
came second), and he and his
younger brother studied at
the Academie Julien in Paris
for two years before returning
to the USA to set up their
own studio. His illustrations
appeared in magazines such as*
Collier's, Success, Up to Date,
and The Saturday Evening
Post. *He also illustrated war
bond posters (during World
War II) and advertisements for
Kellogg's cornflakes, Ivory soap,
Chesterfield cigarettes, and
Arrow collars and shirts. He
originated the Arrow Shirt collar
man, which became the epitome
of elegant style sought after by
the public.*

1 *MAGAZINE:* THE SATURDAY
EVENING POST
DATE: 1940

2 *ADVERTISEMENT: "ARROW
COLLARS"*
DATE: 1913

3 *POSTER*
DATE: c. 1916

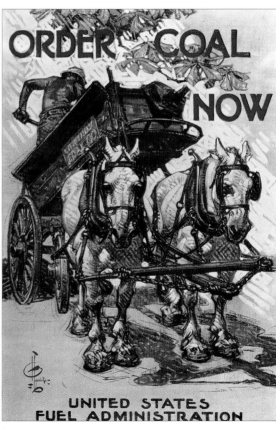

3

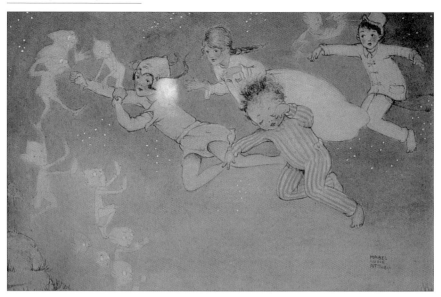

1

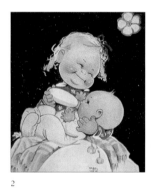

2

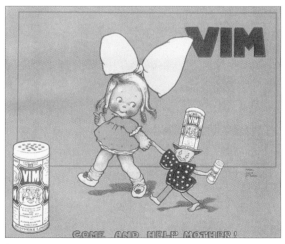

3

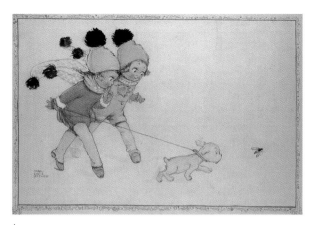

4

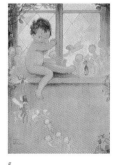

5

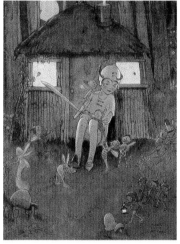

6

Born in London. Studied at the
Regent Street and Heatherley
Art Schools. From 1911 until
the end of her life, Attwell's
work appeared in annuals and
gift books and on countless
advertisements, posters,
calendars, wall plaques,
and greeting cards, which
she designed for Valentine
of Dundee. Her chubby,
mischievous toddlers, often
featured in situations with
adult overtones, conveyed a
sentimental and nostalgic view
of daily life between the wars.
During the first decades of
the century Attwell illustrated
such fairy-tale classics as
Mother Goose (1910), Alice in
Wonderland (1911), and Hans
Andersen's Fairy Tales (1914),
as well as Charles Kingsley's
The Water Babies (1915) and J
M Barrie's Peter Pan and Wendy
(1921). She also contributed
to The Tatler, The Bystander,
Graphic, and The Illustrated
London News.

1, 5, 6 BOOK: PETER PAN AND
WENDY by J M Barrie
DATE: 1921

2 GREETING CARD
DATE: c. 1920

3 ADVERTISEMENT: "VIM
CLEANING POWDER"
DATE: c. 1910

4 POSTER: "WHERE DO FLIES
GO IN WINTER-TIME?"
DATE: c. 1915

Born in Cork, Ireland. His parents wanted him to be a doctor but, after failing at medical school, he was eventually allowed to attend the Slade School of Art in London. His career was then stalled by World War I, during which he served at Gallipoli, and it was not until 1918 that he became a freelance artist, specializing in wood engraving. His early work tended to the simplicity of silhouettes, but in time he developed an extraordinarily precise technique that brought a great richness of detail to his engravings. In 1924 he bought the Golden Cockerel Press and set up as a printer of fine editions. He sold it in 1933 and lectured on book production at Reading University until 1942, when he left to concentrate on his own work and to travel. In all he illustrated 61 books and was the author of 14, including Lovely Is the Lee *(1945),* Coming Down the Wye *(1952),* Sweet Cork of Thee *(1951),* Coming Down the Seine *(1953), and* Trumpets from Montparnasse *(1955). His last work,* Till I End My Song, *was published in 1957, a year before his death.*

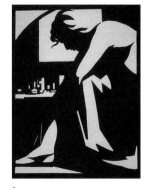

1

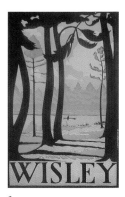

2

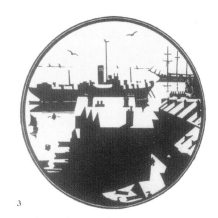

3

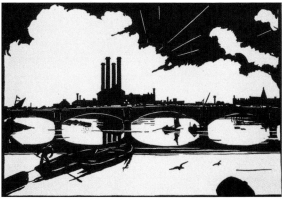

4

1 *BOOK:* THE GIRL IN THE GARRET *by Robert Gibbings*
DATE: 1921

2 *POSTER:* "LONDON TRANSPORT"
DATE: 1922

3 *WOOD ENGRAVING:* FOWEY HARBOUR
DATE: 1921

4 *WOOD ENGRAVING:* CHELSEA BRIDGE
DATE: 1921

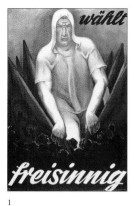

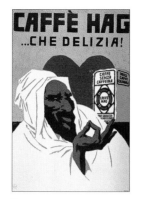

1

2

Born in Munich, Germany, son of the portrait painter Franz Moos. In 1897 he began his career as an illustrator for a Munich daily newspaper. In 1915 he established himself in Munich, where he divided his time between painting mountain landscapes and working for a local design group. His excellent draughtsmanship, combined with gentle but graphic use of color, ensured his success both as an illustrator of posters and as a scenic artist.

1 POSTER: *"VOTE FOR FREEDOM OF THE SPIRIT"* DATE: 1935

2 ADVERTISEMENT: *"CAFFE HAG"* DATE: 1927

3 TRAVEL POSTER: *"ST MORITZ"* DATE: 1929

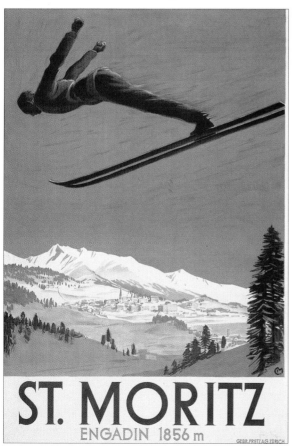

3

GEORGE STUDDY
(1878–1948)

Born in Devon, UK. Studdy developed a childhood interest in drawing while confined to a hospital bed, and later contributed his work to boys' magazines while a student at Dulwich College. On graduating from Heatherley's School of Art he worked as an engineer's draughtsman until 1906, when, after seeing the Royal Academy Summer Show, he was inspired to become a humorous artist. He illustrated regularly for The Sketch *magazine, where he developed the character of "Bonzo," the mischievous puppy which made him famous and which appeared on postcards, jigsaw puzzles, and posters. In fact Bonzo became so popular that he escaped the confines of the media normally available to illustrators and appeared on ashtrays, car mascots, sweets, cigarette cards, and other ephemera, all of which have become collectable items today. He also appeared in books and annuals and became a star of stage and screen. This craze peaked in the 1920s and Bonzo's popularity declined after Studdy's death from lung cancer in 1948.*

1, 2 *BOOK:* A BOX OF TRICKS
DATE: 1922

3, 4 *BOOK:* PUPPY TAILS
DATE: 1922

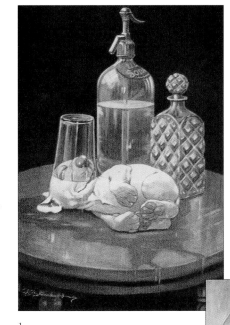

1

2

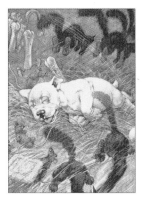

3

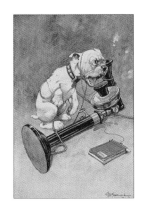

4

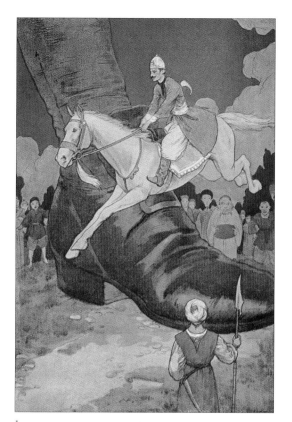

1

Born in Wolstanton, UK. Studied at Burslem School of Art, the Royal College of Art, and in Italy. The range of his work included painting, book illustration, and ceramic and stained glass design. From 1935 to 1938 he held the post of Principal at the Regent Street Polytechnic School of Art in London. As an illustrator he is known for work on children's books such as Charles Kingsley's The Water Babies *(1922),* Stories of King Arthur *(1925), and* Grimm's Fairy Tales *(1930), and he contributed to the periodical* Holly Leaves. *His skill as a water colorist is reflected in the pleasing coloring of his illustrative work.*

1, 2 *BOOK:* GULLIVER'S TRAVELS *by Jonathan Swift*
DATE: 1920

3 *BOOK:* GRIMM'S FAIRY TALES
DATE: 1930

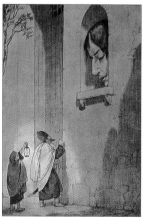

2

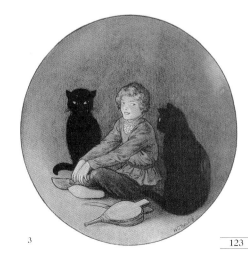

3

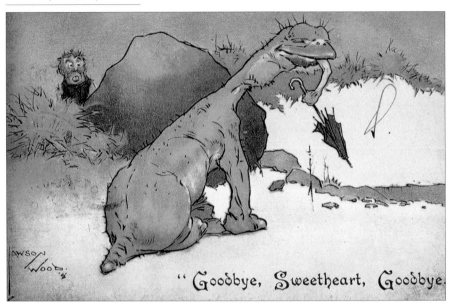

"Goodbye, Sweetheart, Goodbye."

1

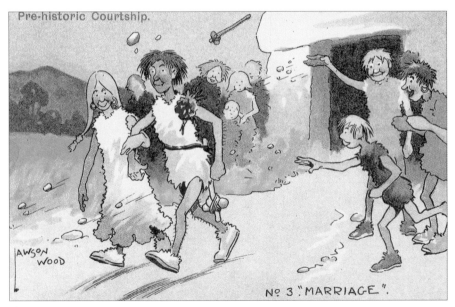

Pre-historic Courtship.

Nº 3 "MARRIAGE".

2

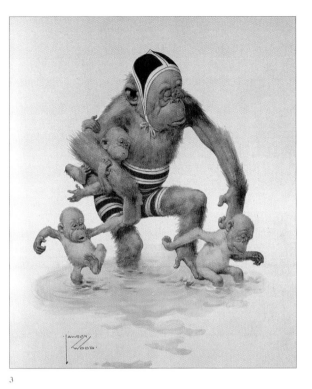

3

*Born in London. Studied at
Heatherly's and the Slade Art
School and at Frank Calderori's
School of Animal Painting.
From 1896 to 1902 he was
chief artist at the magazine
publishers Arthur Pearson Ltd.,
during which time he gained
valuable practical experience in
commercial work and learned
about the printing process
so that he could best ensure
the quality of his published
drawings. During his career
he became very popular with
the public for his witty and
technically brilliant illustrations
of animals and people, and he
contributed to* Graphic, The
Illustrated London News, *and*
Punch. *He also illustrated a
number of books, including* Old
Nursery Rhymes *(1931),* Lawson
Wood's Fun Fair *(1931), and
his famous series* The Merry
Monkeys *(1946). He was a close
friend of Tom Browne and a
fellow member of the London
Sketch Club.*

1 *POSTCARD*
DATE: 1906

2 *POSTCARD*
DATE: 1906

3, 4 *BOOK:* THE MERRY
MONKEYS *by Arthur Groom*
DATE: 1946

5 *BOOK:* BRUSH, PEN AND
PENCIL *by A E Johnson*
DATE: 1910

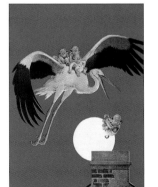

4

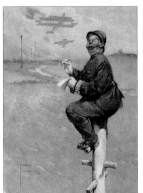

5

Born in London. Studied at the Académie Julien in Paris, Goldsmith's College School of Art in London, and in Italy. An accomplished landscape and architectural painter, he was one of the artists commissioned for poster work by London Midland & Scottish Railways and London Underground during the 1920s and 1930s. Images such as "The Heart of the Empire," an aerial view of Westminster and the Houses of Parliament, "Trafalgar Square," and "Chigwell," a graphic view of a Tudor-style inn, show Taylor's superb grasp of architectural structure and detail and a subtle approach to color. "Hampstead Fair" describes the holiday crowd enjoying the fair in a riot of bold, bright hues. His control of line in black-and-white rendering is equally crisp and immediate.

1 *POSTER: "ENSIGNETTE"*
DATE: c. 1915

2 *POSTER: "LONDON UNDERGROUND"*
DATE: 1920

3 *POSTER: "LONDON & NORTH EASTERN RAILWAY"*
DATE: c. 1923

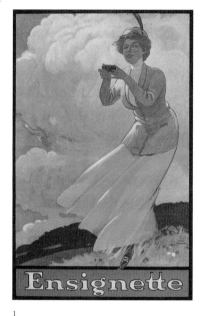

1

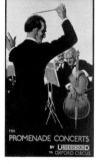

2

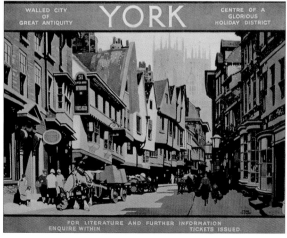

3

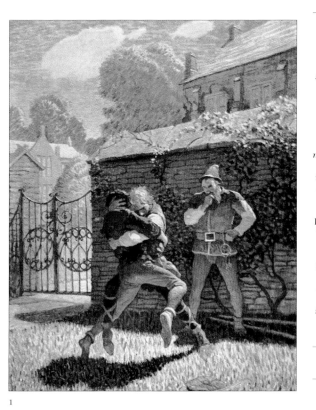

1

Born in Needham, USA. Wyeth was a devotee of his teacher, Howard Pyle. He depicted similar subjects—medieval life, Americana, and pirates—and captured dramatic scenes in rich decorative colors. He was extremely prolific, and during his lifetime produced more than 3,000 illustrations, murals, still lifes, and landscape paintings. Among them were more than 25 books for Charles Scribner's Sons' Classic Series, including J Boyd's Drums *(1928), Stevenson's* David Balfour *(1924), and J F Cooper's* The Deerslayer *(1925), some of which are still in print today. One of the finest examples of his work is J F Cooper's* Last of the Mohicans *(1919). He was an extremely popular figure in America, and his skills were inherited by his extraordinarily talented family—most notable being his son Andrew.*

1, 2 *BOOK:* ROBIN HOOD
DATE: 1921

3 *PAINTING:* INDIAN BRAVE
FISHING
DATE: c. 1900

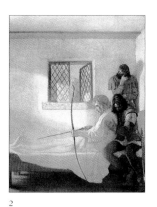

2

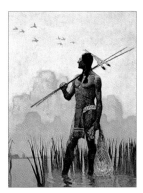

3

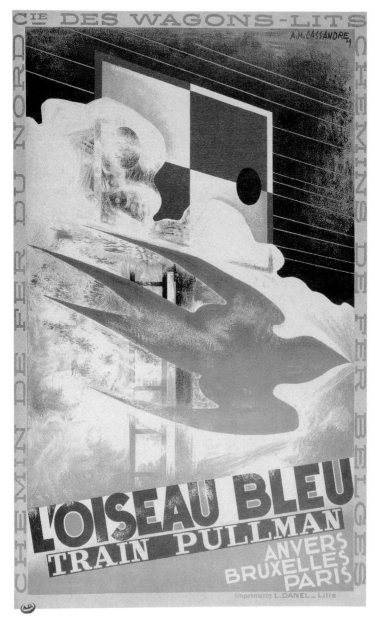

1

Born Adolphe Mouran in Russia. Studied at the Académie Julien in Paris. From 1922 to 1928 he designed posters for Hachard and Co., and in 1930 he founded the Alliance Graphique with Charles Loupot and Maurice Moyrand. Influenced by Léger, Delaunay, and the Italian Futurists, he took elements from avant-garde painting and design and popularized them in his brilliant posters, widely acknowledged as among the best to have come out of France during the 1930s. His designs for the French National Railways, and those for the ocean liners L'Atlantique (1931) and Normandie (1935), are classics of their genre. He also designed theater sets, costumes, and typefaces for Olivetti and ran a small art school where André François was one of his pupils.

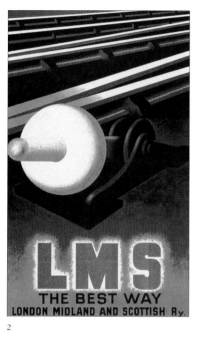

2

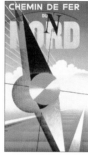

3

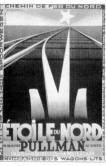

4

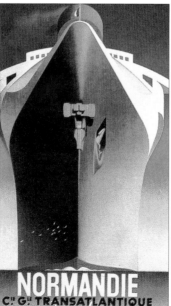

5

1 *POSTER: "BELGIAN RAILWAYS"*
DATE: 1929

2 *POSTER: "LONDON, MIDLAND SCOTTISH RAILWAY"*
DATE: 1928

3 *POSTER: "FRENCH NORTHERN RAILWAYS"*
DATE: 1929

4 *POSTER: "BELGIAN RAILWAYS"*
DATE: 1927

5 *POSTER: "FRENCH TRANSATLANTIC LINE"*
DATE: 1935

WILLY POGANY
(1882–1955)

Born in Szeged, Hungary. He started working while still a child, to help support his family after his father's death, and paid for his own education at the Budapest Technical School, where he studied engineering by giving tuition to fellow students. He later attended the Academy of Art in Budapest and studied art in Paris and Munich. In 1906 he moved to London, where he became a protégé of Edmund Dulac (a fellow member of the London Sketch Club) and where he became a very successful illustrator. Books illustrated include The Rime of the Ancient Mariner *(1910),* The Rubaiyat of Omar Khayyam *(1909), and Goethe's* Faust *(1912). In 1915 he settled in New York, where he continued to illustrate books and also designed hotel interiors and stage sets. He worked in Hollywood as an art director for Warner Studios until the 1930s. Pogany's best illustrations were in pen and ink, a medium in which he was remarkably fluent.*

1 *MAGAZINE:* LE JOURNAL DE LA DECORATION
DATE: c. 1900

2 ORIENTAL MOTIFS NO 4
DATE: c. 1900

3 ORIENTAL MOTIFS NO 3
DATE: c. 1900

4 *BOOK:* LEGENDS OF THE MIDDLE AGES
DATE: 1914

5, 6 *BOOK:* NURSERY RHYMES
DATE: 1919

7 *BOOK:* GULLIVER'S TRAVELS
by Jonathan Swift
DATE: 1919

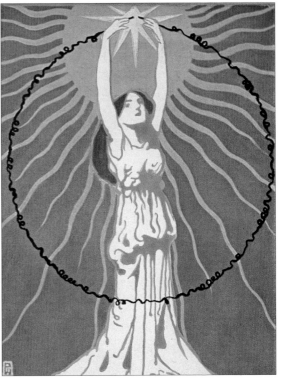

1

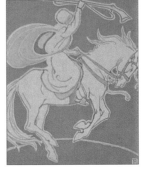

2

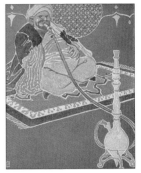

3

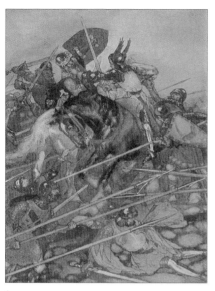

4

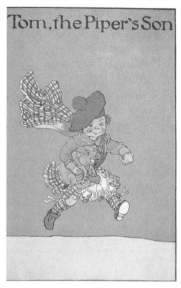

5

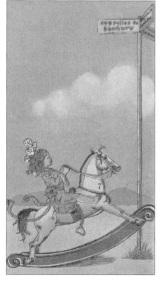

6

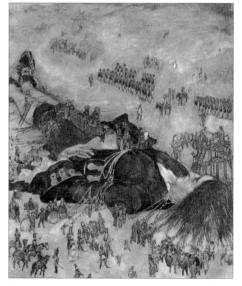

7

Born in London. His father was an artist and Sullivan studied under him until the age of 20, when he joined The Daily Graphic. *Although perhaps overshadowed by Dulac and Rackham, he quickly established himself as a fine draughtsman with two distinct styles—black-and-white work in pen and ink and a looser, gentler treatment with washes and chalk lines. He was a devotee of Phil May and, in his own words, wanted to express "the character the solid body is possessed of—the spiritual essence . . . and the impact made on the whole complex mind and not only upon, or by, the retina." He contributed to many of the publications of his day and illustrated nearly 20 books, including Wells'* Modern Utopia *(1905),* The Pilgrim's Progress *(1901), and* The Rubaiyat of Omar Khayyam *(1913). He was also highly influential as a teacher, lecturing at Goldsmith's College of Art and producing a detailed instruction manual,* The Art of Illustration *(1921).*

1 *BOOK:* DREAM OF FAIR WOMEN *by Alfred Tennyson*
DATE: 1900

2 *ADVERTISEMENT: "SHELL FUELS"*
DATE: 1923

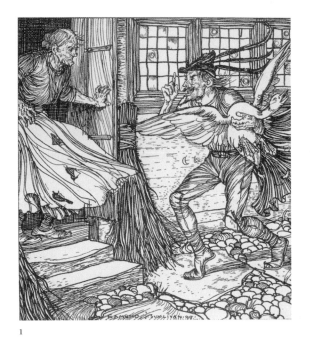

1

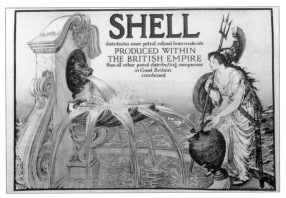

2

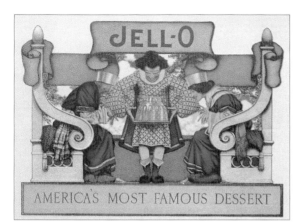

1

*Born in Philadelphia, USA.
Educated at Haverford College
and the Pennsylvania Academy
of Fine Arts and studied under
Howard Pyle at the Drexel
Institute. He illustrated for a
number of magazines, including*
Harper's Weekly, Collier's, *and*
Time. *Books illustrated include*
Dream Days *(1906) by Kenneth
Grahame,* Poems of Childhood
(1889) by Eugene Field, and
The Knave of Hearts *(1925) by
Louise Saunders. His unique
combination of color, exotic
characters, and fanciful settings
won him much popular acclaim
during his lifetime.*

1 *ADVERTISEMENT:*
"JELL-O DESSERT"
DATE: 1924

2 *BOOK:* THE KING ALBERT
BOOK
DATE: 1914

3 *MAGAZINE:* THE CENTURY
DATE: c. 1930

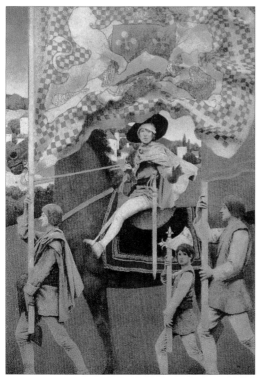

2

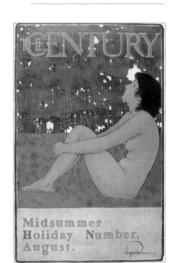

3

ERIC GILL
(1882–1940)

Born in Brighton, UK. Studied at Chichester Art School and the Central School of Arts and Crafts in London. He began his career as a letter-cutter and sign writer, then turned to figure carving in wood and stone. In 1913 he became a Catholic and after World War I, formed the Guild of St. Joseph and St. Dominic—a society of craftsmen dedicated to reviving a religious attitude toward art and craft. A versatile artist, he was a very skilful engraver, illustrating many books for Robert Gibbings at the Golden Cockerel Press from 1924. He was also a sculptor of international repute and played an enormous part in the development of English 20th-century typography.

1 *BOOK:* THE FOUR GOSPELS
DATE: 1931

2 *BOOK:* PASSIO DOMINI
NOSTRI JESU CHRISTI
DATE: 1926

3 *BOOK JACKET:* THE ALDINE
BIBLE
DATE: 1934

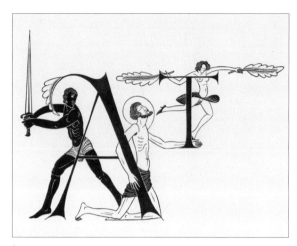

1

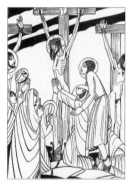

2

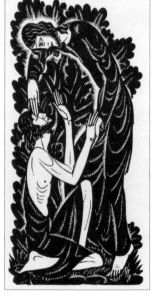

3

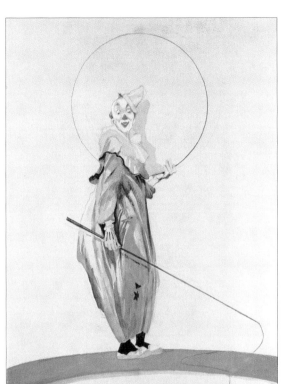

1

*Born in Sheffield, UK. Studied
at the Academy of Art in
Dusseldorf, where he was a
rebellious student, and was
expelled in 1884. He returned to
England before continuing his
studies in Antwerp and Paris,
where French poster art had
a lasting influence on his own
work. His most famous posters
are "The Gaiety Girl," for Sir
Augustus Harris's theatrical
venture, and "The Yellow Girl,"
which advertised Jerome K
Jerome's new publication* Today.
*The latter was particularly
popular and started a craze for
posters in England.*

1 *PROGRAMME DESIGN:*
BERTRAM MILLS' CIRCUS
DATE: 1921

Born in Queenstown, Pennsylvania, USA. In 1886 he drew cartoons for the Pittsburgh Post, *using the trademark of a little racoon. Over the next few years he created other strips, including* Coon Hollow Folks, Bear Creek Folks, *and* Scary William, *for newspapers in Pittsburgh and Philadelphia. Paine had a very individual and decorative style, with sketchy, boldly colored figures drawn inside circles rather than the usual panel format. When he became successful he moved to California, from where he sent* Honeybunch's Hubby *to New York for publication three times a week. However, his fame rests on his classic strip* S'Matter Pop?, *featuring the adventures of Pop, Willyum, and Desperate Ambrose. It was first published in* World *in 1917 and ran for 30 years. After its demise, Paine fell into obscurity and died penniless in New York.*

1 *ADVERTISEMENT: "SHELL OIL"*
DATE: 1928

2 *POSTER: "LONDON TRANSPORT"*
DATE: 1922

3 *PUBLICITY POSTER: "WELWYN GARDEN CITY"*
DATE: 1939

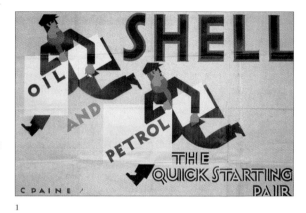

1

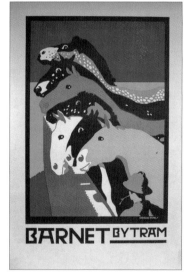

2

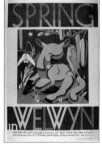

3

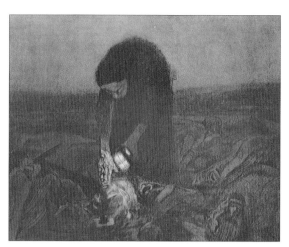

1

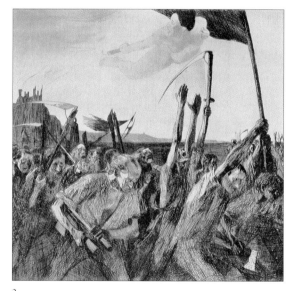

2

Born *Käthe Schmidt in Konigsberg, Germany. Studied painting in Munich, where she discovered what was to become a life-long preference for black-and-white media. She married a doctor and lived in the poor northern area of Berlin, where her husband worked and where she took up etching. Sharing with Gauguin the belief that "ugliness can be beautiful, prettiness never," her art was an expression of her solidarity with the oppressed and poverty-stricken. In the late 1890s she achieved fame as a socialist artist with her illustrations for Hauptmann's* The Weavers' Uprising, *and in 1902 she was much praised for her series* The Peasants' War. *In 1909 she contributed drawings to the satirical magazine* Simplizissimus *and in the following year took up sculpture. In 1919 she began producing woodcuts, a medium whose bold simplicity was well suited to her subjects and themes. Her son was killed in World War I and she remained passionately opposed to war, producing "The War" series of woodcuts in 1923.*

1 *ETCHING:* PEASANTS' WAR
DATE: 1903

2 *ETCHING:* PEASANTS' WAR
DATE: 1907

Illustrator, poster artist, and writer born in the USA. While Lautrec, Mucha, and Cheret were enjoying the "Golden Age of the Poster" in Europe, Penfield was producing some of the best poster work in America. His style was to draw in silhouetted shapes that had been refined from careful preliminary sketches. The effect was deceptive, in that when seen from a distance the simplicity of the treatment made the subject immediately recognizable and yet when seen in close-up the work contained sufficient detail to hold the viewer's interest. In the first two decades of the 20th century his work appeared frequently on the covers of magazines such as Collier's and he illustrated many calendars, the most notable being his redrawing of the Old Farmer's Almanac for the Beck Engraving Company in 1918. He also wrote and illustrated the outstanding Holland Sketches, which was published by Scribner's in 1907. Penfield had a lasting influence on American illustration through his work, his teaching at the Art Students League, and his years as art director of Harper's magazine. He was president of the Society of Illustrators in 1921 and 1922.

1 BOOK: THREE GRINGOS IN CENTRAL AMERICA AND VENEZUELA by Richard Harding
DATE: c. 1900

2 PUBLICITY POSTER: "HARPER'S MAGAZINE"
DATE: c. 1900

3 ADVERTISEMENT: "HART SCHAFFNER & MARX OUTFITTERS"
DATE: NOT KNOWN

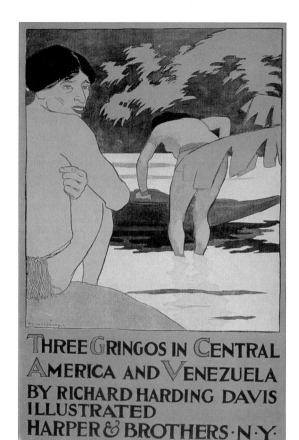

1

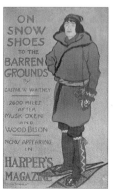

2

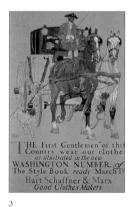

3

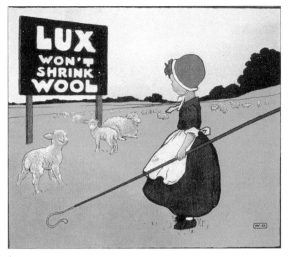

1

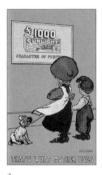

2

Born in Malta. Studied at Lambeth School of Art. He developed a humorous style with heavy outlines that was reminiscent of his contemporaries John Hassall and Tom Browne. His work was very popular and he contributed frequently to magazines such as Punch, The Sketch, Tatler, The Strand Magazine, The Graphic, The Idler, *and the* Humorist. *He developed a working relationship with the humorous writer WW Jacobs and illustrated four of his books, including* Sailor's Knots *(1909) and* Short Cruises *(1920). He also wrote and illustrated five books of his own –* Alleged Humour *(1917),* Three Jolly Sailors and Me *(1919),* Old London Town *(1921),* Mr. Peppercorn *(1940), and* What's the Dope? *(1944). However, his style was best suited to posters, and he produced a great many for such clients as Lux washing powders and Sunlight soap.*

1 ADVERTISEMENT: "LUX SOAP
FLAKES"
DATE: c. 1920

2 ADVERTISEMENT:
"SUNLIGHT SOAP"
DATE: c. 1920

3 PUBLICITY POSTER
DATE: c. 1920

MASKELYNE & DEVANT'S
MYSTERIES

HOUSTON
CHINESE MAGICIAN

ST GEORGE'S HALL, OXFORD CIRCUS, W
DAILY AT 3 & 8

3

Grew up and was schooled in
France. The son of a portrait
painter, Rooke studied at the
Slade in London from 1899 to
1903 and then under Edward
Johnstone at the Central School
of Art, where Eric Gill was one
of his contemporaries. In 1904
he took up wood engraving.
He drew directly on to the
wood block, working in both
black and white line, and
experimented with graduated
tones and wood-cutting.
Although he was familiar with
the techniques of color printing,
he mostly limited himself to
black and white in his book
illustrations.

1 *POSTER: "LONDON
TRANSPORT"*
DATE: c. 1900

2 *POSTER: "LONDON
TRAMWAYS"*
DATE: c. 1900

3 *POSTER: "LONDON
TRAMWAYS"*
DATE: c. 1900

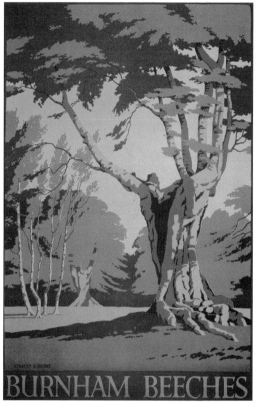

1

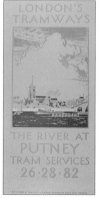

2

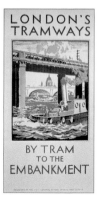

3

ERTÉ
(1892–1990)

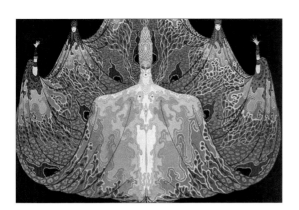

1

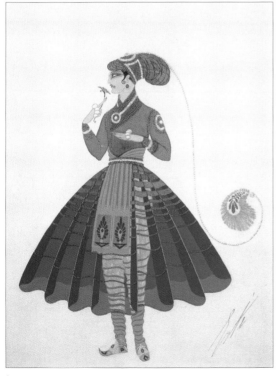

2

*Born in St Petersburg
(Leningrad), Russia. Moving
to Paris in 1912, be became
a designer with the couturier
Paul Poiret. He adopted the
pseudonym Erté from the French
pronunciation of his initials R T
(Remain de Tirtoff). He designed
magazine covers and fashion
plates for* Harper's Bazaar *over
a period of more than 20 years,
and he also contributed to* Vogue
*and others. Erté's designs were
typically elaborate and stylish.
His illustrations, in black and
white or vivid color, ranged
from richly decorative Art Deco
fantasies to fluidly elegant,
practical modern clothing,
and he was frequently able
to combine a graphic visual
economy with careful attention
to descriptive detail.*

1 *COSTUME DESIGN
DATE:* c. 1920

2 *COSTUME DESIGN
DATE:* 1921

Born Georg Ehrenfiied Gro in Germany. Studied at the Dresden Academy of Art and had his first satirical drawings published in the comic magazine Ulk at the age of l7. He also studied in Paris and at the Berlin School of Arts and Crafts, where he made a living by selling his caricatures. By 1919 he was a leading member of the Dada art movement in Berlin, and, with John Heartfield, edited satirical magazines of the political left, which made him unpopular with the Nazis. An opponent of what he called "the slavish copying of nature," he believed in the expressive use of line. At his most brilliant in Ecce Homo (1923), which was confiscated by the police and led to an indecency trial, Grosz's harsh images and startling use of line and color perfectly express his contempt for the decadent bourgeoisie. His illustrations have had an enormous influence on subsequent generations of artists and illustrators. In 1932 he moved to New York, where he taught at the Art Students League.

1–7 *BOOK:* ECCE HOMO
DATE: 1923

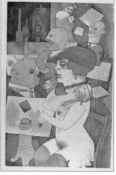

1

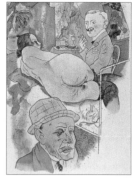

2

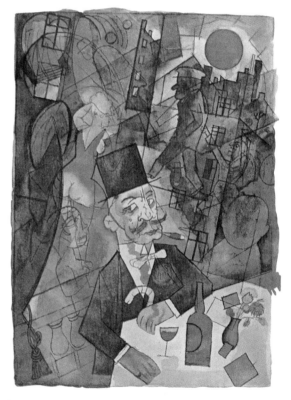

3

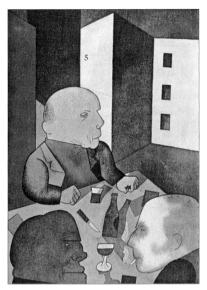

4

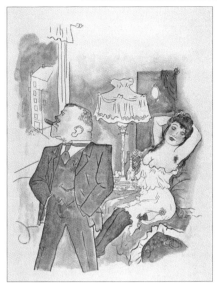

5

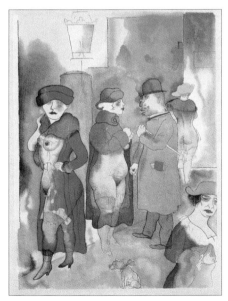

6

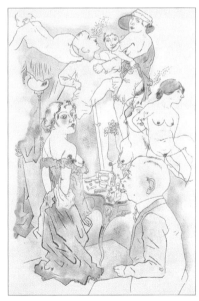

7

HARRISON FISHER
(1875–1934)

*Born in New York. His early
talent for drawing was
encouraged, and he studied at
the Mark Hopkins Institute of
Art in San Francisco. At the age
of 16, and while still a student,
his work was published in
the local newspapers. After
leaving college he returned to
New York and worked as a
staff artist on Puck. By now his
talent for drawing women was
established; his Fisher Body Girl
was a trademark for years, and
led to an exclusive contract to
illustrate the monthly covers for
Cosmopolitan magazine, which
he did for several years.*

1 *MAGAZINE:* COSMOPOLITAN
DATE: 1920

2 *MAGAZINE:* COSMOPOLITAN
DATE: 1920

3 *MAGAZINE:* COSMOPOLITAN
DATE: 1920

4 *MAGAZINE:* COSMOPOLITAN
DATE: 1920

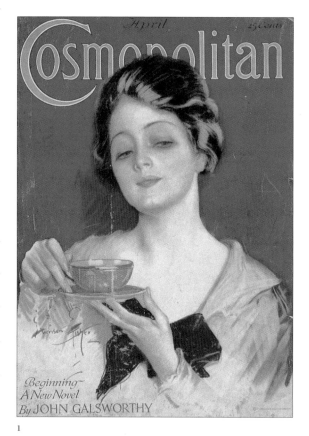

1

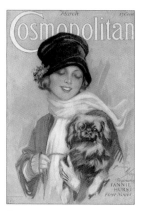

2

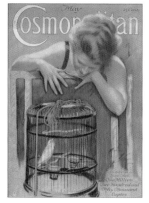

3

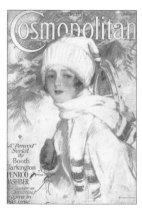

4

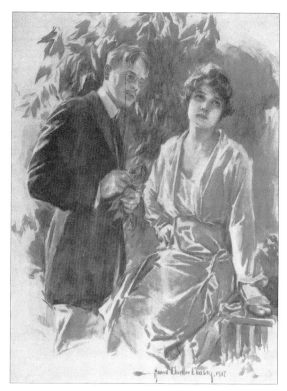

1

*Born in Ohio, USA. Studied
at the Art Students League
and the National Academy in
New York and was taken on
by William Merritt Chase as a
private student at his famous
10th Street Studio. Initially
Christy planned to be a fine
artist, but after selling his
work to Scribner's, Harper's,
and Leslie's Weekly he chose
a more commercial career.
During the Spanish-American
conflict he worked as a war
artist and went with the U.S.
troops to Cuba. However, he
is remembered mostly for
his drawings of women. His
subjects were usually healthy,
outdoor types, who became
known as the "Christy Girls,"
and were popular with
the public and with
magazine publishers.*

1 *MAGAZINE:* COSMOPOLITAN
DATE: 1918

ANNE ANDERSON
(1874–1930)

Born in Scotland but spent her childhood in Argentina before finally settling in England. She worked on over 100 children's books, including treasuries and annuals, sometimes in collaboration with her husband Alan Wright. She produced several titles as both author and illustrator, among them The Funny Bunny ABC *(1912),* The Cosy Corner Book *(1943), and* The Podgy Puppy *(1927). Her decorative line work and delicate coloring showed the influence of Art Nouveau and also owed something to the style of Mabel Lucie Attwell. Her illustrations were particularly popular during the 1920s and she also produced greeting card designs. Her work has proved enduringly popular and her illustrated* Grimm's Fairy Tales *(1928 and 1929) have been reprinted many times.*

1 *CHRISTMAS CARD*
DATE: c. 1930

2 *BOOK:* OLD ENGLISH
NURSERY SONGS
DATE: NOT KNOWN

3 *BOOK:* THE GOLDEN
WONDER BOOK
DATE: 1934

4 *BOOK:* OLD ENGLISH
NURSERY SONGS
DATE: NOT KNOWN

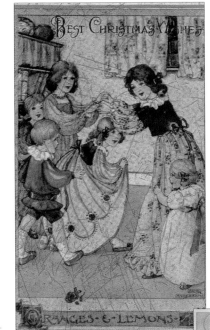

1

2

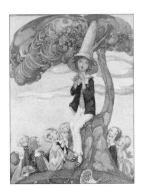

3

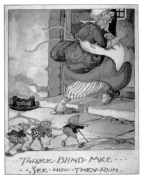

4

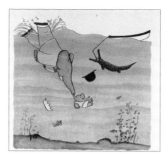

1

2

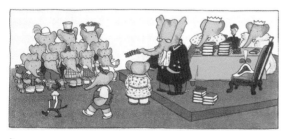

3

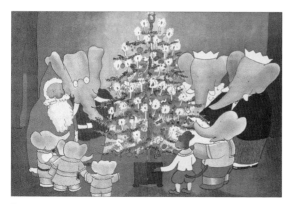

4

JEAN DE BRUNHOFF
(1899–1937)

Born in Paris. Studied under Othon Friesz. De Brunhoff will always be remembered for his stories and illustrations of Babar the Elephant, a character he created for the amusement of his children. The simple water color drawings were accompanied by text in clear but child-like handwriting. The first book, The Story of Babar, *was published in Paris in 1931 and soon after in London and New York, and was an immediate success.* Babar's Travels *and* Babar the King *soon followed, and the stories of Babar and the inhabitants of the town of Celesteville were serialized in* The Daily Sketch *in the UK. In 1936 the books were translated into eight languages, making Babar the internationally famous character that he remains to this day. De Brunhoff died at the age of 38 and the last two books,* Babar and Family *(1938) and* Babar and Father Christmas *(1939), were completed by his brother Michel and son Laurent. In 1988 Babar reached the big screen in* The Babar Story, *an English-speaking animated feature directed by Alan Bunce.*

1–3 *BOOK:* BABAR THE KING
by Jean de Brunhoff
DATE: 1938

4 *BOOK:* BABAR AND FATHER CHRISTMAS *by Jean de Brunhoff*
DATE: c. 1939

HENRY MAYO BATEMAN
(1887–1970)

*Born in New South Wales,
Australia. His family returned
to England when he was a
child and he studied at the
Westminster and New Cross
Art Schools, after which he
worked in the studio of Charles
Van Havenmaet for several
years. In 1906, encouraged by
Phil May (a fellow member of
the London Sketch Club), he
began contributing humorous
drawings to Tatler, Scraps,
Punch, and The Graphic.
After 1911, he revolutionised
humorous art in Britain with
his The Man Who. . . series
of cartoons, which exploited
middle-class mores and the
fear of committing a faux pas.
His barking colonels, haughty
matriarchs, and timid little men
were drawn from his own social
milieu, and the comic situations
focused on the social arenas
of the party, the club, and the
meal table. His books include
Bateman's Booklets (1931), The
Art of the Caricature (1936,)
and H M Bateman by Himself
(1937). He also illustrated
advertisements for the London
tailors Moss Bros, Lucky Strike
cigarettes, and Guinness beer
and designed theater posters.*

1 *WWII POSTER: "UP AND AT
'EM!"*
DATE: c. 1939

2 *BOOK:* BROUGHT FORWARD
DATE: 1932

3 *ADVERTISEMENT:*
"GUINNESS BEER"
DATE: 1937

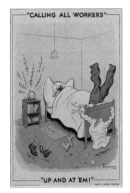

1

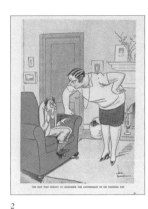

2

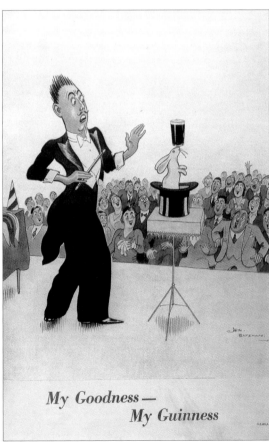

3

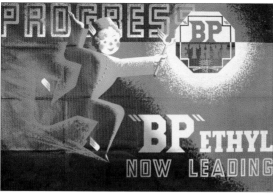

1

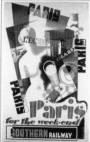

2

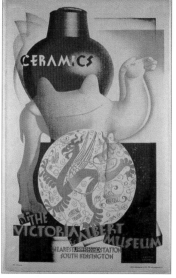

3

Born in Souris, Canada. His family moved to Wales in 1896 and he studied at art schools in Cardiff and Scotland, continuing evening studies after he moved to London to begin his career. After work in Canada as a commercial artist, interrupted by a period of service in Europe during World War I, he settled in London in 1922, where he developed a strong and colorful graphic style. Work for London Transport posters and his design for the Natural History Museum in London (1928) led to similar commissions from the Royal Mail shipping company, BP Oil, and many others. In 1943 he began to develop his painting skills independently of commercial work and became known as a painter of abstracts.

1 *ADVERTISEMENT: "BP OIL"*
DATE: 1933

2 *POSTER: "SOUTHERN RAILWAY"*
DATE: 1930

3 *POSTER: "VICTORIA AND ALBERT MUSEUM"*
DATE: 1934

Born in New York. Trained as an architect but later studied art in New York with Robert Henri, Abbott Thayer, and William Chase. He was one of a breed of American illustrators who combined artistic endeavor with a life of adventure. He spent the winter of 1918 on Fox Island in Alaska and his diaries and drawings were the source material for his own publication Wilderness *(1920). This experience was still evident ten years later in his portrayal of* Moby Dick *(1930). However, neither work is really typical of his style. His architect's precision is better represented in* Salamina *(1935) and his interest in Art Deco in* Candide *(1928). His achievements went beyond illustration and he became famous as an engraver, lithographer, mural painter, writer, and lecturer. Throughout his life he remained a controversial left-wing activist. He was blacklisted during the McCarthy era, in response to which he later refused the title of National Academician.*

1– 3 BOOKPLATES
DATE: c. 1937

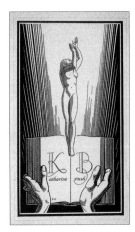

1

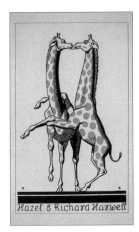

2

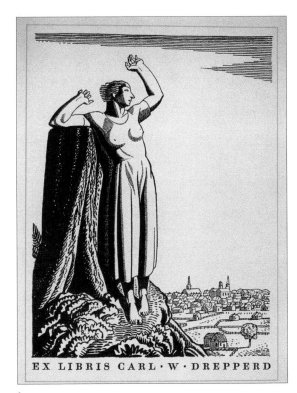

3

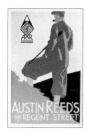

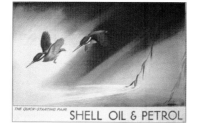

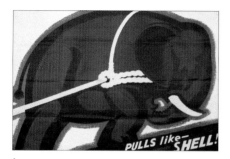

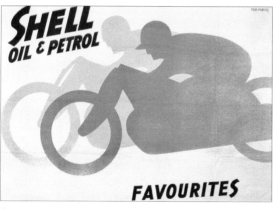

Born in Bristol, UK. Studied at Camberwell School of Art and after graduating worked for six years in advertising before deciding to set up his own studio. He quickly became successful as a poster artist and from 1920 to 1950 his prolific output could be seen on billboards and hoardings all over the UK. His style was characterized by the use of bold colors and minimal detail, and his many clients include Dewar's whiskey, Bovril, the LNER, Shell-Mex, BP, and Austin Reed. In 1935 he helped organize the "British Art in Industry" exhibition at the Royal Academy, and in 1940 to 1945 he was an official war artist, attached to the Ministry of Supply, where he produced posters that boosted British morale and encouraged material economies.

1 ADVERTISEMENT: "AUSTIN REED"
DATE: c. 1930

2 ADVERTISEMENT: "SHELL OIL"
DATE: 1931

3 ADVERTISEMENT: "SHELL OIL"
DATE: 1930

4 ADVERTISEMENT: "SHELL OIL"
DATE: 1928

Born in Folkestone, UK. Studied at the London and Byam Shaw Schools of Art, then attended the Académie Julien in Paris. He worked a great deal in pen and ink, drawing caricatures very much in the style of the 1920s, and also developed a strong graphic style with flat colors that was extremely effective on posters. He illustrated several books, including The Diary of Mr. Niggs (1922), Lewis Melville's The London Scene (1926), and Peter Traill's Under the Cherry Tree (1926). He also worked as a scenic artist and taught commercial and theatrical design at the Westminster School of Art.

1 POSTER: "LONDON TRANSPORT"
DATE: 1923

2 POSTCARD: "CHARLES LAUGHTON"
DATE: 1928

3 ADVERTISEMENT: "'232' GREY FLANNELS"
DATE: c. 1928

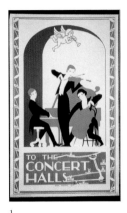

1

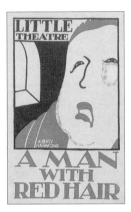

2

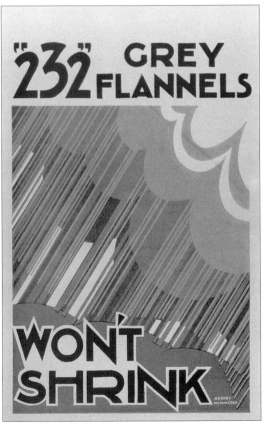

3

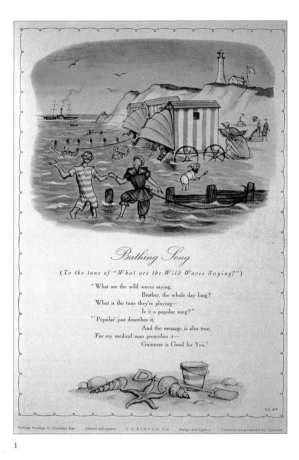

1

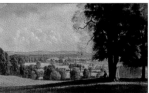

2   3

Born in Eltham, UK. He was
an artistically gifted child
and studied for a year at the
Royal Academy Schools before
enrolling at the Slade School of
Fine Arts at the age of 17. Here
he was encouraged by Professor
Tonks and in 1926, when he
was just 21, was commissioned
to paint a mural in the tea room
at the Tate Gallery. Inspired by
the Temple Gardens of Stowe
and Wilton, Whistler created
an architectural fantasy, called
The Pursuit of Rare Meats,
that brought him immediate
recognition and success. One
of his earliest publications
was Children of Hertha (1929),
written by his brother Laurence.
Whistler went on to illustrate
three further books by his
brother, Armed October (1932),
The Emperor Heart (1936), and
Oho (1946). However, his classic
work is undoubtedly Gulliver's
Travels (1930), which contained
full-plate drawings in pen and
ink with color washes applied
by hand. Whistler's work was
always witty, and during the
1930s he produced a Guinness
advertising campaign consisting
of faces drawn in pen and ink
which changed character when
viewed upside down. He also
designed for stage productions,
including The Rake's Progress,
Victoria Regina, Fidelio, and The
Marriage of Figaro.

1 *ADVERTISEMENT:
"GUINNESS BEER"
DATE:* c. 1937

2 *BOOK:* FAIRYTALES AND
LEGENDS *by Hans Christian
Andersen
DATE:* 1935

3 *POSTER: "SHELL FUELS"
DATE:* 1933

Born in Kölliken, Switzerland. From 1906 to 1907 he studied in Florence and Paris, where he was a student of E Grasset at the Académie de la Grande Chaumière. He then returned to Switzerland, where he exhibited his landscapes and lithographs and where his graphic style made him a successful designer and illustrator of posters.

1 *POSTER: "WORLD CYCLE CHAMPIONSHIP"*
DATE: 1923

2 *TRAVEL POSTER*
DATE: 1937

3 *TRAVEL POSTER*
DATE: 1930

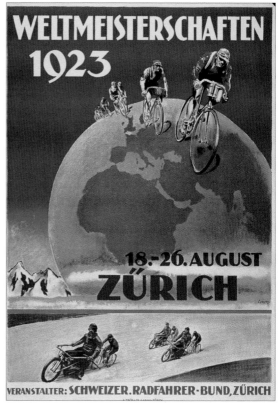

1

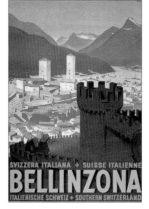

2

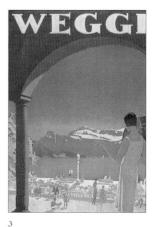

3

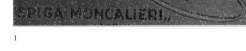

1

MARCELLO DUDOVICH
(1878–1962)

Born in Trieste, Italy. Educated in Bologna, where he later worked as a commercial artist. His mastery of line and use of strong color and simple graphic designs made him a much sought-after poster artist, and he worked regularly for the Ricordi publishers in Milan and for advertising clients such as Gitane cigarettes in France. His work was exhibited in the Milan International Exhibition in 1905. He became a political caricaturist during the 1911 Tripoli War and was later a professor at the Brera Academy in Milan.

1 *ADVERTISING POSTER:*
"SPIGA TYRES"
DATE: 1931

2 *POSTER*
DATE: c. 1925

3 *POSTER*
DATE: c. 1920

4 *ADVERTISING POSTER:*
"STREGA LIQUEUR"
DATE: 1911

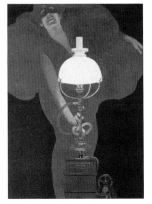

2

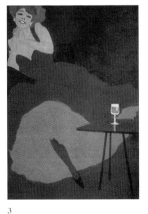

3

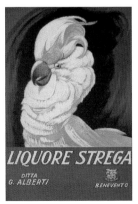

4

Born in London. Studied etching
and engraving at Goldsmith's
College of Art. In 1932 he took
up painting mainly semi-
abstract landscapes of Wales,
Cornwall, and Pembrokeshire.
An official war artist during
World War II, his illustrations
of the devastation helped secure
his developing reputation.
From 1927 to 1940 he taught at
Kingston and Chelsea Schools of
Art and designed stained glass
and tableware decoration as
well as illustrating for clients
such as Jack Beddington at
Shell. In 1942 he published his
Pembrokeshire Sketchbook in
Horizon magazine. He remains
most famous for his paintings,
which were influenced by
Samuel Palmer. In the late
1940s he began to concentrate
on portraiture and painted
Somerset Maugham in 1949
and Winston Churchill in 1954.
This latter portrait caused
a controversy and was later
destroyed by Churchill's family.
In 1956 he moved to the south
of France and the following
year received his most famous
commission, the Christ In Glory
Tapestry at Coventry Cathedral.

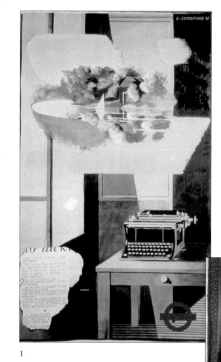

1

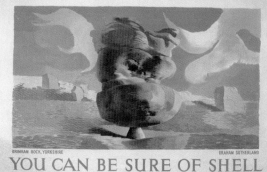

2

1 POSTER: "LONDON
TRANSPORT"
DATE: 1938

2 POSTER: "LONDON
TRANSPORT"
DATE: 1935

3 ADVERTISEMENT: "SHELL
OIL"
DATE: 1937

3

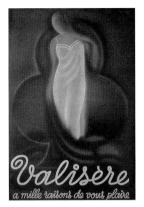

1

2

Born in Nice, France. Trained at the Ecole des Beaux-Arts, Lyon. He first practiced as a graphic artist in Switzerland before settling in Paris. From 1922 he designed advertising materials for a number of French firms, including Voisin, Monsavon, and Vichy-Celestin. Loupot's major contribution to a totally new approach to poster advertising came with the commission in 1938 to redesign the St. Raphael-Quinquina poster. He devised a strongly graphic representation of the St. Raphael name. Once established in the public eye, this was broken up into formal patterns and abstract designs which, though no longer displaying the full name, remained instantly identifiable with it. This work extended over almost 20 years, but Loupot's output was varied and extended into different styles and contexts. In 1931, he shared an exhibition of poster art with Cassandre and his work was include in exhibitions of advertising art worldwide. He contributed work to, among others, La Gazette du Bon Ton, Femina, and Art et Industrie.

1 ADVERTISEMENT: "CAILLER CHOCOLATE"
DATE: 1921

2 ADVERTISEMENT: "VALISÈRE LINGERIE"
DATE: 1937

3 ADVERTISEMENT: "VALENTINE PRINT"
DATE: 1929

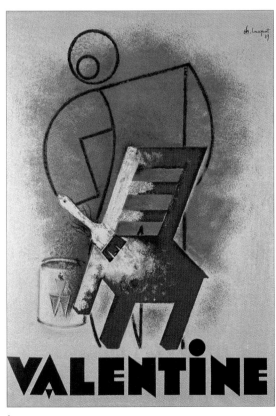

3

ERNEST HOWARD SHEPARD
(1879–1976)

Born in London. Educated at St Paul's School, where his early talent for drawing was encouraged. He took extra classes at Heatherley's Art School and in 1897 won a scholarship to the Royal Academy Schools, where he was the Landseer scholar in 1899. He began drawing for Punch *in 1907, and in 1945 became their chief cartoonist, which he remained until he was fired by Malcolm Muggeridge in 1953. He produced some impressive political cartoons during World War II, but his sensitive pen and ink style was more suited to childhood scenes. He is best remembered for his illustrations for A A Milne's* Winnie-the-Pooh *(1926) and Kenneth Grahame's* The Wind in the Willows *(1931).*

1–2 *BOOK:* THE WIND IN THE WILLOWS *by Kenneth Grahame*
DATE: 1931

3 *BOOK:* WHEN WE WERE VERY YOUNG *by A A Milne*
DATE: 1924

4–5 *BOOK:* WINNIE-THE-POOH *by A A Milne*
DATE: 1926

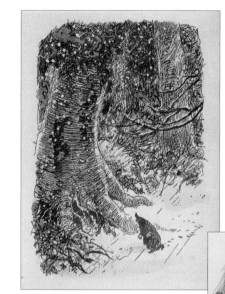

1

2

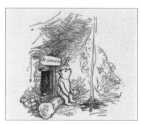

3

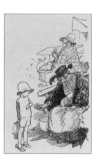

4

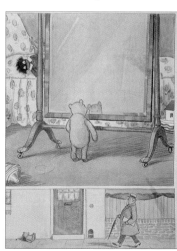

5

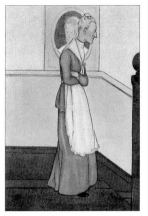

1

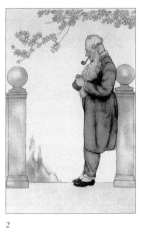

2

SUSAN B PEARSE
(1878–1980)

Born in Fair Oak, UK. Studied at New Cross Art School and the Royal College of Art, London. Married W E Webster, portrait painter and illustrator. Her distinctive style of children's book illustration shows a charmingly decorative approach to form and composition coupled with a sturdy sense of realistic detail. She illustrated several books, including Dickens' Captain Boldheart *(1927), and contributed to the periodical* Little Folks *and to* Playbox Annual, *but is particularly known for her series of* Ameliaranne *books, in which her illustrations were provided with texts by various writers, including Eleanor Farjeon and M Gilmour. Her 1920 poster illustration for Start-Rite shoes has become a classic graphic image.*

1, 2 *BOOK:* AMELIARANNE AT THE FARM *by M Gilmour*
DATE: 1937

3 *BOOK:* AMELIARANNE GIVES A CONCERT *by M Gilmour*
DATE: PUBLISHED 1944

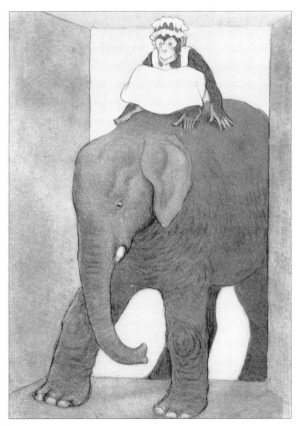

3

Born Hans Schleger in Kempen, Germany. Studied in Berlin and worked for five years in the USA, initially as a freelance designer and then as director of a New York advertising agency, where he adopted the name "Zero" when signing his work. In 1932 he moved to London and became a British citizen in 1938. He established his own studio and design consultancy and his work covered the full spectrum of graphic and commercial art. He was influenced by the Bauhaus, A M Cassandre, and his close friend E McKnight Kauffer. As well as designing posters for clients such as Shell, MacFisheries, London Transport, and the Post Office, he pioneered the concept of corporate identity in the UK, illustrated book jackets, designed exhibitions and packaging, and created the symbol for London bus stops and the trademark for Penguin books. He lectured at Chelsea School of Art and his work has been exhibited worldwide.

1 POSTER: *"LONDON PASSENGER TRANSPORT BOARD"*
DATE: 1936

2 POSTER: *"LONDON TRANSPORT"*
DATE: 1936

3 POSTER: *"LONDON UNDERGROUND"*
DATE: 1935

4 POSTER: *"SHELL FUEL"*
DATE: 1938

5 POSTER: *"LONDON TRANSPORT"*
DATE: 1939

6 PUBLIC INFORMATION POSTER
DATE: c. 1938

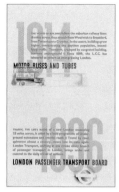

1

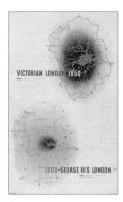

2

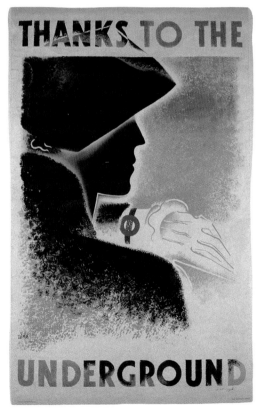

3

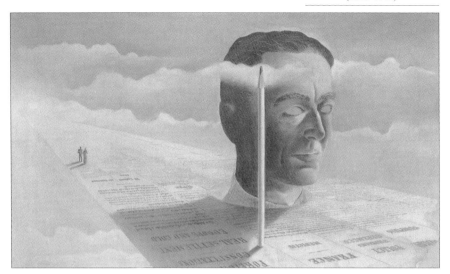

4

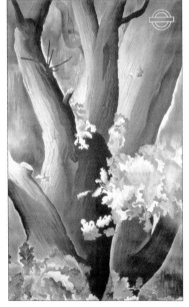

5

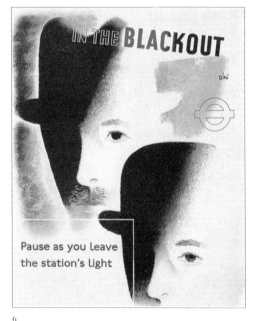

6

Born in Basle, Switzerland.
Studied at the German
School of Art in Basle and the
Conservatory of Art in Zurich
under Dr. Oskar Bätschmann.
He taught for three years before
traveling to Paris in 1894,
where he began painting, and
subsequently to Munich, where
he mastered the technical
skills of lithography. In 1900
he returned to Basle and began
producing posters with a
graphic artist called Anstalten
Wassermann. Mangold was
extremely versatile and
employed a broad range of
styles to suit differing subjects.
In 1905 an exhibition of his
work was held in Zurich and
over the following 15 years he
established himself as one of the
most important poster artists of
his generation, producing some
of his finest work in the years
before World War I. In 1915 he
returned to the German School
of Art in Basle to study stained
glass design and lithography
and was president of the school
from 1918 to 1929.

1 ADVERTISEMENT
DATE: 1902

2 ADVERTISEMENT
DATE: 1916

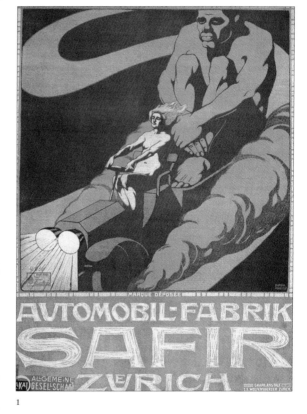

1

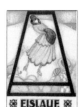

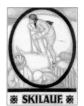

2

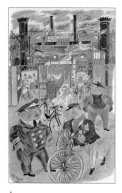

1

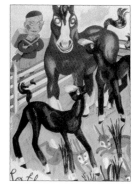

2

Born in London. Studied at Goldsmith's College School of Art, The Royal College of Art, and the Central School of Arts and Crafts in London. Her books as author and illustrator include The Cross-Purposes *(1945),* Ella's Birthday *(1946), and* Beauty and the Burglar *(1958). She contributed to* Country Fair *and* The Strand Magazine. *Her quirky, faux-naif style was used to good effect in London Transport posters during the late 1930s, including* "London Transport for all occasions," *depicting a wedding in which the bride and groom are upstaged by several pale bridesmaids and five angular black cats. Animals were favorite subjects and another London Transport poster,* "To the fields," *shows a complex pattern of horses and frolicking rabbits, typically combining an aura of innocence with a sharp visual wit.*

1 *POSTER: "LONDON TRANSPORT"*
DATE: NOT KNOWN

2 *POSTER: "LONDON TRANSPORT"*
DATE: 1938

3 *POSTER: "LONDON TRANSPORT"*
DATE: 1938

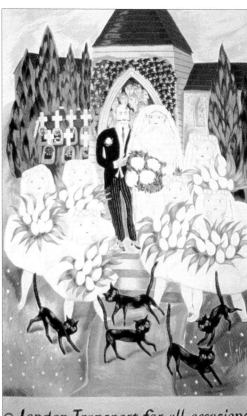

⊖ London Transport for all occasions

3

WILLIAM HEATH ROBINSON
(1872–1944)

Born in London. After studying at the Royal Academy Schools he began illustrating books, including two children's books of his own, Uncle Lubin *(1902) and* Bill the Minder *(1912). During World War I he emerged as one of the greatest comic artists of his time with his whimsical pen and ink drawings of incredibly complicated contraptions usually designed to solve very simple problems. These drawings can be seen in* The Saintly Hum *(1917),* Humours of Golf *(1923),* Absurdities *(1934), and the Professor Branestawm books (1933), which finally made him the most famous of the three Robinson brothers, the others being Tom and Charles. Between the wars he contributed to such periodicals as* The Bystander, The Sketch, The Humorist, The Graphic, *and* The Strand *and exhibited a mural for the liner* Empress of Britain. *He worked mainly in black-and-white and had a highly developed eye for detail and characterization.*

1 *BOOK:* THE INCREDIBLE ADVENTURES OF PROFESSOR BRANESTAWM
DATE: 1933

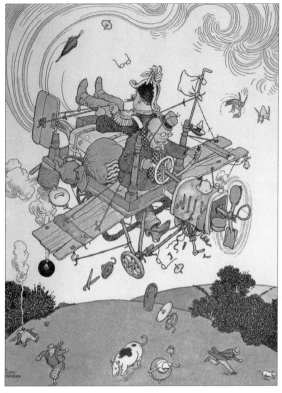

1

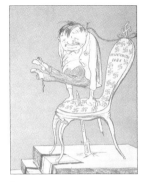

1

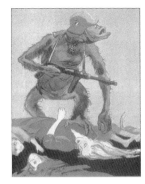

2

A group of Russian artists comprising Mikhail Kupriyanov (1903–1991), Porfiry Krylov (1902–1990), and Nikolai Sokolov (1903–2000). They studied at Vkhutemas in Moscow, where they were pupils of David Moor. During the 1920s they began to collaborate on student publications, first as "the Kukryniks," and after 1927 as "the Kukryniksy." From 1933 their cartoons began to appear regularly in Pravda *and their satirical drawings were much in demand by leading newspapers and magazines. Their poster "We shall mercilessly defeat and destroy the enemy" was one of the first to appear within a few days of Hitler's invasion, and throughout World War II they made a significant contribution to Soviet political poster design. They were also prominent book illustrators.*

1 *CARICATURE: (published in Moscow)*
DATE: c. 1940

2 *CARICATURE: (published in Moscow)*
DATE: c. 1940

3 *CARICATURE: (published in Moscow)*
DATE: c. 1940

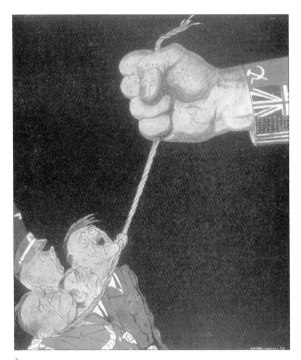

3

*Born Helmut Herzfelde in Berlin.
Studied at the School of Applied
Arts in Munich and the Arts and
Crafts School in Berlin. Later he
Anglicized his name as a protest
against German militarism. In
1911 he was one of the founders
of the Berlin Dada group, and
is renowned as the greatest
exponent of photomontage—
the technique of combining
strikingly incongruous
photographic images to surreal
effect. An active member of the
Communist Party from 1918, he
co-edited the satirical journals
Jedermann Sein Eigener Fussball
and Die Pleite with Grosz and
his brother Wieland Herzfelde,
and in 1923 to 1927 was editor
of the satirical magazine Der
Knüppel. His anti-Nazi images,
which appeared in most of the
newspapers and magazines of
the political left in Germany
from the 1920s, lost him his
German nationality in 1934. He
was eventually forced to move
to Czechoslovakia and then
to Britain, where he worked
for Picture Post and Lilliput
magazines and Penguin Books.
He returned to East Berlin in
1950. In 1956 he was nominated
by Bertolt Brecht to the German
Academy of Arts, where he
became a professor.*

1 *ORIGINAL PHOTOMONTAGE:*
"BLOOD AND IRON"
DATE. c. 1935

2 *ORIGINAL PHOTOMONTAGE*
DATE: 1933

3 *ORIGINAL PHOTOMONTAGE*
DATE: 1934

4 *ORIGINAL PHOTOMONTAGE*
DATE: c. 1935

5 *MAGAZINE:* ARENA
DATE: 1927

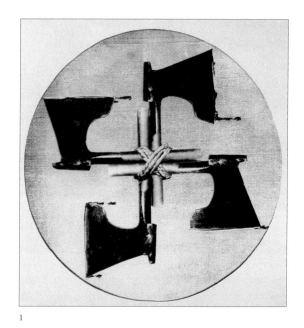

1

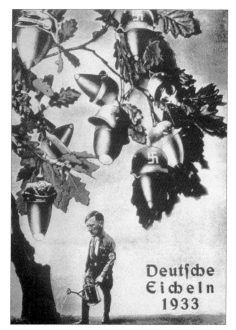

Deutſche
Eicheln
1933

2

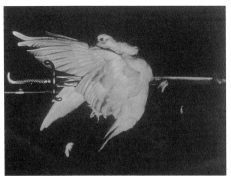

3

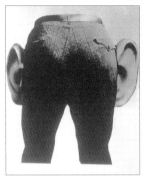

4

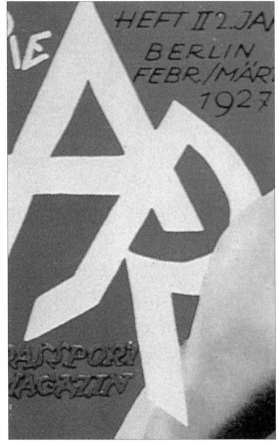

5

EDWARD McKNIGHT KAUFFER
(1890–1954)

Born in Montana, USA. He attended evening classes at the Mark Hopkins Institute, where he met Professor Joseph McKnight, who sponsored him to study art in Paris and whose name Kauffer adopted in tribute. From 1926 to 1931 he was involved in theater and exhibition design, interior design, and book illustration.

A great fan of T S Eliot, he illustrated several of his books, including A Song for Simeon (1925), Ariel Poems (1927), and Marina (1930). Such was Eliot's satisfaction that he wrote to Kauffer, "Yours is the only kind of decoration I can endure." According to the art historian Anthony Blunt, Kauffer's posters and illustrations took the conventions of super-realism and cubism and broadened their appeal to an otherwise uninterested public. He spent two years in Paris before settling in London in 1914, where his posters for the Underground Railways and Shell Petroleum made him a national figure by the 1920s.

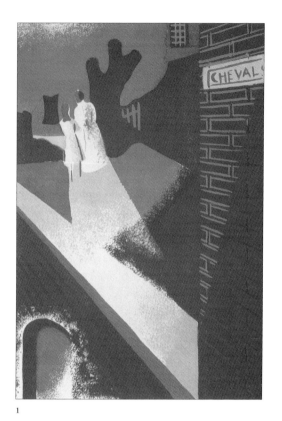

1

1 *BOOK:* ELSIE AND THE CHILD *by Arnold Bennett*
DATE: 1924

2 *POSTER: "LONDON TRANSPORT"*
DATE: 1932

3 *TRAVEL POSTER*
DATE: c. 1924

4 *POSTER: "LONDON TRANSPORT"*
DATE.1954

5 *POSTER: "LONDON TRANSPORT"*
DATE: 1932

6 *ADVERTISEMENT: "SHELL FUEL"*
DATE: 1939

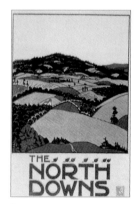

2

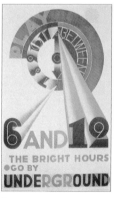

3

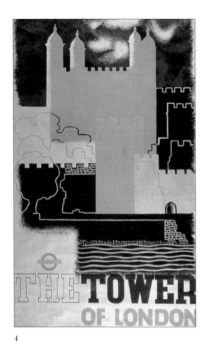

4

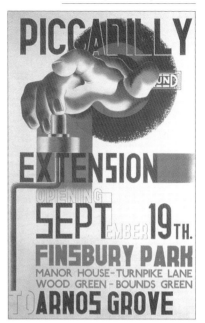

5

6

MAURITS CORNELIS ESCHER
(1898–1972)

*Born in Leeuwarden, Holland.
Studied graphics at the
Technical School of Architecture
and Ornamental Design in
Haarlem. Between 1922 and
1935 he experimented with
various graphic techniques,
producing about 70 woodcuts
and 40 lithographs during this
period. From 1938 he developed
highly decorative designs that
involved transformations of
form through mathematically
precise progressions. He
also produced a series of
geometric drawings, with
such titles as "The Regular
Division Of A Plane" and
"Cubic Space-division," which
were of particular interest to
mathematicians: a large number
of them were exhibited at the
International Mathematical
Congress in Amsterdam in 1964.
His hyper-realistic style had the
surreal effect of confusing the
real with the imaginary, as in
his complex and highly detailed
visual illusions which use
tricks of line and perspective to
create images of the impossible.
Since his death, his work has
frequently been used to illustrate
album covers, books, and
magazine articles and his visual
ideas have been a source of
inspiration to photographers as
well as illustrators.*

1 *WOODCUT:* DAY AND NIGHT
DATE: 1938

2 *WOODCUT:* DEVELOPMENT 1
DATE: 1937

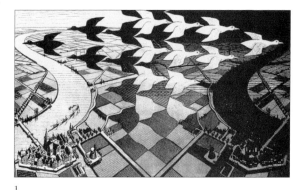

1

2

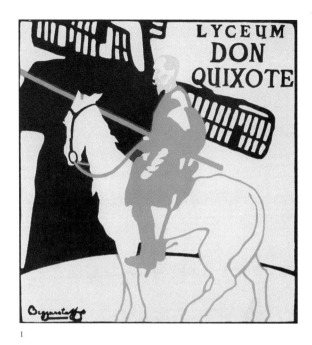

1

*Sir William Nicholson
(1872–1949) and James
Pryde (1886–1941). Although
referred to as "The Beggarstaff
Brothers," William Nicholson
and James Pryde were in fact
brothers-in-law. Nicholson was
born in Newark-on-Trent, UK
and studied at the Académie
Julien in Paris. Pryde, born
in St. Andrews, Scotland,
studied at the Royal Scottish
Academy School in Paris
under Bouguereau and then
also at the Académie Julien.
Their collaboration started
when they entered a poster
competition at the Westminister
Aquarium. For economy's sake
they worked in one color and
painted in silhouette for ease
of reproduction. The ensuing
success in the competition and
the style that emerged from its
constraints made them the most
popular artists in Britain. As
well as designing posters they
both worked in theater design,
and Nicholson was also a
landscape, still-life, and portrait
painter. He illustrated* An
Alphabet *(1898) and Siegfried
Sassoon's Memoirs of a Fox-
Hunting Man (1929).*

---

1 *THEATER POSTER*
DATE: c. 1900

---

2 *PUBLICITY POSTER:*
"HARPER'S MAGAZINE"
DATE: c. 1900

---

3 *POSTCARD:* CELEBRATED
POSTERS SERIES
DATE: c. 1900

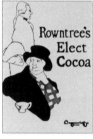

3

2

DAVID MOOR
(1883–1946)

Born Dmitri Stakhievich Orlov in Russia. Studied law at Moscow University and dreamed of being an opera singer. However, after joining an insurgent group during the Moscow uprising of 1905, he helped to set up an underground print store. The following year, an idle sketch he had made of a Tsarist minister was discovered by the editor of an evening newspaper and led to his first commission. He became a political cartoonist and produced a satirical review called Volynka that never passed the censors. After the October Revolution, Moor concentrated on poster art and throughout the civil war years produced over 50 political posters. He always signed them, originally with the name Dor (an abbreviation of his real name), then Mor (to avoid confusion with a prominent journalist), and finally Moor (after a character in Schiller's play The Robbers). He was strongly influenced by French painting, German graphic art, and the cartoonist Olaf Gulbransson.

1 POSTER: "TSARIST REGIMENTS & THE RED ARMY: WHAT THEY FOUGHT FOR BEFORE / WHAT THEY FIGHT FOR NOW"
DATE: 1919

2 POSTER: "RED SOLDIER UNCLOAKS WRANGEL TO REVEAL CONSPIRACY OF WESTERN NATIONS AGAINST RUSSIA"
DATE: 1920

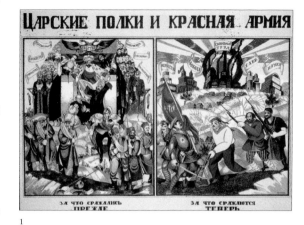

1

2

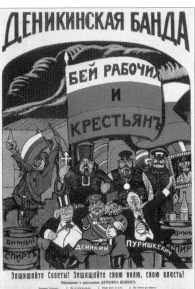

1

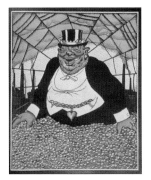

2

Born Viktor Denisov in Moscow. At the age of 17 he had his first drawings published in the satirical journal Budilink, for which his older brother wrote poetry. In 1913 he moved to St. Petersburg, where his work appeared regularly in the satirical journals Solntse Rossii, Vesna, and Satirikon, and became art director of the humorous weekly Bich. When the magazine was closed down after the October Revolution, Deni began working for the artistic section of the Volga military district, making nearly 50 political posters between 1918 and 1921 and becoming one of the leading figures in Soviet poster art (the other was David Moor), particularly admired for his satirical eye. From 1921 he concentrated on drawing newspaper cartoons, contributing regularly to Pravda, the Party newspaper, until World War II, when he went back to making posters.

1 POSTER: "DEMKEN'S BAND"
DATE: 1919

2 POSTER: "AT THE GRAVE OF COUNTER-REVOLUTION"
DATE: 1920

3 POSTER: "CAPITAL"
DATE: 1919

4 POSTER: "CONSTITUENT ASSEMBLY MEETING"
DATE: 1921

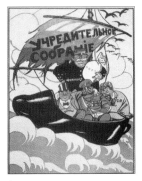

3

4

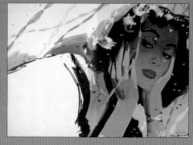

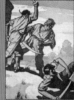

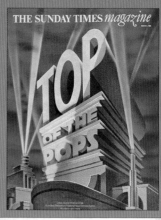

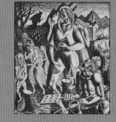

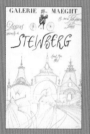

GALERIE MAEGHT

Dessins STEINBERG

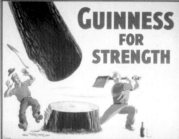

GUINNESS
FOR
STRENGTH

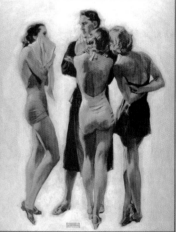

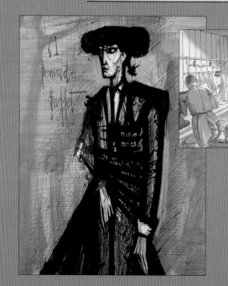

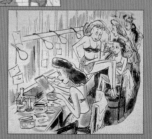

CHAPTER THREE
1940-1969

AS FAR AS ILLUSTRATION WAS CONCERNED, the onset of World War II presented a set of opportunities as well as a set of limitations. The need for propaganda, morale boosting, and public-information material generated a great deal of work. Surprisingly, advertising also thrived during this period. Many manufacturers were concerned that the public would forget them while their production was limited and so ran long-term branding campaigns that stressed their own efforts in the war and assured customers that both quality and supply would be restored as soon as the war had ended.

But while the conflict kept artists busy, the shortages of working materials had a direct effect on their style and methods of working. Paper shortages necessitated that magazines be printed on thinner stock, and art directors advised their illustrators to avoid heavy contrast in their images, as the darker areas would print through and appear on the other side of the page. It also became common to print on the reverse side of unused posters, and this encouraged artists to use darker colors to ensure that the old image could not be seen.

With the end of the war, the mid-1940s became boom years for the illustrator in America. During this period of social reconstruction, publishers placed a great emphasis on "lifestyle" and developed a close relationship with the American housewife through magazines such as *Cosmopolitan* and *Ladies' Home Journal,* which featured the work of artists such as John La Gatta and Jon Whitcomb. At the same time, Norman Rockwell was becoming famous for his portraits of American life, which were featured regularly on the covers of the *Saturday Evening Post.* Advertising budgets rocketed, and the hyper-realistic effect of the airbrush challenged photography in the multitude of campaigns mounted by the fast-growing automobile industry. Even the illustrated novel enjoyed a revival with the arrival of the book club.

The 1950s, however, saw a reaction against slick, photograph-oriented realism. The invention of television had a disastrous effect on the publishing business, and several national periodicals folded. There was also a sharp decline in the sale of illustrated books, owing to the prevalent belief that a novelist's imagination should be interpreted by the reader and not by an illustrator. In aesthetic terms these problems created a very positive energy and response as publishers adopted a more progressive attitude and took artistic risks in the hope of regaining their fickle public. The result was a diversity of styles, which was encouraged also by the presence of European artists such as George Grosz, who had emigrated to America at the end of World War II.

Throughout this time in Britain, the illustrator's life had been running on a parallel course to that on the other side of the Atlantic. During the war years, government spending had encouraged the work of many artists, including Abram Games, Tom Eckersley, McKnight, Kauffer, and Fougasse, and with the return of peace, advertising clients clamored for their services. In their hands, and with the sponsorship of major companies such as Shell, the poster regained its status as an art form.

There was also something of a revival of book illustration within the Neo-Romantic style. This lasted for about 12 years and began with the publication in 1943 of Mervyn Peake's illustrations for Coleridge's *Rime of the Ancient Mariner.* However, the introduction of television in the 1950s damaged the UK publishing industry in much the way it had done in America, although it led to an increased circulation of *Radio Times* magazine, which was then, and remains, a particularly good medium for the introduction of new illustrator's work.

The complacency, born of prosperity, that suffused this period could never have prepared either artists or the public for the style revolution that was to take place in the 1960s.

Pop Art actually began its life in 1956, not in America but in Britain, with Richard Hamilton's photomontages parodying the domestic and materialistic lifestyle of the time. His work, and that of others in the Independent Group, was further developed in the early 1960s by artists such as David Hockney, Patrick Caulfield, and Allen Jones in the UK and Andy Warhol in America. Simultaneously, Bridget Riley, Peter Sedgley, and Piero Dorazio were exploring the optical effects of line and color first seen in the paintings of the Spanish artist Victor Vasarely. The philosophies and aesthetics of these artists then meshed with the emergence of a counter-culture that expressed its anarchic sensibilities through every conceivable medium: paintings, sculpture, music, illustrations, fashion, underground magazines, poster art, festivals, and "happenings."

What followed was an explosion of aesthetic extravagance never seen before. Naturalistic colors were replaced with day-glow psychedelia in the works of Victor Moscoso and Martin Sharp. Michael English's rock 'n' roll posters, which revealed the influence of Art Nouveau, featured convoluted and virtually unreadable hand-rendered lettering. Eclecticism was the guiding principle of the day: Eastern imagery, mysticism, and hallucinatory experience were major creative influences in all branches of the arts.

This revolution was not confined to the "underground." It affected every level of society and, through the work of artists such as Milton Glaser and the influential Push Pin Studios, it reached every level of mainstream media. If ever there was a lingering question about the status of the illustrator as artist, it was answered in the 1960s.

CHAPTER THREE
1940–1969

Studied at the Slade School of Fine Art. Marshall developed a very fluid black-and-white style in charcoal and pen and ink which earned him many commissions for fashion illustrations in the 1950s. His drawings were full of movement and captured the energy and elegance of the catwalk models and of the era, and his work dominated the pages of Vogue, Harper's Bazaar, *and* Woman's Journal. *In 1950 he wrote and illustrated* Sketching the Ballet, *and later produced similar volumes entitled* Fashion Drawing *and* Drawing the Female Figure. *In his manual* Magazine Illustration *(1959), he encouraged the use of photographs as reference material and recommended the special "incident" studios that were then producing images for illustrators. He was also an accomplished watercolorist and landscape artist and exhibited several times at London's Walker Galleries.*

1 *MAGAZINE:* WOMAN'S
MAGAZINE
DATE: c. 1950

2 *MAGAZINE:* WOMAN'S
MAGAZINE
DATE: 1950

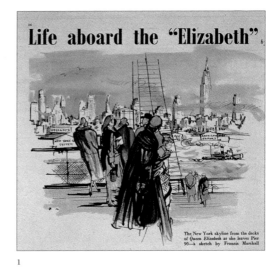

Life aboard the "Elizabeth"

The New York skyline from the decks of *Queen Elizabeth* as she leaves Pier 90—a sketch by Francis Marshall

1

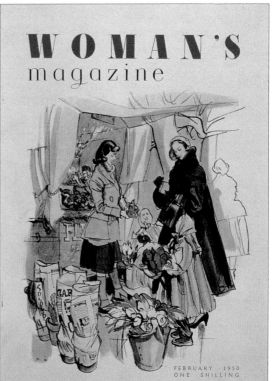

WOMAN'S
magazine

FEBRUARY 1950
ONE SHILLING

2

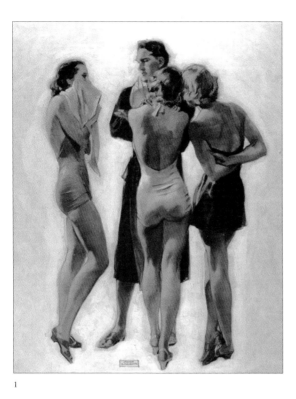

1

Born in Naples, Italy. Emigrated to America and studied at the Chase School, New York School of Applied and Fine Arts, Parsons, and the Art Students League. He began his career in advertising illustration before establishing his own studio in Woodstock, where he specialized in illustrations of beautiful women. Advised by his wife and model Florence, his drawings of romantic interludes among the upper classes regularly illustrated the stories in magazines such as Redbook, Ladies' Home Journal, and Cosmopolitan, and he received many commissions in the early years of World War II. In 1941 he moved to California, where he took up portraiture and landscape painting.

1 MAGAZINE: REDBOOK
DATE: c. 1940

2 MAGAZINE: COSMOPOLITAN
DATE: 1949

3 MAGAZINE: REDBOOK
DATE: c. 1940

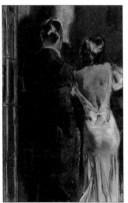

2

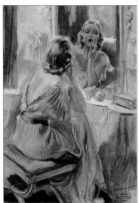

3

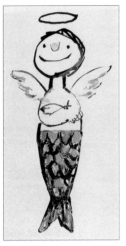

1

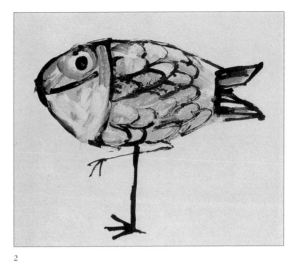

2

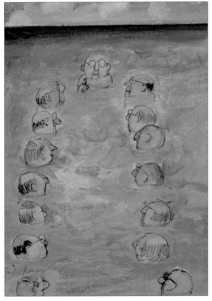

3

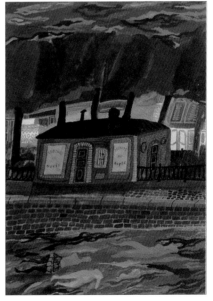

4

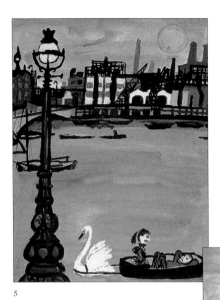

5

*Born in Timisoara, Hungary.
Studied in Budapest, then
under Cassandre in Paris. From
1944 he established himself
as a humorous artist, and his
distinctive, satirical images
appeared in magazines such
as Punch, Vogue, and The New
Yorker. His advertising posters
for Citroën and Kodak are
among the most innovative and
influential of the 20th century.
Francois was also a sculptor
and poster artist and designed
stage sets and costumes for
the theater and ballet. His own
illustrated books included
The Tattooed Sailor and Other
Cartoons from France (1953),
The Half-naked Knight (1958),
The Biting Eye (1960), and
Les Rhumes (1966). He also
illustrated Ubu Roi by Alfred
Jarry (1957).*

6

1 *ADVERTISEMENT: "CITROËN
CARS"*
DATE: 1960

2 *ADVERTISEMENT: "CITROËN
CARS"*
DATE: 1960

3 *MAGAZINE:* THE NEW
YORKER
DATE: 1965

4 FIRST AID FOR THE
DROWNED *(unpublished)*
DATE: 1947

5 *MAGAZINE:* PUNCH
DATE: 1955

6 *MAGAZINE:* PUNCH
DATE: 1960

7 BIG RED BICYCLE
(unpublished)
DATE: 1955

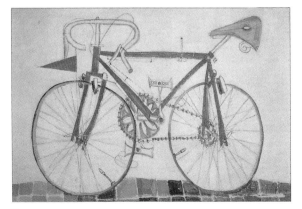

7

Born in Lancashire, UK. Trained at Salford School of Art under Martin Tyas. He moved to London in 1934 and set up in partnership with Eric Lombers. In 1935 he won the Heywood Medal of Merit for poster design and in 1937 to 1939 he taught poster art at Westminster School of Art. Like his contemporary Abram Games, Eckersley produced posters with simple graphic imagery, integrated typography, clean lines, and strong colors. During World War II he produced cartographical drawings for the Royal Air Force, returning to freelance design in 1945. His style attracted many advertising clients, including Gillette, Guinness, British Aluminium, Eno's, and various cigarette brands. In 1948 he was awarded the Order of the British Empire for his services to British poster design and in 1958 became Head of Graphic Design at the London College of Printing.

1 *PUBLIC INFORMATION POSTER: "ROYAL SOCIETY FOR THE PREVENTION OF ROAD ACCIDENTS, LONDON"*
DATE: 1944

2 *WWII POSTER: "POST OFFICE SAVINGS BANK"*
DATE: 1943

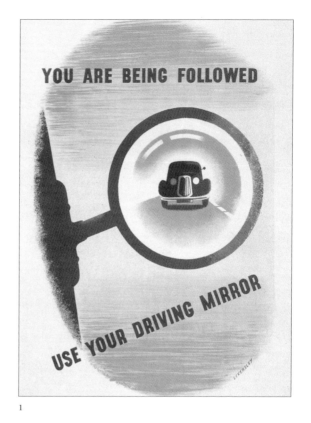

1

2

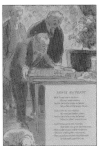

1

Born in Haiphong, Vietnam. His family moved to England when he was five. Attended life classes at Westminster School of Art, under Bernard Meninsky, while employed as a clerk in London. At the age of 27 he gave up his job to become an artist, and around 1930 began illustrating regularly for the Radio Times. His books Little Tim and the Brave Sea Captain (1936) and Lucy Brown and Mr. Grimes (1937), which he wrote and illustrated to entertain his own children, were a great success in England and America. Tim All Alone (1956), was the first book to win the British Library Association's Kate Greenaway Medal. He is best known as a children's illustrator, but his fluid and expressive style, either drawn with cross-hatching or painted in simple watercolors, was equally suited to serious subjects. He cited Bernard Meninsky, Doré, Daumier, and Caldecott as his main influences. He was an official war artist during World War II, and the drawings he made remain a powerful record of the atrocities of war.

1 ADVERTISEMENT: "PUNCH MAGAZINE"
DATE: 1954

2 ADVERTISEMENT: "GUINNESS BEER"
DATE: 1955

3 ADVERTISEMENT: "GUINNESS BEER"
DATE: 1955

4 BOOK: TIM ALL ALONE by Edward Ardizzone
DATE: 1956

2

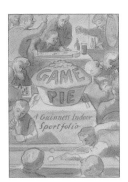

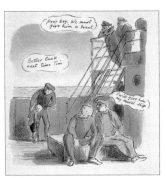

3

4

Born in Kuling, China, the son
of medical missionaries. The
family returned to England
in 1923 and he was educated
at Eltham College, Kent and
the Royal Academy Schools in
London. His first illustrated
book, Captain Slaughterboard, a
humorous fantasy for children,
was published in 1939.
Invalided out of the forces in
1943, he visited Germany in
1946 to record the devastation
for Leader magazine. He was
also sent to make drawings at
Belsen, an experience which
profoundly affected his later
work. Peake illustrated many
books, including Alice Through
the Looking Glass (1954),
Grimm's Fairy Tales, and
Treasure Island. He also wrote
and illustrated his own novels
and poems, including Rhymes
Without Reason (1944), Captain
Slaughterboard Drops Anchor
(1945), Shapes and Sounds
(1941), and The Glassblowers
(1950). His most famous work,
Gormenghast (part two of a
gothic fantasy trilogy written
between 1946 and 1959),
won the W J Heinemann
Foundation Prize (Royal Society
of Literature) in 1950. In many
of Peake's works a lively humor
is merged with an instinct for
the macabre and the grotesque,
as seen in the facial caricatures
that were a recurring element in
his work.

1,4–6 BOOK: RIDE-A-COCK
HORSE & OTHER NURSERY
RHYMES
DATE: 1945

2, 7 BOOK: FIGURES OF
SPEECH by Mervyn Peake
DATE: 1952

3 BOOK: TITUS ALONE by
Mervyn Peake
DATE: 1959

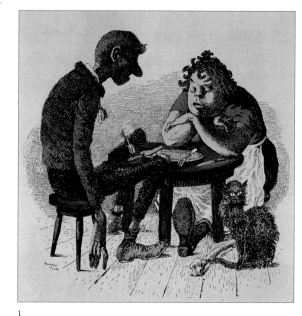

1

Coming up to scratch

2

3

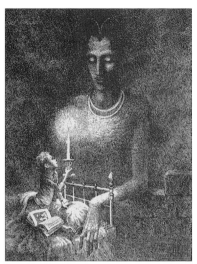

4

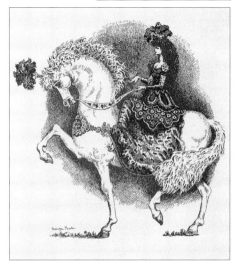

5

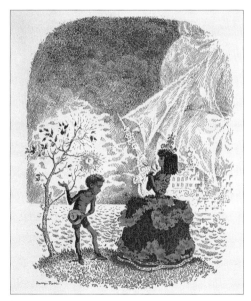

6

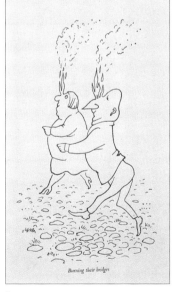

Burning their bridges

7

*Born in Warrington, Cheshire,
UK. Studied at art schools
in Liverpool, London, and
Penzance and trained as a
stage designer in Liverpool. In
1928 he designed the sets for
A Midsummer Night's Dream at
Liverpool Repertory Theatre and
in 1929 designed the sets for the
original production of Toad of
Toad Hall. Moving to London,
he worked in a commercial
studio for two years and then
began designing for the London
theaters, working on over 25
productions until after World
War II, when he turned to book
and magazine illustration.*

1 *BOOK:* THE NEW BOOK OF
DAYS
DATE: 1941

2, 3 *BOOK:* HANS CHRISTIAN
ANDERSEN'S FAIRY TALES
DATE: 1946

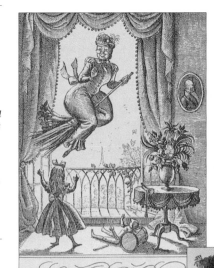

1

2

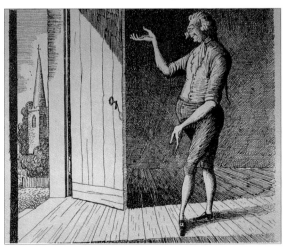

3

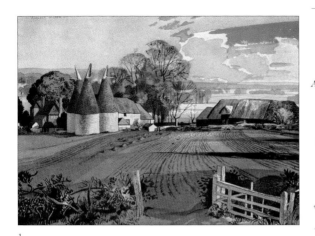

1

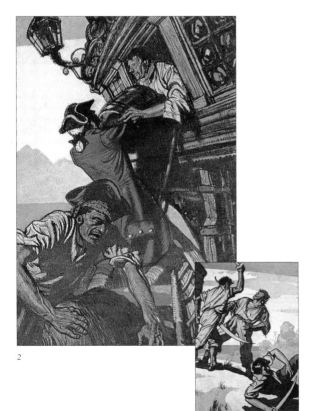

2

3

Born in Long Island, USA but settled in England during childhood. Studied at Goldsmith's College School of Art, London and won a traveling scholarship which he applied to studying marine art in the Netherlands. From 1925 he received commissions from publishers, many with marine themes, including Moby Dick *(1926) and* The Adventures of a Trafalgar Lad *(1926). His landscape drawings for Mary Webb's* Precious Bane *(1929) were later marketed as greeting cards. Other significant titles were* The Midnight Folk *(1931), a personal commission from poet laureate John Masefield,* The Bible for Today *(1938), and, with his wife Edith Wider, the* Shell Guide to Flowers of the Countryside. *His prolific output of greeting card designs for the Medici Society and Ward Gallery established his widespread popularity, but after World War II he published his designs through his own Heron Press. From the 1960s he became increasingly dedicated to painting for non-commercial reasons, though his work continued to be widely reproduced.*

1 *MAGAZINE:* PUNCH
DATE: 1952

2–3 *BOOK:* TREASURE ISLAND
by Robert Louis Stevenson
DATE: 1946

Born in Basel, Switzerland. Studied at art schools in Munich and Basel. He was a major figure in the development of Swiss poster art, which had already achieved high standards by the 1920s. His work produced a refinement of design concepts, ranging from stylized, two-dimensional, almost purely symbolic images to more detailed and realistic representations, married to clean, unfussy typographic presentation. Examples can be seen in museums in Basel and Zurich, and Stoecklin's work has gone into private collections worldwide. Another important interest was postage stamp design, and he produced a number of detailed designs for this purpose, mainly featuring plants and animals. He also illustrated books, including Hermann Hesse's Knulp (1945).

1 *ADVERTISEMENT: "BINACA TOOTHPASTE"*
DATE: 1941

2 *ADVERTISEMENT: "META MATCH STRIKERS"*
DATE: 1941

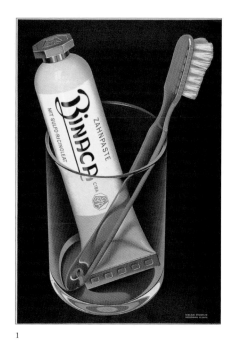

1

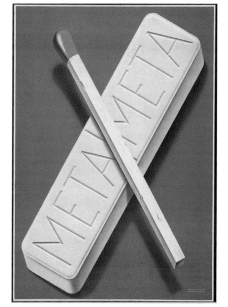

2

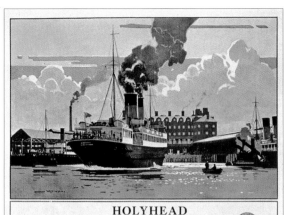

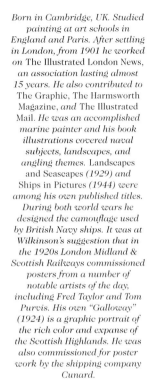

1

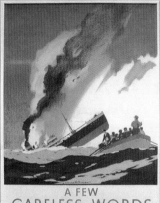

2

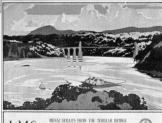

3

Born in Cambridge, UK. Studied painting at art schools in England and Paris. After settling in London, from 1901 he worked on The Illustrated London News, an association lasting almost 15 years. He also contributed to The Graphic, The Harmsworth Magazine, and The Illustrated Mail. He was an accomplished marine painter and his book illustrations covered naval subjects, landscapes, and angling themes. Landscapes and Seascapes (1929) and Ships in Pictures (1944) were among his own published titles. During both world wars he designed the camouflage used by British Navy ships. It was at Wilkinson's suggestion that in the 1920s London Midland & Scottish Railways commissioned posters from a number of notable artists of the day, including Fred Taylor and Tom Purvis. His own "Galloway" (1924) is a graphic portrait of the rich color and expanse of the Scottish Highlands. He was also commissioned for poster work by the shipping company Cunard.

1 TRAVEL POSTER: "LONDON MIDLAND & SCOTTISH RAILWAY COMPANY"
DATE: 1940

2 PUBLIC INFORMATION POSTER
DATE: 1940

3 TRAVEL POSTER: "LONDON MIDLAND & SCOTTISH RAILWAY COMPANY"
DATE: NOT KNOWN

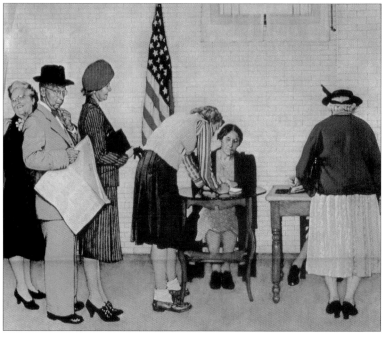

1

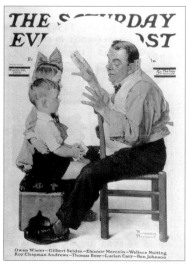

2

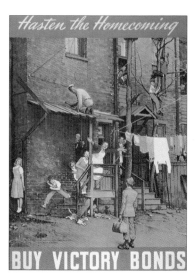

3

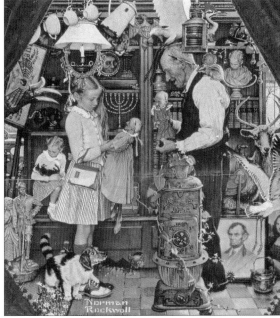

4

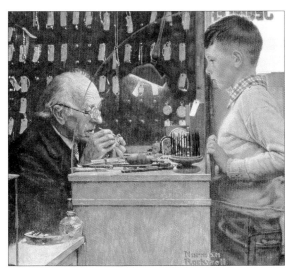

5

Born in New York. Studied at Chase Art School, the National Academy of Design, and the Art Students League in New York under Thomas Fogarty and George Bridgman. At the age of 17 he was already illustrating for McBride and Nast publications, and later became editor of a boy scouts' magazine. His covers for The Saturday Evening Post, *spanning more than 40 years from 1916, made him one of America's best-known and most-loved illustrators. His superbly crafted portrayals of American life were done with a warmth and humor that touched the hearts of millions and reflected the spirit of the country at the time. During World War II the essence of Franklin D Roosevelt's war aims was captured in Rockwell's powerful "Four Freedoms" posters, one of which is on permanent display at the Metropolitan Museum of Art in New York.*

1 *MAGAZINE*: THE SATURDAY
EVENING POST
DATE: 1940

2 *MAGAZINE*: THE SATURDAY
EVENING POST
DATE: c. 1940

3 *POSTER*
DATE: c. 1945

4 *MAGAZINE*: THE SATURDAY
EVENING POST
DATE: 1940

5 *MAGAZINE*: THE SATURDAY
EVENING POST
DATE: 1949

Born in Kovno, Russia. His family emigrated to America in 1904 and he studied biology at New York University and attended the National Academy of Design. In the 1920s he traveled in Europe and North Africa and during World War II he designed posters for various government departments. His work, which used heavy outlines to expressive effect and which brought to mind the illustrations of Francois and Buffet, won numerous awards. He illustrated several children's books, including A Partridge in a Pear Tree (1949), which featured illustrations in a style that was most unusual for the world of the nursery rhyme. His adult publications include The Sorrows of Priapus (1957) by E Dahlberg and Thirteen Poems (1956) by Wilfred Owen. His work also appeared in advertising campaigns and in publications such as Fortune Magazine, Harper's Bazaar, and Town and Country. He was a painter as well as an illustrator and had one-man shows in Boston, New York, and Chicago.

1 *WW II POSTER*
DATE: 1943

2 *WW II POSTER*
DATE: 1943

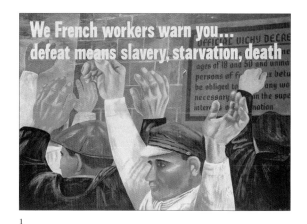

1

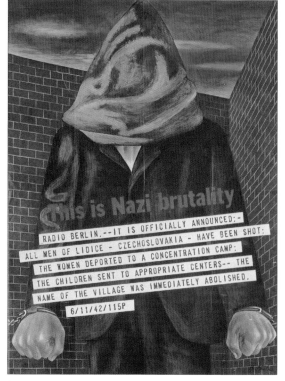

2

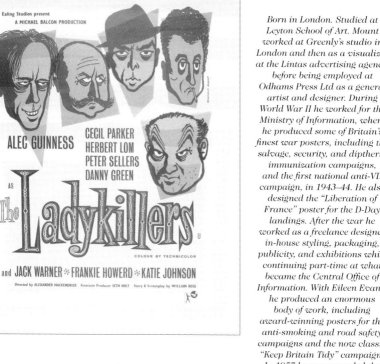

1

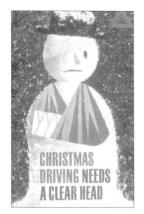

2

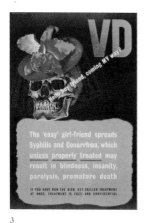

3

Born in London. Studied at
Leyton School of Art. Mount
worked at Greenly's studio in
London and then as a visualizer
at the Lintas advertising agency,
before being employed at
Odhams Press Ltd as a general
artist and designer. During
World War II he worked for the
Ministry of Information, where
he produced some of Britain's
finest war posters, including the
salvage, security, and diptheria
immunisation campaigns,
and the first national anti-VD
campaign, in 1943–44. He also
designed the "Liberation of
France" poster for the D-Day
landings. After the war he
worked as a freelance designer
in-house styling, packaging,
publicity, and exhibitions while
continuing part-time at what
became the Central Office of
Information. With Eileen Evans,
he produced an enormous
body of work, including
award-winning posters for the
anti-smoking and road safety
campaigns and the now classic
"Keep Britain Tidy" campaign.
In 1957 he was awarded the
OBE for services to government
publicity.

1 MOVIE POSTER:
"LADYKILLERS"
DATE: 1955

2 GOVERNMENT INFORMATION
POSTER
DATE: 1962

3 GOVERNMENT INFORMATION
POSTER
DATE: 1943

Born Cyril Kenneth Bird in
London and educated at
Cheltenham College and King's
College, London. From 1916 his
work was published in Punch
and in 1937 he became Art
Editor, then Editor (1949–52).
He illustrated a number of
books, including The Luck of the
Draw (1936), Drawing the Line
Somewhere (1937), and The
Good Tempered Pencil (1956).
During World War II he designed
posters for various government
ministries, including the
famous "Careless Talk Costs
Lives" series for the Ministry of
Information. Fougasse was a
master of the expressive line.
Over the years he developed
a highly individual graphic
shorthand in his drawings of
humorous figures, the hands
and feet often represented by a
single line.

1 WW II POSTER
DATE: 1940

2 WW II POSTER
DATE: 194 0

3 POSTER: "LONDON
UNDERGROUND"
DATE: c. 1940

4 POSTER: "NATIONAL
SOCIETY FOR THE
PREVENTION OF CRUELTY TO
CHILDREN"
DATE: c. 1940

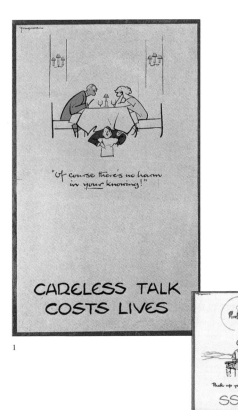

1

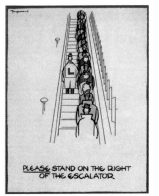

2

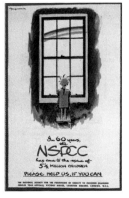

3

4

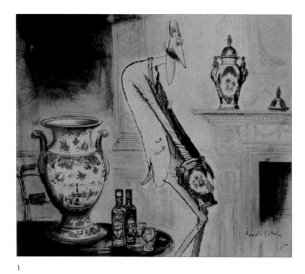

RONALD SEARLE
(b. 1920)

*Born in Cambridge, UK. Studied
at Cambridge School of Art and
first started drawing for the
Cambridge Daily News in 1935.
In 1939 he fought in Malaya
and was imprisoned by the
Japanese from 1942 to 1945,
something he cites as a major
formative experience. His first
published book after the war,
Forty Drawings of Ronald Searle
(1946), was a sobering record
of this bleak interlude in his life.
However, he is more famous for
having created the St Trinian's
schoolgirls in his books Hurrah
for St Trinian's (1948), The
Female Approach (1948), Back
to the Slaughterhouse (1952),
and The Terror of St Trinian's
(1952). In 1956 he joined the
staff of Punch magazine, a
perfect platform for his witty
observations on social behavior.
His work also has a serious
side and he was a member of
the Association of International
Artists, a political group. In
1969 he produced The Secret
Sketchbook: The Backstreets of
Hamburg, which contained no
text but a series of expressive
sketches of prostitutes which
owe something to the influence
of George Grosz. His work has
appeared in many major British
publications and was frequently
published in America's Saturday
Evening Post.*

1 *ADVERTISEMENT*
DATE: 1960

2 *CARTOON: "THE COMING OF
THE GREAT CAT GOD"*
DATE: 1968

3 *BOOK:* ST TRINIAN'S
DATE: c. 1948–1952

1

2

3

NOEL FONTANET
(1898–1982)

Born in Germany. Studied at the Geneva Art School and later drew for local newspapers including caricatures for the Nebelspalter. He was an excellent draftsman and developed a strong graphic style, which earned him the position of art director in a design company and fame as a poster artist.

1 POSTER: "GENEVA INTERNATIONAL AUTOMOBILE SHOW"
DATE: 1930

2 ADVERTISEMENT: "VELOSOLEX"
DATE: 1950

3 POSTER: "GIVE BOOKS"
DATE: 1943

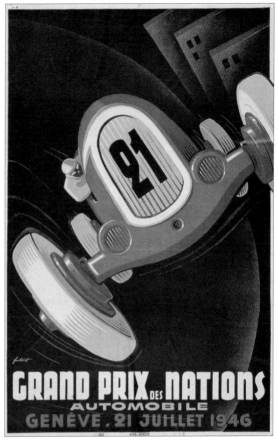

1

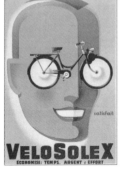

2

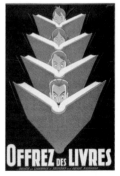

3

KEITH VAUGHAN
(1912–1977)

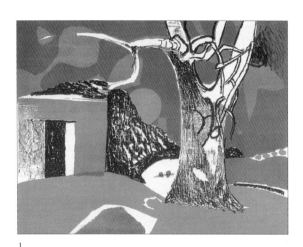

1

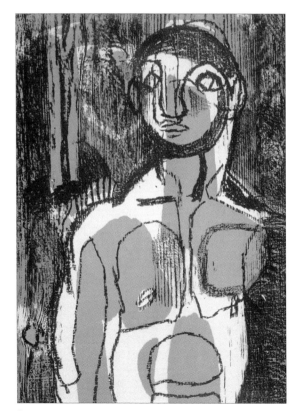

*Born in Sussex, UK. He received
no formal art training but
during the 1930s he developed
an interest in modern art,
particularly the work of
Cezanne, Picasso, and the
French Impressionists. During
World War II he worked as a
clerk and German interpreter
in London and produced a huge
volume of powerful gouaches
and ink drawings which were
displayed as part of a war
exhibition at the National
Gallery. His first one-man show
was in 1944, and it was at
this time that he met Graham
Sutherland and John Minton.
During the 1950s his work,
although essentially figurative,
became more abstract and
revealed the influence of
De Staël and the Abstract
Expressionists. He had several
major exhibitions and taught
periodically at the Camberwell,
Central and Slade schools of
art. In 1964 he was made an
Honorary Fellow of the Royal
College of Art and in 1965 was
awarded the CBE. His* Journals
and Drawings *were published the
following year and in 1989 there
was a major retrospective of
his work at the Austin/Desmond
Gallery in London.*

1 LANDSCAPE *(unpublished)*
DATE: 1949

2 THE WOODMAN
(unpublished)
DATE: 1949

2

Born in London. The son of a
professional boxer, he grew up
around the street markets of
south London. After World War
II he studied drawing, etching,
engraving, and lithography at
the Regent Street Polytechnic,
where he returned in 1956 as a
lecturer. Keeping worked mostly
in pen and ink. He illustrated
over 50 books, including
Charlie, Charlotte and the
Golden Canary, which won the
Kate Greenaway Medal in 1967,
and The Wildman, which won
the Francis Williams Prize in
1976. Joseph's Yard (1969), The
God Beneath the Sea (1970),
and The Railway Passage (1974)
were all commended for the Kate
Greenaway Medal. He taught
at Camberwell School of Art in
the 1980s and his work was
represented at the Victoria &
Albert Museum in London.

1 COSTER CART
(unpublished)
DATE: 1956

2 DERELICT CITY CARTS
(unpublished)
DATE: 1954

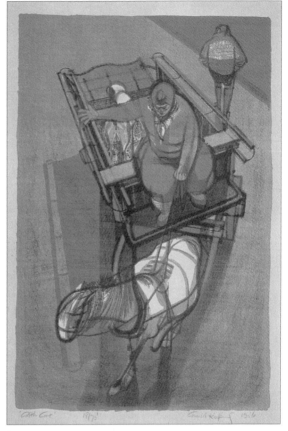

1

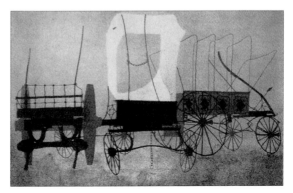

2

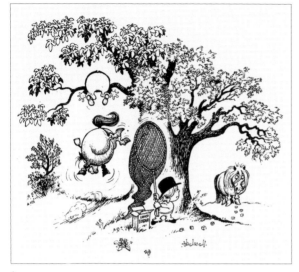

1

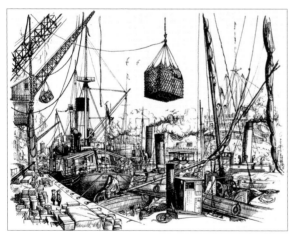

2

Born in Birkenhead, UK. He drew from childhood but was not encouraged to consider a career in art and started work in 1939 as a junior office clerk. After World War II a special government grant awarded to ex-servicemen enabled him to study at Liverpool College of Art, and after graduating in 1950 he taught at Wolverhampton College of Art. In 1952 he sent his first cartoon to Punch magazine and in 1956 he left teaching to take up illustration full-time. Over the next 25 years he produced over 60 covers and 1,500 illustrations for Punch, reflecting the English way of life. He also drew a pony cartoon strip, "Penelope and Kipper," for the Sunday Express. Although he is most famous for his humorous cartoons of endearingly scruffy, barrel-chested ponies ridden by tubby little girls, he also drew cartoons on a wide range of serious moral and political issues, but always with his characteristically gentle eye. His books were sold all over the world and his autobiography, Wrestling with a Pencil, was published in 1986.

1 ACQUIRING A PONY IS NOT AS EASY AS IT SOUNDS
DATE: 1962

2 I NEVER TIRE OF LOOKING AT THE SEA
DATE: 1952

*Born in Brooklyn, New York. At
the age of only eight, he enrolled
at the Brooklyn Academy of
Fine Arts. He started his career
working in comics, was an
assistant to Al Capp on Li'l
Abner, and developed his own
strip called Johnny Comet, as
well as contributing to Mad and
Playboy. During the 1960s and
1970s his cover illustrations
for the Conan series of heroic
fantasy stories by R E Howard
brought him to the forefront
of science-fiction art. After
illustrating the covers for a
series of Tarzan paperbacks
his style changed direction as
he became more involved in
sword and sorcery illustrations.
From this genre Frazetta has
emerged as an artist with a
cult following. He now has
the freedom to choose his own
subjects, and the originals of
his calendars, posters, and
paperback covers are valuable
collectors' pieces. His style,
characterized by exotic settings,
sex, violence, and exaggerated
physiques, is definitive of
fantasy art and has been
enormously influential. The
Fantastic Art of Frank Frazetta
was published in 1975.*

1 *POSTER: "FRANKENSTEIN
AND DRACULA" (non-
commissioned)*
DATE: 1969

2 *POSTER: "REASSEMBLED
MAN" (non-commissioned)*
DATE: 1965

3 *POSTER: "THE RETURN OF
JOUGAR" (non-commissioned)*
DATE: 1967

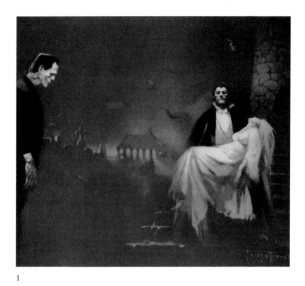

1

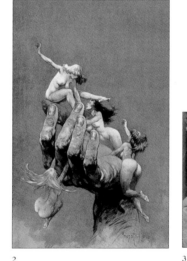

2

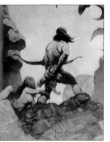

3

BERNARD BUFFET
(1928–1999)

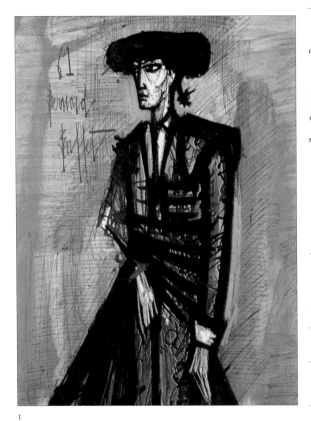

Born in Paris. At 15 he took evening classes in art and spent a year at the Ecole des Beaux-Arts in Paris. In 1947 he held his first exhibition, in a book shop in the Rue des Ecoles, and in 1948 shared the Grand Prix de la Critique. Seven years later his distinctive style won him recognition by the Connaissance des Arts as the leading post-war artist. His illustrated books included Cocteau's La Voix Humaine *(1957), Cyrano de Bergerac's* Les Voyages Fantastiques *(1958), and* Les Chants des Maldoror *(1952). He also designed stage sets for two ballets:* La Chambre *for Roland Petit and* Le Rendezvous Manque, *based on a story by Francoise Sagan. His work is held in permanent collection by the Tate Gallery, London and the Museum of Modern Art, New York.*

1 *CATALOG:* NICOLAS WINE
DATE: 1961

2 *POSTER:* "YOUNG PAINTER
IN FRANCE"
DATE: 1955

3 *PAINTING:* PIETA
DATE: 1946

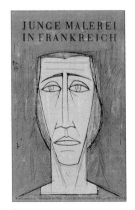

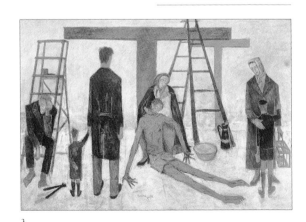

Born in London, daughter of the
illustrator John Hassall. She
studied at the Royal Academy
Schools and subsequently
attended the London County
Council School of Photo-
engraving and Lithography.
Her first commission after
graduating was for a wood-
engraved title page for her
brother Christopher's book of
poems Devil's Dyke (1936).
Other books included A Child's
Garden of Verses by Robert Louis
Stevenson (1947) and Jane
Austen's Mansfield Park (1959),
Northanger Abbey (1960),
Persuasion (1961), and Emma
(1962). She also illustrated for a
number of magazines, including
Argosy, London Mystery
Magazine, Picture Post, and The
Periodical, and designed the
invitation for the coronation of
Queen Elizabeth II in 1953. Her
wood-engraved illustrations
were worked in a meticulous
style influenced by Thomas
Bewick.

1 BOOK: CRANFORD by Mrs
        Gaskell
    DATE: 1940

2 BOOK: SEALSKIN TROUSERS
        by Eric Linklater
    ·DATE: 1947

3 BOOK: URANIA by Ruth Pitter
    DATE: 1950

4 BOOK: COLLECTED POEMS
        OF ANDREW YOUNG
    DATE: 1950

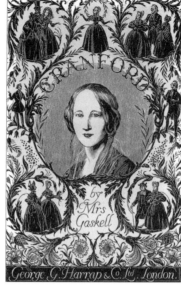

1

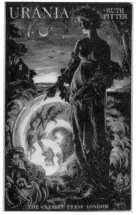

3

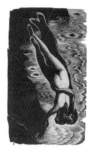

2

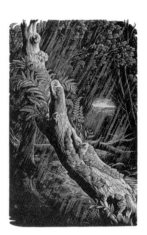

4

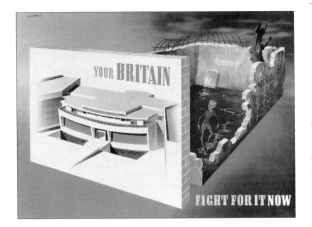

1

Born in London. Mainly self-taught as an artist, his first job was in a commercial studio from 1932 to 1936, and it was during this period that he developed an interest in poster design. His work, features striking color, bold graphic ideas, and beautifully integrated typography, communicated clearly and effectively. In 1940 he became the official War Office poster designer. At the end of the war he produced posters and stamps for British, Irish, Israeli, and Portuguese government departments and designed murals and advertising poster campaigns for clients such as Guinness, BOAC, Shell, and Capstan cigarettes. In 1951 he designed the official emblem for the Festival of Britain and in 1953 the symbol of BBC Television. From 1946 to 1953 he taught at the Royal College of Art in London. He was awarded the OBE in 1958 for his services to graphic design.

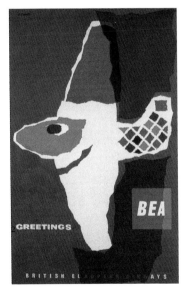

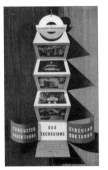

3

1 POSTER: "FINSBURY HEALTH CENTRE"
DATE: 1943

2 POSTER: "BRITISH EUROPEAN AIRWAYS"
DATE: 1960

3 POSTER: "LONDON TRANSPORT"
DATE: 1953

Born in Beckenham, UK. Studied at Dulwich College and Goldsmith's College of Art under Ed Sullivan. After graduation he designed scenery and costumes for the Everyman Theatre in Hampstead, London, then worked briefly in advertising before becoming a freelance illustrator. In 1934 he designed and executed a huge mural at the Museum of the Chartered Insurance Institute of London. From 1936 to 1937 he lived in New York, where he began writing and illustrating children's books. He specialized in historical reconstructions, and the publication of Shakespeare's Theater *won him the Kate Greenaway Medal for best British book illustration in 1964. In 1966 he was runner-up for the Carnegie Medal for* Namesake. *His love of the stage was quite evident in his work, and in 1951 he was involved in the design of the Mermaid Theatre in London.*

1 *MAGAZINE:* RADIO TIMES
DATE: 1950

2 *MAGAZINE:* RADIO TIMES
DATE: 1950

3 *MAGAZINE:* RADIO TIMES
DATE: 1950

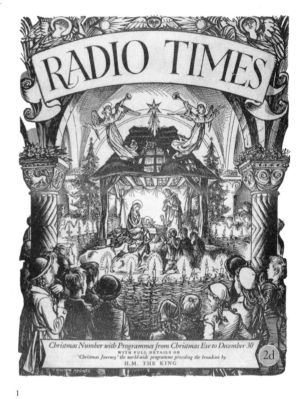

1

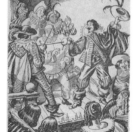

2

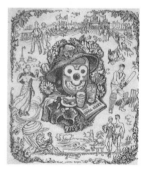

3

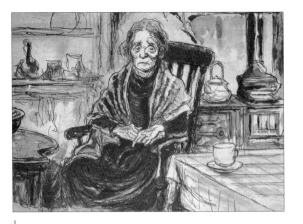

1

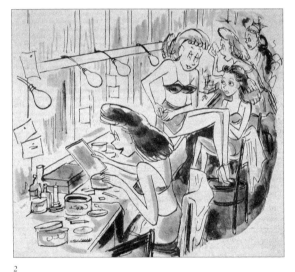

2

Born Victor Weisz in Berlin, of
Hungarian parentage. He left
school at the age of 14 to help
support his family and began
selling caricatures of public
figures to the local newspapers.
With the rise of Nazism he
turned to political cartoons
in 1929 and in 1935 he left
Germany to settle in London,
eventually becoming a British
citizen. He worked for the News
Chronicle as a staff artist and,
in the years after World War II,
his drawings illustrated stories
and articles in publications
such as Cosmopolitan, Woman's
Own, The Leader, and The Daily
Mirror. In 1958 he joined the
staff of the Evening Standard.

1 MAGAZINE: THE LEADER
DATE: 1950

2 MAGAZINE: THE LEADER
DATE: 1950

LEONARD BASKIN
(1922–2000)

Born in New Brunswick, USA. Studied at Yale University of Fine Arts and the New School for Social Research, and also in Paris and Florence. A sculptor and graphic artist, he also made an important contribution to book illustration as publisher and printer for his own Gehenna Press. The first title of this imprint, On a Pyre of Withered Roses *(1942), was produced while Baskin was still a student at Yale. The range of his subsequent work included strongly graphic linoleum and wood engravings in* A Little Book of Natural History *(1951) and highly detailed etchings in* Horned Beetles and Other Insects *(1958).*

1 TOBIAS AND THE ANGEL
(unpublished)
DATE: 1958

2 MAN WITH SPRING PLANTS
(unpublished)
DATE: 1953

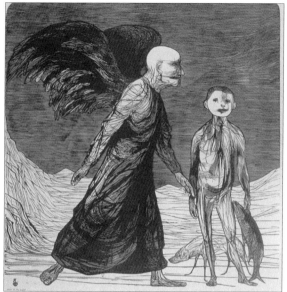

1

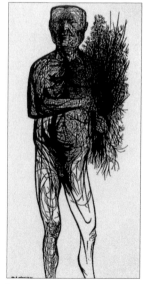

2

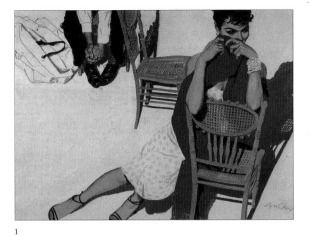

1

Born in Ohio, USA. Trained at
the Dayton Art Institute and the
Chicago Art Institute, where
he took evening classes while
serving an apprenticeship in
a local art studio. He worked
briefly for the Herald Examiner
before moving to New York. In
common with his contemporary
Jon Whitcomb, his primary
interest was in depicting
glamorous and beautiful
women, but his softer use of
color was more definitively
romantic and his compositions
explored the subtler nuances of
the relationships between men
and women.

1 *MAGAZINE:* LADIES' HOME
JOURNAL
DATE: 1947

2 *ILLUSTRATION:* (unpublished)
DATE: NOT KNOWN

3 *MAGAZINE:* THE SATURDAY
EVENING POST
DATE: NOT KNOWN

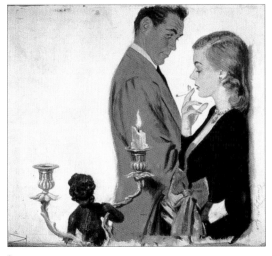

2

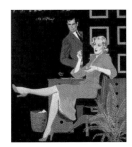

3

Born in Memphis, USA. He was
a student of Burton Callicott,
whom he cited as his greatest
influence, before attending
the American Academy of Art
in Chicago. He then became
a freelance illustrator at the
studio partnership of Sundblom,
Stevens and Stultz. Although
one of the "Sundblom Circle,"
he developed his own highly
individual approach to the
problems of illustration. His
method was to work out his
compositions with quick,
rough sketches and then pose
and photograph models in the
positions that he had drawn.
Later, when preparing the
final illustration, he used the
photographs to provide the
details of lighting and minutiae
that would otherwise remain
unseen. The technique was
extremely successful, and he
was commissioned frequently
by The Saturday Evening Post,
Cosmopolitan, Redbook, and
Good Housekeeping. During the
early 1950s he traveled to India,
Japan, Hong Kong, and Hawaii
recording the activities of
the U.S. Air Force. Later, he
concentrated on commissioned
portrait painting.

1 *MAGAZINE:* SPORTS AFIELD
DATE: 1959

2 *MAGAZINE:* THE SATURDAY
EVENING POST
DATE: 1962

3 *MAGAZINE:* THE SATURDAY
EVENING POST
DATE: 1958

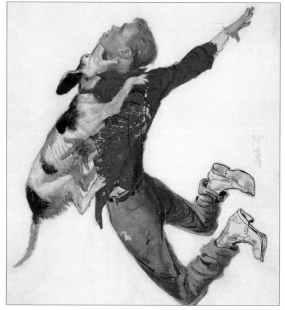

1

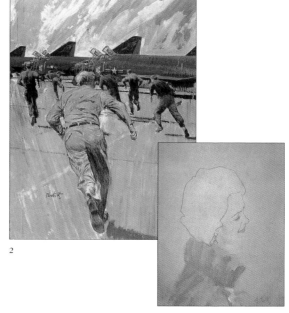

2

3

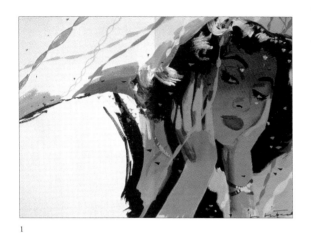

1

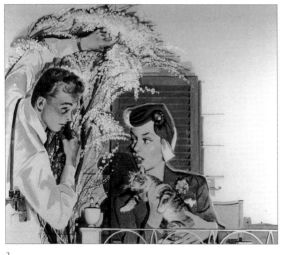

2

Born in Oklahoma, USA. Studied art at Ohio Wesleyan University, then worked as a poster artist and produced drawings for local advertising agencies. In 1934 he moved to New York and concentrated on freelance illustration. He specialized in depicting romantic interludes and portraits of beautiful, glamorous women, and achieved popularity through publication in such magazines as Collier's *and* Good Housekeeping. *He spent some time as a combat artist during World War II, returning to gentler themes after his discharge in 1945. His style was perfectly suited to the editorial content of* Redbook Magazine *and* Cosmopolitan, *for whom he wrote and illustrated a monthly column on movie stars. He also wrote two children's books,* Coco *and* Pom Pom's Christmas, *and a book on beautiful women,* All about Girls.

1 BROWN-HAIRED GAL
(unpublished)
DATE: c. 1940

2 *MAGAZINE:* WOMAN'S HOME
COMPANION
DATE: 1941

EDWARD BAWDEN
(1903–1989)

Born in Braintree, UK. Studied at Cambridge School of Art and the Royal College of Art under Paul Nash. He was an official war artist during World War II and traveled to France and the Middle East. His strong graphic style, economy of line, and sardonic wit perfectly captured the spirit of the places he visited. Influenced by Nash, Beardsley, Cézanne, and Picasso, he also designed and executed murals for the liner SS Orcades and for the Lion and the Unicorn Pavilion at the Festival of Britain. His illustration clients were many, and included Shell, London Transport, and Penguin Books. He tended to draw in pen and ink with washes on non-absorbent paper. He was also a highly accomplished watercolorist, and won the Francis Williams Book Illustration Award in 1977 and 1982. He taught design and book illustration for many years, first at Goldsmith's College and later at the Royal College of Art, and as of 1951 was a trustee of the Tate Gallery, where his work is represented. In 1956 he was made a Royal Academician.

1 *POSTER: "LONDON TRANSPORT"*
DATE: 1952

2 *POSTER: "LONDON UNDERGROUND"*
DATE: c. 1950

3 *BOOK:* LIFE IN AN ENGLISH VILLAGE
DATE: 1949

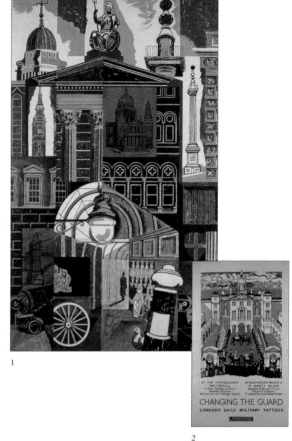

1

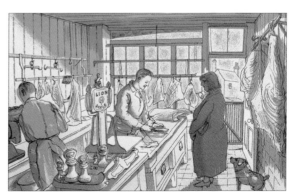

2

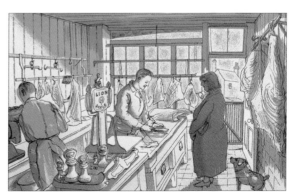

3

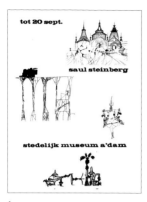

1

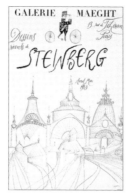

2

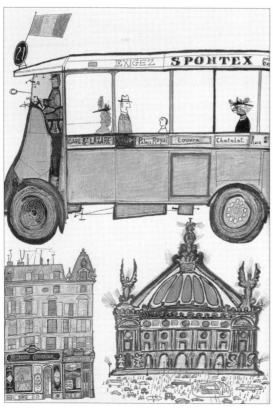

3

*Born in Ramnic Sarat,
Romania. Studied psychology
and sociology at Bucharest
University and in 1933 moved
to Milan, where he studied
architecture. In 1942 he
emigrated to America and joined
the staff of* The New Yorker
*magazine. During the war he
served with the U.S. Navy and
then returned to New York,
where he lived for the rest of his
life. He was a prolific artist, well
known for his witty cartoons,
or "graphic parodies," as they
were called. His illustrated
books included* All in Line
(1945), The Art of Living
(1945), The Passport *(1954),*
and The Labyrinth *(1961). An
enormously influential artist, his
reputation was international,
and he had exhibitions at the
Museum of Modern Art, New
York; the ICA, London; and in
Paris and Amsterdam.*

1 *EXHIBITION POSTER*
DATE: 1953

2 *EXHIBITION POSTER*
DATE: 1953

3 *MAGAZINE:* VOGUE
DATE: 1951

ALFRED BESTALL
(1892–1986)

Born in Burma. Studied at Birmingham School of Art. After World War I he joined a commercial studio and also worked as a freelance illustrator. In 1936 he took over the Rupert Bear *strip in the* Daily Express *from its original illustrator, Mary Tourtel (1897–1940). He was subsequently identified with Rupert until his retirement in 1965, when he left a great deal of material still to be published. As well as in the newspaper strip, "Rupert" was published in annuals, the first in 1936; at the height of their popularity during the 1940s and 1950s, they sold over 1.5 million copies a year. Bestall followed the graphic style developed by Tourtel but introduced more humor and action into the story lines, sometimes developing a slightly surreal element to the adventures of the intrepid bear and his playmates.*

1, 2 *BOOK:* DAILY EXPRESS ANNUAL
DATE: 1956

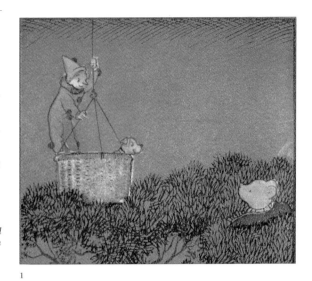

1

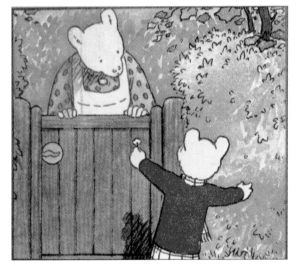

2

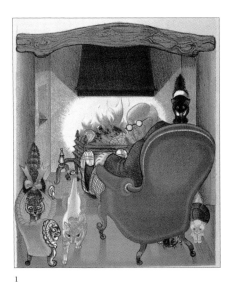

1

*Born in Scotland. Attended
life classes at Manchester Art
School, then studied art at
Reading University. In 1917 she
moved to London, where she
attended the Central School of
Art and Crafts whilst designing
book jackets, posters and
illustrating children's stories.
She is most famous for her
Orlando books, a series of stories
based on the adventures of a
large marmalade cat which
she wrote for her own children.
Although his adventures were
flights of fantasy, the character
of Orlando, like that of Jean de
Brunhoff's Babar (of which Hale
was a great admirer), remains
perfectly plausible – in keeping
with her belief that fantasy
should always have some basis
in reality. She was awarded the
OBE in 1976.*

1 *BOOK:* ORLANDO BUYS A
COTTAGE *by Kathleen Hale*
DATE: 1963

2, 3 *BOOK:* ORLANDO: THE
FRISKY HOUSEWIFE *by
Kathleen Hale*
DATE: 1956

2

3

PETER BLAKE
(b. 1932)

Born in Dartford, UK. Studied at Gravesend Technical College and School of Art and attended the Royal College of Art from 1953–56. He spent a year studying folk art in Europe, an experience clearly reflected in his early work. Other influences have been the popular Victorian realists and American Symbolic Realists such as Ben Shahn. Although a brilliant draftsman, he was best known during the 1960s for his collage work, incorporating everyday consumer items, advertisements, photographs of pin-up girls, and other ephemera, and was very much part of the British Pop Art movement. His illustrative work includes Summer with Monica *by Roger McGough, several covers for the* Arden Shakespeare *series published by Methuen, album sleeves, posters, and magazines. He has held several one-man exhibitions in London, Europe and Japan, exhibited with "The Ruralists" in 1981, and is represented in major public collections throughout the world.*

1 *RECORD ALBUM COVER:* SGT PEPPER'S LONELY HEARTS CLUB BAND
DATE: 1967

2 *PERIODICAL:* THE TIMES LITERARY SUPPLEMENT
DATE: 1966

3 *MAGAZINE:* THE SUNDAY TIMES MAGAZINE
DATE: 1969

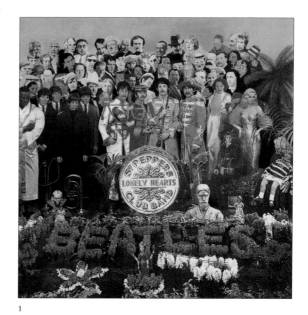

1

2

3

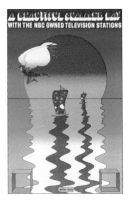

1

2

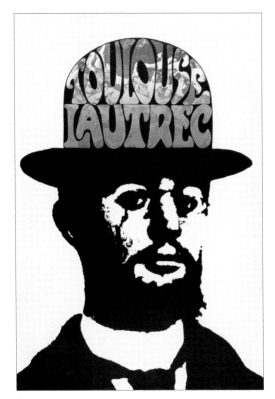

3

Born in Berlin, Germany. Spent his childhood in Shanghai, where he developed his interest in Eastern art and philosophy. When he was 12 his family moved to Israel, where he studied art and astronomy. In the mid-1950s his family took him to New York, where he attended the Art Students League, the Pratt Institute, and the School of Visual Arts. In 1962 he set up a design studio with his friend Daly, which over the next two years won an astonishing 68 awards for excellence in illustration, design, and typography. Max's personal art form, "Cosmic Art," took its inspiration from nature, as he believes that "it is in nature that the most beautiful things are to be found." Religion, mythology and oriental symbolism are all important components of his designs, which to epitomize the aesthetics of the 1960s.

1 POSTER: "USA LIBERAL PARTY, NEW YORK"
DATE: 1969

2 POSTER: "NBC TELEVISION"
DATE: 1969

3 POSTER: "TOULOUSE LAUTREC"
DATE: 1967

DR SEUSS
(1904–1991)

Born Theodor Seuss Geisel in Massachusetts, USA. He was educated at Dartmouth College and did a postgraduate year at Oxford University in England. His intention was to become a professor of English Literature. However, after traveling in Europe for a year he returned to America, where he spent 15 years working in advertising. In 1937 he published his first book, And to think that I saw it on Mulberry Street, *and went on to publish 27 children's books featuring strange creatures of his own design—hybrids of cats, bears, and human beings. This strange menagerie has proven to be enduringly popular.*

1,2 *BOOK:* THE SLEEP BOOK *by*
Dr Seuss
DATE: 1962

3 *BOOK:* THE FOOT BOOK *by*
Dr Seuss
DATE: 1968

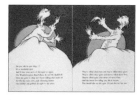

1

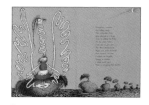

2

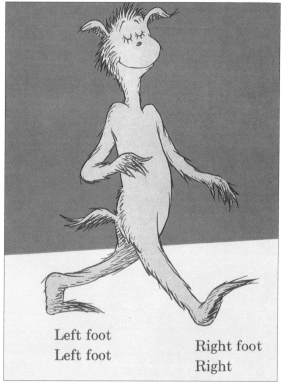

Left foot
Left foot

Right foot
Right

3

BRIAN WILDSMITH
(b. 1930)

Born in Penistone, UK. After abandoning a promising career in chemistry, he studied at the Barnsley School of Art and then at the Slade School of Fine Art. He became a freelance illustrator at the age of 27 and his illustrations were featured in two books published in 1959, The Story of Jesus *by Eleanor Graham and* The Daffodil Bird *by Ruth Tomalin. Since then he has written and illustrated nearly 20 books, including* Brian Wildsmith's ABC, *which won the Kate Greenaway Medal in 1962. Within all of his drawings, both black-and-white and full color, he uses a wide variety of media and techniques to create a striking array of textures, and his style was extremely influential throughout the 1960s.*

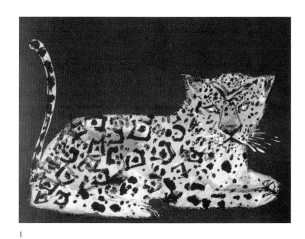

1

1–2 *BOOK:* BRIAN WILDSMITH'S ABC
DATE: 1962

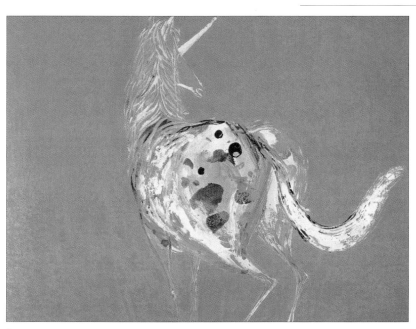

2

MARTIN SHARP
(b. 1942)

Born in Sydney, Australia. He studied at the East Sydney Art School, and after graduating in 1963 produced cartoons and graphics for Richard Neville's magazine Oz. In 1966 these illustrations were published under the title Martin Sharp Cartoons and in the same year, he, Neville, and Oz moved to London. Over the next three years Sharp's psychedelic, day-glow paintings became icons of underground art and, as well as working prolifically for Oz, he produced posters for the Big O poster company and illustrated album covers for Cream's Disraeli Gears and Wheels of Fire. In 1969 he returned to Australia and has since concentrated on paintings and posters. In 1972 he published Artbook, a collection of his work which reveals such diverse influences as Rene Magritte and Vincent van Gogh. He spent ten years making a movie about the life of Tiny Tim, "Street of Dreams." In 1988 he exhibited his posters in Brighton, UK.

1 MAGAZINE: OZ
DATE: 1968

2 MAGAZINE: OZ
DATE: 1968

3 POSTER: "BOB DYLAN"
DATE: 1967

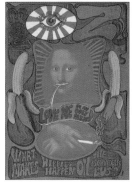

1

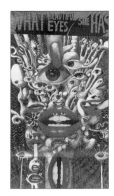

2

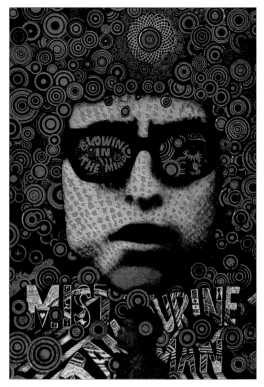

3

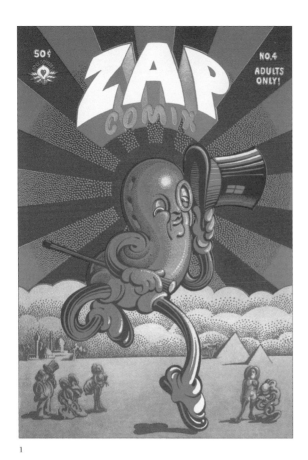

Born in Spain. Moscoso lives
and works in America, where
during the 1960s he achieved
eminence as an underground
artist. His earliest works are a
series of posters in 1967 for the
Avalon and Fillmore ballrooms
in San Francisco, where bands
such as the Grateful Dead were
playing. In the late 1960s he was
a staff artist on Rolling Stone
magazine, then in the 1970s he
became more involved in comic
book illustration. His work
appears in All Stars (1970), his
own book Color (1971), and
science-fiction comics which
also featured the drawings
of Robert Crumb and Gilbert
Shelton. His most notable comic
work is featured in the Zap
Comix series, which is still in
print. Moscoso's definitively
psychedelic style made him
popular with underground
publications around the world
and he was featured heavily in
London's Oz and International
Times. His pictures have also
appeared in Playboy and in
advertisements for Levi jeans.

1 COMIC: ZAP
DATE: c. 1969

JOHN BURNINGHAM
(b. 1936)

Born in Farnham, UK. Studied at the Central School of Art. After graduation, he wrote his own stories to get his work published. His first book, Borka: The Adventures of a Goose with no Feathers, *won the Kate Greenaway Medal in 1963.* Mr Gumpy's Outing *won the medal again in 1970 as well as the Boston Globe* Horn Book Award *for illustration in 1972. Burningham works in full color, using an array of media— india ink crayons, gouache, cellulose, montage, printer's ink, pastel, and photostats. He says of children's illustration: "A beautiful picture is not enough; a mixture of action, detail, and atmosphere is important." He lives and works in London.*

1 *POSTER: "LONDON TRANSPORT"*
DATE: 1963

2 *POSTER: "LONDON TRANSPORT"*
DATE: c. 1960

3 *BOOK:* MR GUMPY'S OUTING
by John Burningham
DATE: 1970

4 *BOOK:* TROUBLOFF
by John Burningham
DATE: 1964

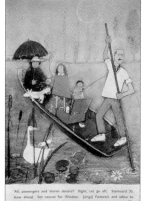

1

2

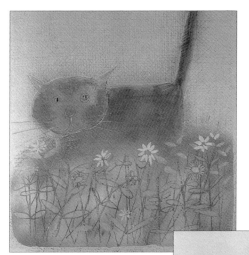

3

4

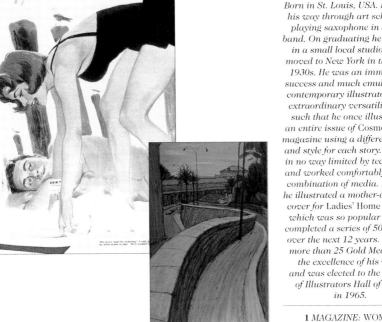

Born in St. Louis, USA. He paid his way through art school by playing saxophone in a jazz band. On graduating he worked in a small local studio, then moved to New York in the mid-1930s. He was an immediate success and much emulated by contemporary illustrators. His extraordinary versatility was such that he once illustrated an entire issue of Cosmopolitan magazine using a different name and style for each story. He was in no way limited by technique, and worked comfortably in any combination of media. In 1939 he illustrated a mother-daughter cover for Ladies' Home Journal which was so popular that he completed a series of 50 of them over the next 12 years. He won more than 25 Gold Medals for the excellence of his work and was elected to the Society of Illustrators Hall of Fame in 1965.

1 *MAGAZINE:* WOMAN
DATE: 1960

2 *MAGAZINE:* SPORTS ILLUSTRATED
DATE: 1964

3 *ADVERTISEMENT:* "AMERICAN AIRLINES"
DATE: 1965

1

2

3

MICHAEL ENGLISH
(b. 1943)

Born in London. Studied at Ealing College of Art. In 1967 he formed a design company, Haphash and the Coloured Coat, with Nigel Waymouth, the co-owner of the cult King's Road store, Granny Takes a Trip. Over the next two years they produced many psychedelic posters advertising underground events in London. English's work also appeared in the counter-culture's foremost magazine, International Times. *His paintings, which are definitive of the psychedelic era, were the product of an extraordinarily eclectic style. His influences embraced the Art Nouveau period of Beardsley and Mucha, Art Deco, Hindu symbolism, Japanese and Islamic decoration, Surrealist imagery, and cartoon-style typography. English was also interested in the ephemera of the late 1960s, designing T-shirts and sunglasses decorated with the Union Jack. With the arrival of the 1970s his work changed dramatically and he abandoned the esoteric in favor of an exploration of the minutiae of urban life through his airbrushed hyper-realistic illustrations.*

1 *POSTER: "LIVERPOOL LOVE FESTIVAL"*
DATE: 1968

2 *POSTER: "LOVE ME FILM PRODUCTIONS"*
DATE: 1969

3 *POSTER: "JIMI HENDRIX CONCERT"*
DATE: 1968

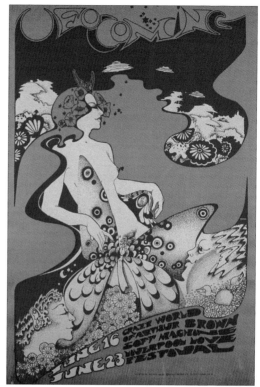

1

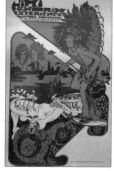

2

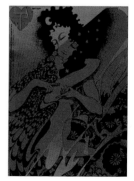

3

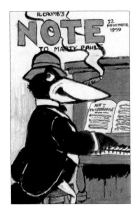

1

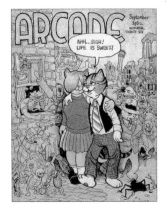

2

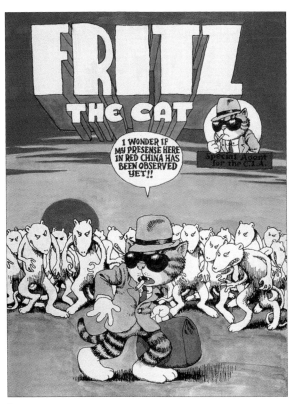

3

Born in Philadelphia, USA.
He started drawing cartoons
as a child and drew comic
books with his brother as a
teenager. This is when he first
created Fritz the Cat the cartoon
character for which he is most
famous and which was made
into an X-rated animation
movie in 1971. In 1962 he
moved to Cleveland, Ohio, and
from 1964 started drawing for
the underground newspapers
Yarrowstalks and East Village
Other. In 1966 he moved to San
Francisco, where he started the
hugely popular Zap and Snatch
comics. His fluid expressive
cartoons, executed in pen and
ink, brilliantly reflected the
hippy drug culture of the 1960s
and early 1970s, when his
Schuman the Human and Mr.
Natural characters, and his
sexually explicit cartoons, often
starring himself as the unlikely
victim of sex-starved women,
reached the peak of their
popularity. His books include
The Snatch Sampler (1977) and
Head Comix (1968).

1 COMIC: NOTE
DATE: 1959

2 COMIC: ARCADE
DATE: 1962

3 COMIC: FRITZ THE CAT
DATE: 1962

Born in London. Brother of the actress Hattie Jacques, he was educated in Hertfordshire and worked in an advertising agency while submitting illustrations to the Radio Times. After the war he became a full-time freelance illustrator, his first commissions being Dickens' Doctor Marigold (1945) and Cross' The Angry Planet (1945). In 1948 he was appointed art editor of The Strand Magazine and contributed to many other magazines, including The Leader, The Listener, Punch, Vogue, The Sunday Times, Nova, and The Observer. His drawings were meticulously detailed and usually executed in line, sometimes with an ink or watercolor wash. He had a particular interest in 19th-century literature and placed a great emphasis on research to ensure the accuracy of his drawings.

1 MAGAZINE: THE LEADER
DATE: 1950

2 MAGAZINE: THE LEADER
DATE: 1950

3 MAGAZINE: THE LEADER
DATE: 1950

4 BOOK: FORTY-TWO STORIES
by Hans Christian Andersen
DATE: 1953

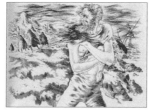

1

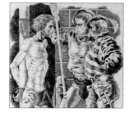

2

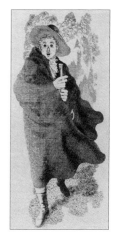

3

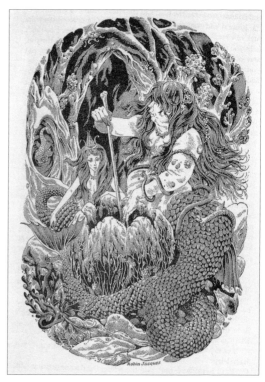

4

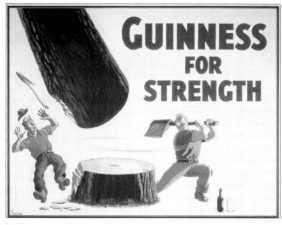

1

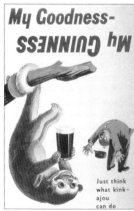

2

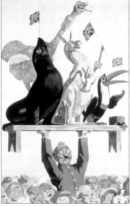

3

Born in Newcastle, UK. Educated at King Edward VI College in Newcastle, he went on to study at the Royal College of Art, London. On returning from a traveling scholarship to the continent, he became a teacher at the Royal College of Art, designing advertising posters in his spare time. He joined the staff of S H Benson Ltd in 1925 and began a long and distinguished career in advertising art. His posters for Guinness beer, stylized but realistic humorous images with accompanying slogans such as the famous "My goodness, my Guinness," were produced prolifically during the 1930s, when new ideas were required continuously. He also contributed illustrations to Radio Times throughout the 1930s. After World War II, Gilroy concentrated seriously on portrait painting, working on commissions that included portraits of Sir Winston Churchill as well as several members of the British royal family.

1 ADVERTISEMENT:
"GUINNESS BEER"
DATE: 1940

2 ADVERTISEMENT:
"GUINNESS BEER"
DATE: 1956

3 ADVERTISEMENT:
"GUINNESS BEER"
DATE: 1953

BRUCE BOMBERGER
(1918–1980)

Born in California. With the exception of one year in New York, Bomberger spent his life and varied career on the west coast of America. He started work in an art studio and at one point had a studio of his own, but eventually returned to freelancing. He worked for many different advertising clients, his most notable work being his wildlife drawings for the Weyerhaeuser Timber Company. His drawings also illustrated the stories and the editorial pages of such magazines as True, The Saturday Evening Post, Cosmopolitan, Good Housekeeping, *and* This Week. *He was at one time President of the San Francisco Society of Illustrators.*

1 *PAINTING*
DATE: 1962

2 *MAGAZINE:* THE SATURDAY
EVENING POST
DATE: 1954

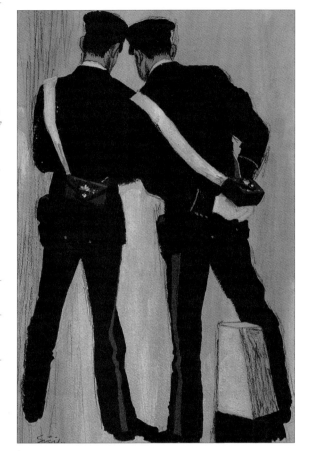

1

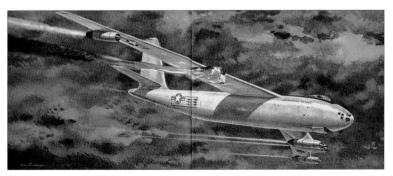

2

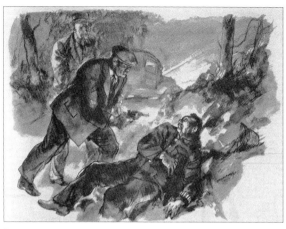

1

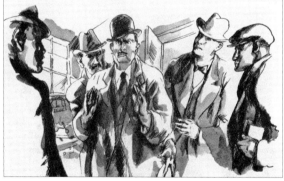

2

Born in London. Studied at London art schools before taking up a career as a freelance illustrator. He was particularly associated with The London Illustrated News *and also worked for* The Graphic *and* Radio Times*. His illustrations were typically line or line-and-wash but he was also an accomplished oil painter and watercolorist, and was elected Royal Academician in 1952. His lively approach to literary themes is exemplified by illustrations to Wycherley's* The Country Wife *(1934), conceived as scenes on stage with a strong sense of movement and dramatic lighting. He brought a fresh character to Dickens' classic* Nicholas Nickleby *(1940), but was equally attuned to the work of contemporary novelists, as in* The Circus is Coming *(1938) by Noel Streatfield and* The Valley of Song *(1951) by Elizabeth Goudge.*

1 *MAGAZINE:* THE LEADER
DATE: 1950

2 *MAGAZINE:* THE LEADER
DATE: 1950

Born in Denver, Colorado, USA. Studied geology at Wichita State University, then enrolled at the Art Center College of Design in Los Angeles. In 1953 he moved to New York, where he was much in demand owing to his ability to work in a broad range of styles using different media and techniques. His first movie poster was for West Side Story *in 1960. Since then he illustrated posters for many box office successes, including* Camelot, *for which he won a Society of Illustrators gold medal,* Hair, The Missouri Breaks, *and* The Last Emperor. *Although he denied having a particular style, he admitted to being influenced by Art Nouveau and had a passion for Egon Schiele, Degas, Matisse, and the French Impressionists. His clients included* Life, Look, Esquire, Cosmopolitan, Sports Illustrated *and,* Playboy *magazines, Coca-Cola, the U.S. Postal Service, and a number of major movie companies, including MGM and Walt Disney. He won numerous gold and silver medals, was voted Artist of the Year in 1961 by the Artists Guild of New York, won the Hamilton King Award in 1968, and was elected to the Society of Illustrators Hall of Fame in 1977.*

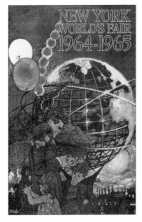

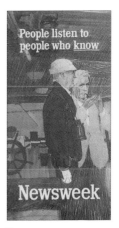

1   2

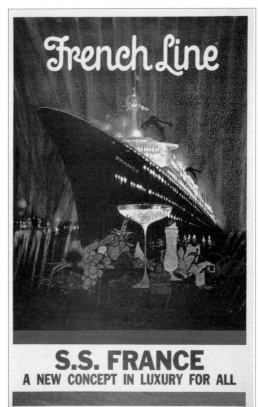

3

1 *ADVERTISEMENT: "NEW YORK WORLD'S FAIR"*
DATE: 1964

2 *ADVERTISEMENT: "NEWSWEEK MAGAZINE"*
DATE: 1964

3 *ADVERTISEMENT: "SS FRANCE"*
DATE: 1964

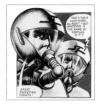

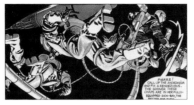

1

2

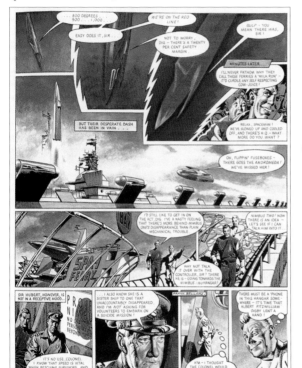

3

Born in Kettering, UK. Bellamy was one of the first Englishmen working in comic books to achieve international recognition as an illustrator. In the early 1950s he drew advertising campaigns for The Daily Telegraph, World Press Agency, and Ad Weekly as well as illustrations for Home Notes, Boy's Own Paper, Men Only, and covers for Lilliput. His first comic strip was an advertisement for a toothpaste company and was called "Commando Gibbs v Dragon Decay." In 1957 he joined the Eagle comic and illustrated the life of Winston Churchill in a strip called The Happy Warrior. It was the first time that the biography of a living individual had been drawn in this style and it was serialized on the back page. In 1960 he was asked to redesign Dan Dare for the front page and in 1962 he created Heros The Spartan, which won him the Academy of Comic Book Arts award in America as Best Foreign Comic Book Artist. He was an immaculate draftsman whose work had an almost photographic realism. He inked directly onto the art board and colored in with gouache and waterproof inks, creating artwork that was as perfect as the printed page. In the latter part of his life he gave up comics, but continued to draw a black-and-white newspaper strip called Garth until his death in 1976.

1 MAGAZINE: EAGLE
DATE: 1960

2 MAGAZINE: EAGLE
DATE: 1960

3 MAGAZINE: EAGLE
DATE: 1963

BRIAN LOVE
(b. 1942)

Born in London. Studied at Gravesend and Walthamstow schools of art and the Royal College of Art. From the mid 1960s his obsession with American and British popular culture, and his collection of popular magazines and juvenile literature, became the prime source of reference for his illustration work, much of which attempted to pastiche the color and compositional arrangement found in such publications. His work as a printmaker greatly influenced the way in which he assembled and designed his illustrations. In many cases he produced line-separated artwork which only formed the completed image when printed. His work has appeared in Town, Nova, Radio Times, The Sunday Times, The Observer, *and* Vogue *magazines and he illustrated* The Beatles' Lyrics *in 1968. Even more prolific as a fine artist, he has had one-man exhibitions of his sculptures in Holland and Germany. In 1978 he mounted a touring exhibition entitled "Aerial Drop"—a never-before-seen collection of propaganda leaflets dropped from airplanes. He has also compiled two books on board games,* Play the Game *(1978) and* Great Board Games *(1979).*

1 *MAGAZINE:* RADIO TIMES
DATE: 1969

2 *MAGAZINE:* THE SUNDAY
TIMES MAGAZINE
DATE: 1969

3 *MAGAZINE:* THE SUNDAY
TIMES MAGAZINE
DATE: 1969

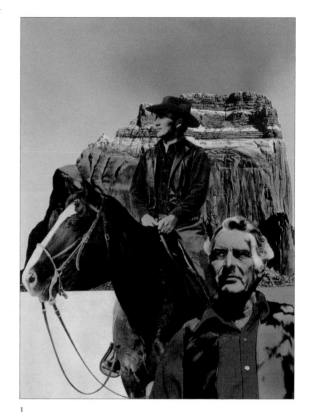

1

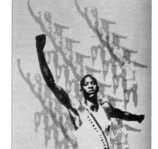

2

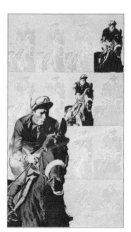

3

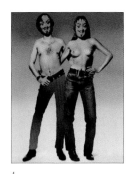

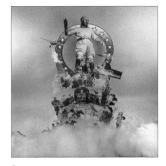

4 *AIRBRUSHED BLACK-AND-
WHITE PHOTOGRAPH:* DAVID
BAILEY AND MARIE HELVIN
(unpublished)
DATE: 1969

5 *MAGAZINE:* THE SUNDAY
TIMES MAGAZINE
DATE: 1969

6 *MAGAZINE:* THE SUNDAY
TIMES MAGAZINE
DATE: 1968

4   5

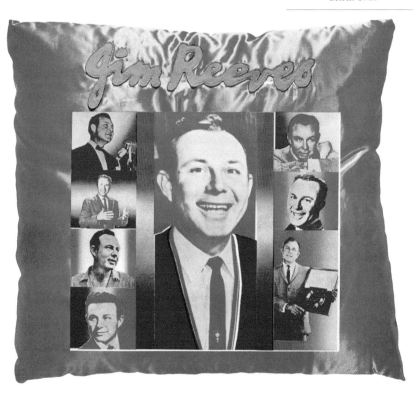

6

RICHARD WEIGAND
(b. 1942)

Born in London. Trained as a typographer at the London College of Printing and then worked as assistant to Hans Neuberg. In 1965 he became a freelance illustrator and graphic designer, and over the next four years worked regularly for magazines such as The Sunday Times *and* Radio Times. *In 1969 he moved to America and from 1970 to 1975 was art director of* Esquire *magazine. He received numerous awards for his work, which he says was never inspired by other illustrators but by the movies and the pop and montage art of the time. From 1975 to 1979 he was director of the Children's Television Workshop, an educational development of the Sesame Street Muppets. He still lives and works in New York, where he is freelance consultant and planner to the magazine publishing industry.*

1 *MAGAZINE:* THE SUNDAY TIMES MAGAZINE
DATE: 1968

2 *MAGAZINE:* THE SUNDAY TIMES MAGAZINE
DATE: 1968

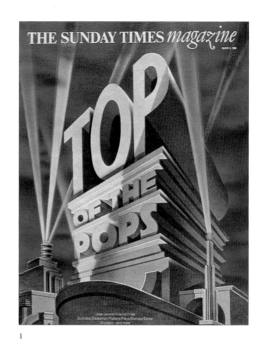

1

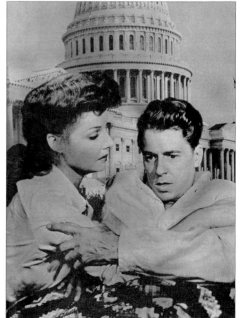

2

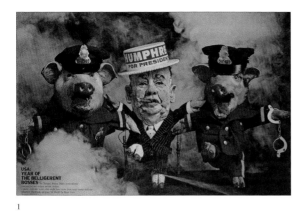

1

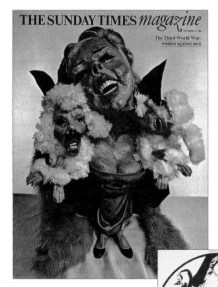

2

Born near Cambridge, UK.
Studied at Cambridge School of
Art, where he met Peter Fluck,
with whom he later formed the
partnership responsible for the
Spitting Image TV series. After
leaving college he worked with
Peter Cook on a satirical strip
for the Observer, and also drew
giant topical cartoons for the
walls of Cook's nightclub, The
Establishment where he met
Lenny Bruce and other stand-up
comics who influenced his later
work. In 1963 he joined the art
department of The Sunday Times
magazine as an illustrator and
collaborated with David King
on a series of record covers
and posters. In 1967 he was a
Rockefeller Foundation winner
and was artist-in-residence at
Reed College, Oregon for six
months. He spent the following
two years in America. He
did fashion drawings and
illustration in San Francisco
and worked at Push Pin Studios
in New York. On his return to
England he became features
editor of The Sunday Times
magazine and in 1975 formed
the Luck and Flaw partnership
with Peter Fluck. Together they
created the hit British comedy
TV show Spitting Image.

1 *MAGAZINE:* THE SUNDAY
TIMES MAGAZINE
DATE: c. 1968

2 *MAGAZINE:* THE SUNDAY
TIMES MAGAZINE
*DATE.*1969

3 *MAGAZINE:* NOVA
DATE: c. 1967

Born in Detroit, Michigan, USA. Studied at the Wicker Art School. He began his art career as assistant to an automobile illustrator, then drew for the Dearborn Independent *before enrolling at the Art Students League in New York. During the Depression he did a variety of jobs, including ghosting the* Flash Gordon *strip and doing pulp illustrations for* Blue Book *magazine. He had an unlimited repertoire of techniques, sometimes reducing his drawings to the barest line and at other times illustrating in delicate colored washes. Most prolific at a time when photography was making real inroads into magazine publishing, he specialized in the candid pose, mimicking the camera's ability to freeze the moment and often seeming to catch his subject unawares. His work appeared in* Collier's, McClure's, Cosmopolitan, Redbook, *and* The Saturday Evening Post, *and his advertising clients included Douglas PC Airliners. He was elected to the Society of Illustrators Hall of Fame in 1969.*

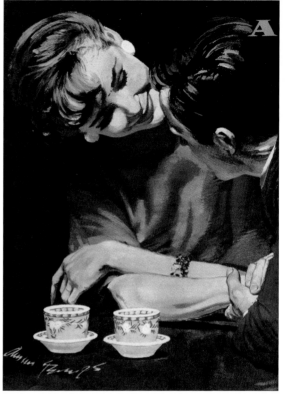

1

1 *MAGAZINE:* WOMAN
DATE: 1960

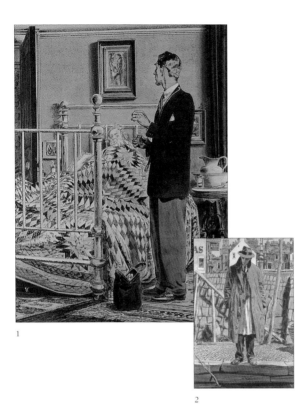

1

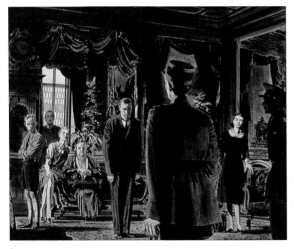

2

Born in London. The son of a keen amateur artist, he grew up in Canada and New York. At the age of 19 he returned to London to study at the Slade School of Fine Art, then in 1924 returned to America and embarked on a career as a freelance illustrator. His superb draftsmanship and compositions quickly earned him a reputation as one of America's finest illustrators, and he worked prolifically on editorial and advertising commissions. During the 1950s he limited his work to reportage and in 1958 he wrote and illustrated On the Art of Drawing. *He returned to London in 1960 to paint a series of murals for the Commonwealth Institute and in 1967 was elected to the Society of Illustrators Hall of Fame.*

1. *MAGAZINE:* COLLIER'S
DATE: 1951

2 *MAGAZINE:* COLLIER'S
DATE: 1951

3 *MAGAZINE:* THE SATURDAY
EVENING POST
DATE: 1945

3

ROWLAND EMETT
(1906–1995)

Born in London. Trained at Birmingham College of Arts and Crafts. Emett was known as the latter-day Heath Robinson, both for his graphic work and for his working models of the eccentric machines described in his illustrations. His fascination for railways was seen in 12 books produced between 1943 and 1958, including Engines, Aunties and Others *(1943),* Sidings and Suchlike *(1946), and* Buffer's End *(1949). His figures frequently seemed as endearingly antiquated as his machines. He contributed illustrations to* Punch, Life, Vogue, *and* Harper's Bazaar, *among others, and created advertising images for Shell and Guinness. He converted antique railway drawings into a full-size, passenger-carrying model for the Festival of Britain in 1951 and produced the Edwardian-style vehicles featured in the 1968 movie* Chitty Chitty Bang Bang. *He created smaller models for window displays and commercial exhibitions.*

1–4 *BOOK:* BELLS AND GRASS
by Walter De La Mare
DATE: 1941

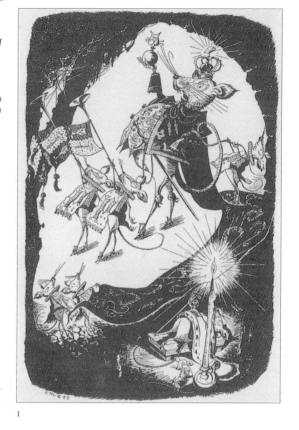

1

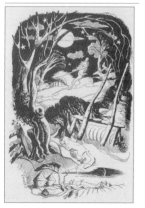

2

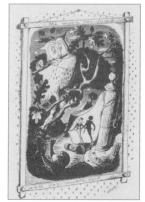

3

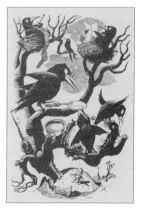

4

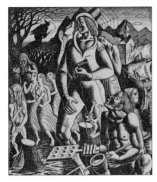

1

Born in London. Studied at
Westminster School of Art
under Walter Sickert, then
at Goldsmith's School of Art,
where he was influenced by
the line draftsman Edmund
Sullivan and the painter Clive
Gardiner. In 1924 he exhibited
etchings at the Royal Academy
and from 1930 to 1938 was a
fashion designer for Harper's
Bazaar. Although perhaps best
remembered for the strong
black-and-white illustrations
he produced for the BBC, and
which appeared frequently
in the Radio Times, he was
also a stained glass artist
and designed murals for the
Glasgow Exhibition in 1938
and the Festival of Britain in
1951. He taught lithography at
Goldsmith's and graphic design
at Camberwell School of Art. His
illustrated books include English
Legends (1951), The Book of
a Thousand and One Nights
(1958), and Sir William and the
Wolf (1960).

1 *MAGAZINE:* RADIO TIMES
DATE. c. 1940

2 *MAGAZINE:* RADIO TIMES
DATE: c. 1940

3 *MAGAZINE:* RADIO TIMES
DATE: c. 1940

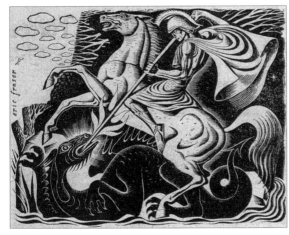

2

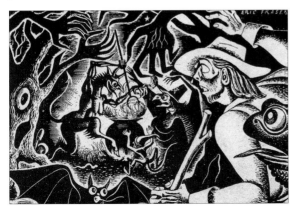

3

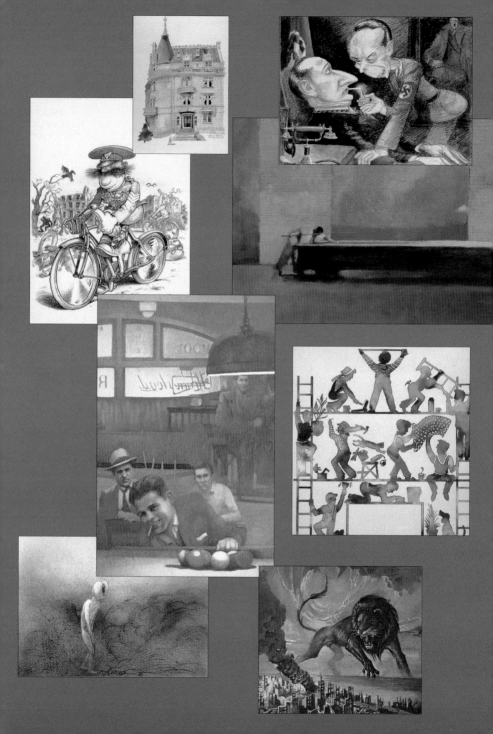

CHAPTER FOUR
1970–1990

OVER THE PAST 150 YEARS politics and war have created an important field of activity for the illustrator. However, the period since 1970 has been one of relative stability, and the ensuing prosperity in the West has had a subtle but profound effect on artists' lives.

The psychedelic 1960s actually ended in about 1972, by which time most of the excesses of the decade had been softened and absorbed into mainstream culture. The next style revolution was that of Punk rock, which took place about three years later. Its effect was most noticeable in the worlds of fashion and music, but it did make an impact on graphic design and particularly on typography. Its effect on illustration was less noticeable. The 1960s had enabled illustrators to develop such a diversity of styles that there was no predominant school for Punk aestheticism to assail, and therefore no obvious reaction took place.

The main influences on illustration have in fact come from developments within the publishing industry. It is a common belief that book illustration went into decline during the period between the wars and that it has never recovered. This is not entirely true. One has only to look through the examples in this chapter to see that children's book illustration is still booming in the hands of such artists as Helen Oxenbury, Wayne Anderson, Nicola Bayley, and Michael Foreman. In fact this market is so healthy that many illustrators, like Maurice Sendak in the USA, have taken to writing their own stories as opposed to reinterpreting the commercial classics. An interesting consequence of this has been the opportunity for artists such as Raymond Briggs to then diversify into animation by selling story rights to a movie company.

What has changed is the range of activities within book publishing. The gift book, in the Edwardian sense, has all but disappeared. Modern novels and poetry are rarely illustrated. The craze for coffee-table books has focused on popular education subjects that have been best documented by photography.

However, the book industry as a whole continues to expand and provide a plentiful supply of work in the form of paperback covers and dust jackets. And, perhaps to carve a niche within this market, it seems increasingly common for illustrators to specialize within a literary genre. This is particularly true of science fiction, a field which is now dominated by the styles of artists like Jim Burns, Chris Foss, and Peter Jones.

As far as the illustrator is concerned, the magazine business has never been so promising. Prosperity creates increased leisure time and with it the proliferation of special interest magazines. These in turn create interesting possibilities for younger artists: Production budgets are often low while a magazine struggles to establish itself, and consequently art departments are prepared to experiment with less proven but less expensive talent.

Advertising, too, is going from strength to strength, and provides artists with a major source of work. It also encourages a diversity of styles, as the very nature of its business is to differentiate, both practically and aesthetically, one product from another. This has led many illustrators to find work at agencies and, because advertising is the most plagiaristic of skills, it has proven especially lucrative for artists like Mick Brownfield in the UK, who can accurately parody bygone styles.

The current diversity of media opportunities has led to a correspondingly wide range of illustration styles. But no real "stars" have emerged. Illustrators, unlike their counterparts of the 1920s, are no longer household names. The artist Bernie Fuchs said in his introduction to a book on American illustration that the illustrator today is more like a businessman than the artist of old. But if that's the case, one has to say that business is good.

*Born in Kent, UK. Studied
industrial design (furniture)
at the Canterbury School of Art
(1961–64), then spent three
years at the Royal College of
Art. His first assignment was to
design the seating for Upstairs
Bar at Ronnie Scott's jazz club in
London. Between 1968 and 1973
he worked prolifically, designing
stage sets, posters, furniture,
hotels, and office towers. His
record-sleeve designs for the
rock groups Osibisa, Yes, Asia,
and the Rolling Stones quickly
established him as the foremost
illustrator of record-album
covers in Britain. With his
brother Martyn he formed the
company Dragon's Dream in
1975 to publish his book* Views,
*featuring Roger's fantasy and
science fiction designs for record
sleeves. Packed with hundreds
of color plates and selling for
the price of a record album,
it went straight to the top of*
The Sunday Times *best-seller
list and sold 500,000 copies
worldwide. In 1976 the Deans
set up a second company, with
Hubert Schaafsma, to publish
books under the Paper Tiger
imprint. In 1979 he became a
director of the Magnetic Storm
design company, specializing
in product research and
development. He worked on
a movie, "Floating Islands,"
which featureed animated 3D
renderings of his classic images.*

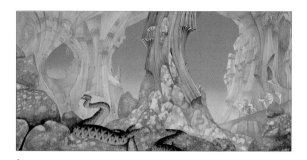

1

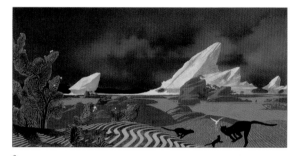

2

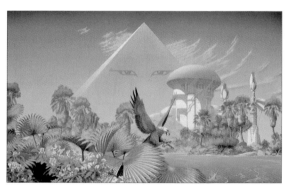

3

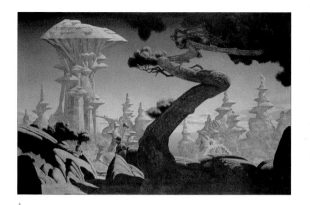

4

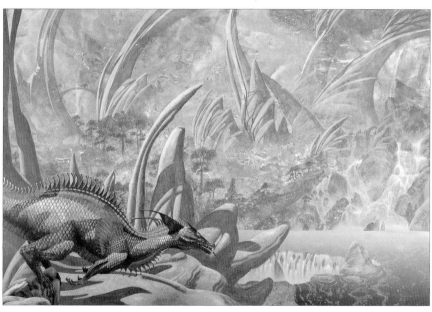

5

MAURICE SENDAK
(b. 1928)

*Born in Brooklyn, New York.
Studied at the Art Students
League. In 1952 he illustrated*
A Hole is to Dig *by Ruth Krauss.
It was a huge success, and
revolutionary in its day because
there was no storyline; the
book consisted of a series of
illustrated children's definitions,
such as "dogs are to kiss
people," and so on. Although
Sendak's illustrations appeared
in many books by other authors,
his most significant books
were those he wrote himself,
including* Where the Wild Things
Are (1962), *which won both
the Hans Christian Andersen
and the Caldecott awards,* In
the Night Kitchen (1970), *and*
Higglety Pigglety Pop! (1967),
*written in dedication to his
dog Julie, who had died shortly
before. Increasingly Sendak
began to link his art to music.
He co-wrote, with Carole King,
an animated TV musical,* Really
Rosie, *and wrote the libretto and
designed the sets for an opera
version of* Where the Wild Things
Are *in 1979. He later worked
on children's opera* Brundibar
in 2003. A movie version of
Where the Wild Things Are *was
released in 2009.*

1–2 BOOK: WHERE THE WILD
THINGS ARE *by Maurice Sendak*
DATE: 1962

3 BOOK: IN THE NIGHT
KITCHEN *by Maurice Sendak*
DATE: 1970

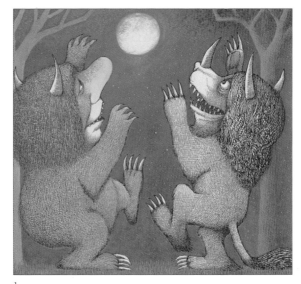

1

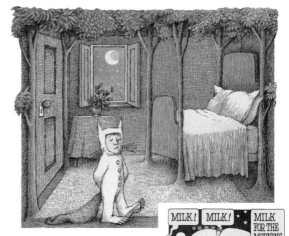

2

3

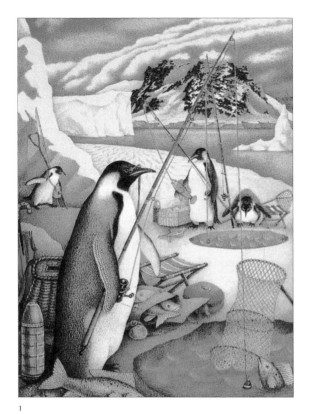

*Born in Singapore. Studied
graphic design at Saint Martin's
School of Art and then entered
the Royal College of Art, where
she studied illustration and
developed a style that is rich
in detail and color and that
uses a fine stippling technique
to create a range of distinctive
textures. Her illustrations of old
nursery rhymes were spotted
by a publisher in her diploma
show and were later published
in a book,* One Old Oxford Ox
(1976). She followed this with
Nicola Bayley's Book of Nursery
Rhymes *and Richard Adams'*
The Tyger Voyage *(both 1976)
and* The Patchwork Cat *(1981).
All were extremely successful
and have been translated into
seven languages. She lives in
London and works in Arthur
Rackham's old studio. She has
worked on* The Moglie Stories,
taken from The Jungle Book.

1, 2 *BOOK:* ONE OLD OXFORD
OX *by Nicola Bayley*
DATE: 1977

3, 4 *BOOK:* THE TYGER
VOYAGE *by Nicola Bayley &
Richard Adams*
DATE: 1976

1

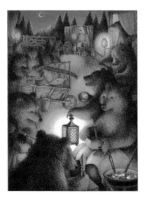

2

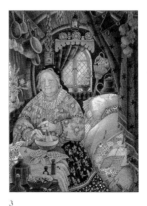

3

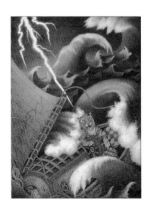

4

QUENTIN BLAKE
(b. 1932)

Born in Sidcup, UK. Studied at Downing College, Cambridge, London University, and Chelsea College of Art. He began drawing for Punch while still at school, and after leaving university also became a regular cover artist for The Spectator and designed book jackets for Penguin Books. His first illustrations for children's books appeared in 1960, since when he has illustrated over 150 books, most of them for children, and has had extended collaborations with Roald Dahl, Russell Hoban, Joan Aiken, Michael Rosen, and John Yeoman. His How Tom Beat Captain Najork and his Hired Sportsmen was joint winner of the Whitbread Award (1974) and Mister Magnolia won the Kate Greenaway Medal (1980). He is now a visiting professor at the Royal College of Art, of which he is a Senior Fellow, and where he was Head of Illustration between 1978 and 1986. He was awarded the OBE in 1988. He was appointed Children's Laureate of Great Britain in 1999, and received the international Hans Christian Anderson Award for Illustration in 2002.

1 BOOK: RUMBELOW'S DANCE by John Yeoman
DATE: 1982

2 MAGAZINE: PUNCH
DATE: 1980

3 BOOK: A FEAST OF TRUE FANDANGLES by Patrick Campbell
DATE: 1979

4 BOOK: THE BIRDS by Aristophanes
DATE: 1971

5 BOOK: THE HISTORY OF TOM THUMB
DATE: 1979

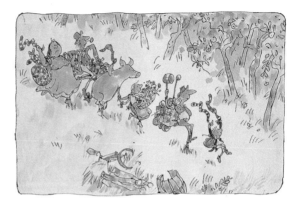

1

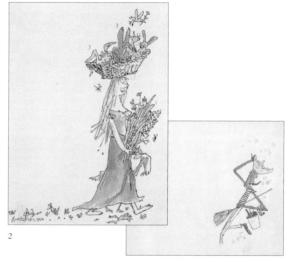

2

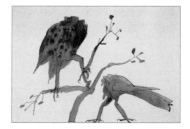

3

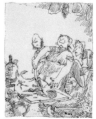

4

5

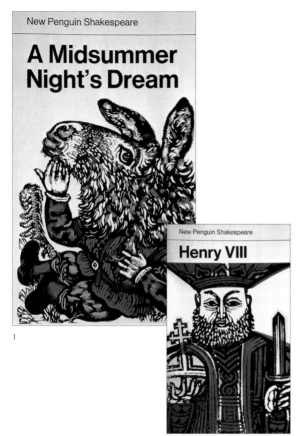

1

2

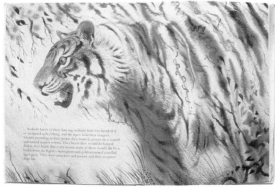

3

Born in London. Studied at
St. Albans School of Art and
the Royal College of Art, where
he taught for two years. Since
1955 he has concentrated
on his own work, which has
included lithography, wood-
engraving, graphic design, and
watercolor painting. His work
ranges in scale from postage
stamps to the platform-length
murals on the Underground
at Charing Cross station
in London. His publishing
clients include Penguin Books,
Cambridge University Press,
Limited Editions Club of New
York, Cape, and Weidenfeld.
He has produced several books
of his own, including David
Gentleman's Britain (1982),
David Gentleman's London
(1985), David Gentleman's
Coastline (1988), A Special
Relationship (1987), and, with
Russell Hoban, The Dancing
Tigers (1979). He has also
written and illustrated several
children's books and one book
on design.

1 BOOK: A MIDSUMMER
NIGHT'S DREAM by William
Shakespeare
DATE: 1975

2 BOOK: HENRY VIII by William
Shakespeare
DATE: 1975

3 BOOK: THE DANCING TIGERS
by David Gentleman & Russell
Hoban
DATE: 1979

BRUCE PENNINGTON
(b. 1944)

*Born in Somerset, UK. Studied at
Beckenham and Ravensbourne
schools of art in Kent. After
graduating in 1964 he worked
for two years as a commercial
artist before becoming a
freelance illustrator in 1967,
entering the science fiction
field with his cover design for
Robert Heinlein's* Stranger in
a Strange Land. *This marked
a turning point in his career
and, finding science fiction an
excellent medium through which
to express his imaginative ideas,
he went on to produce covers for
several Ray Bradbury novels for
Corgi Books. Many of his works
were reproduced in* Science
Fiction Monthly.

1–3 *BOOK:* ESCHATUS *by Bruce
Pennington*
DATE: 1976

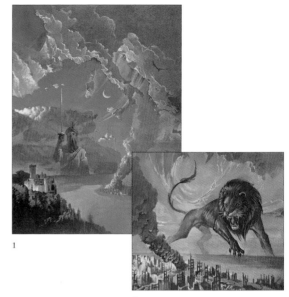

1

2

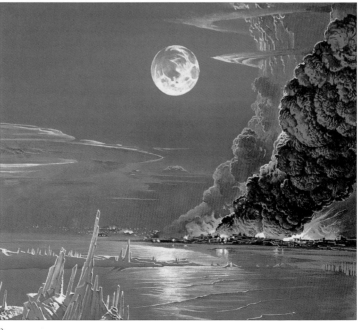

3

PETER ANDREW JONES
(b. 1951)

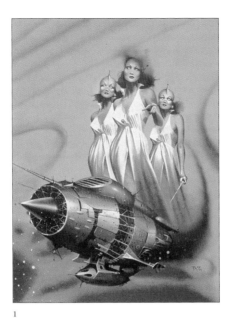

1

*Born in London. Studied at
Saint Martin's School of Art,
where, inspired by the novels
of Isaac Asimov and Larry
Niven, he became interested
in science fiction imagery. His
freelance career took off while
he was still at college, with some
commissions for Puffin Books.
In 1979 he designed a book,
Solar Wind, with Roger and
Martyn Dean. In the same year,
Solar Wind Ltd was formed
to market his career, and he
branched out into movies, TV,
and video productions. In 1982
he launched a highly successful
series of Fighting Fantasy games
books for Puffin. He has also
designed news title sequences,
backdrops, and inserts for BBC
Television and has exhibited in
England, France, and Japan.*

1 *BOOK:* THE QUEST OF THE
DNA COWBOYS *by Mick Farren*
DATE: 1975

2 *BOOK:* THE COMPLETE
ENCHANTER *by L Sprague de
Camp and Fletcher Pratt*
DATE: 1979

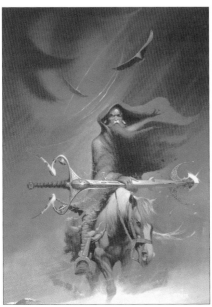

2

JEAN-MICHEL FOLON
(1934–2005)

Born in Brussels, Belgium. Initially studied architecture but abandoned it in favor of becoming an illustrator. Since the mid 1960s he produced a vast body of work and his wistful, poetic watercolors, particularly those featuring his "blue man," appeared in many media. He produced advertising posters for Olivetti, movie posters for Woody Allen, and record covers for Michele Colombier and Steve Kahn. He illustrated the works of Kafka and Lewis Carroll (1973) and the short stories of Jorge-Luis Borges (1974); and he created frescoes for the Belgian Metro and the London Underground. In addition, he designed theater scenery for the operas of Frank Martin and Puccini; and produced animated movies for Cadbury's chocolate in the UK and title sequences for French TV. He held one-man shows around the world.

1 *POSTER: "AMNESTY INTERNATIONAL"*
DATE: 1977

2 *POSTER*
DATE: 1975

3 *POSTER*
DATE: 1977

4 *EXHIBITION POSTER*
DATE: 1977

5 *SOURCE:* NOT KNOWN
DATE: NOT KNOWN

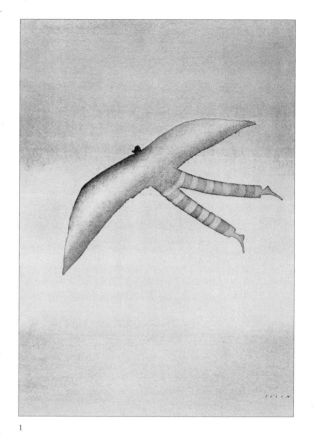

1

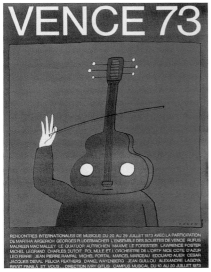

2

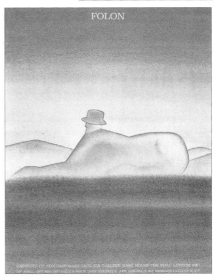

3

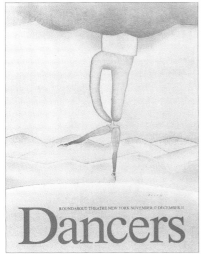

4

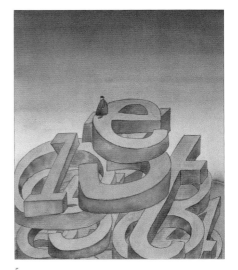

5

JAN PIENKOWSKI
(b. 1936)

Born in Warsaw, Poland. He read English and the Classics at Cambridge and in 1961 was a co-founder of Gallery Five, a greeting card company through which many of his books have been published. In 1967 he illustrated Jessie Townsend's Annie, Bridget and Charlie *and in 1968 formed a collaboration with Joan Aiken which led three years later to the publication of* The Kingdom Under The Sea and Other Stories *(1972). It won the Kate Greenaway Medal. Since 1972 he has produced the* Meg and Mog *series, featuring simplified drawings using strong, fat colors and highly elaborate pop-up books such as* Haunted House *(1979), a masterpiece of paper engineering which won him the Kate Greenaway Medal for a second time. He has done most of his work on computer, producing a CD ROM version of* Haunted House *in 1996, and has worked on several theater productions.*

1, 2 *BOOK:* HAUNTED HOUSE
by Jan Pienkowski
DATE: 1979

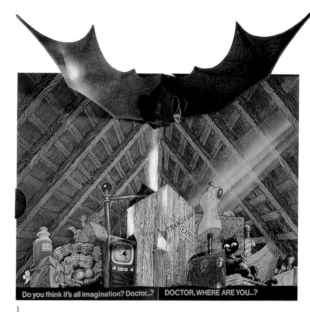

Do you think it's all imagination? Doctor...? | DOCTOR, WHERE ARE YOU...?

1

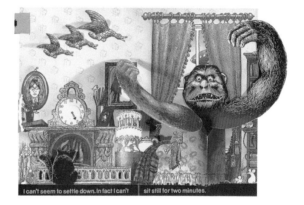

I can't seem to settle down. In fact I can't | sit still for two minutes.

2

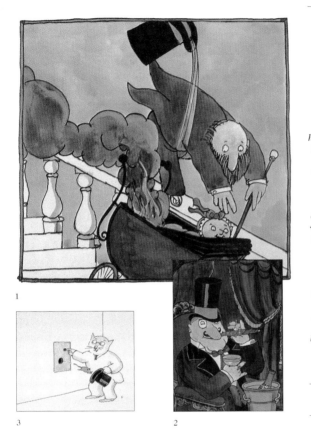

1

3

2

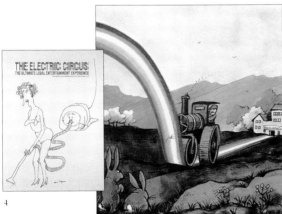

4

5

Born in Strasbourg, France. Spent his early adulthood traveling and doing odd jobs, including a brief stint as a camel-rider with the Sahara Police Force. At the age of 24 he taught himself to draw and paint, and in 1957 moved to New York and established himself as a freelance illustrator. He was immediately successful and his exquisite pen-and-ink drawings with colored washes appeared in Life, Esquire, McCalls, The New York Times, *and in many advertising campaigns. At the same time he was writing and illustrating his own stories, and published* The Mellops Go Diving for Treasure *(1957),* The Mellops Go Flying *(1957), and* Emile *(1960). He won the New York Society of Illustrators Gold Medal in 1960 and the New York Times Best Book of the Year in 1971. Since then he has illustrated many books, including* I am Papa Snap and these are my favorite no-such stories *(1973),* Moon Man *(1980), and* The Hat *(1986).*

1–2 *BOOK:* THE HAT
DATE: 1986

3 *CALENDAR DESIGN FOR* NIXDORF COMPUTERS
DATE: 1979

4 *POSTER: "THE ELECTRIC CIRCUS"*
DATE: 1973

5 *CALENDAR DESIGN FOR* REGENSDORF
DATE: 1979

BERNARD D'ANDREA
(b. 1923)

Born in Buffalo, New York. During World War II he spent three years as a war artist attached to the Quartermaster Corps and the Office of Strategic Services. He began his career as an illustrator in New York in 1950. His first major commission was for The Saturday Evening Post, *and between 1950 and 1970 he also illustrated for* Good Housekeeping, Cosmopolitan, Ladies' Home Journal, *and* Woman's Home Companion, *as well as a number of advertising clients. Since 1970 he has concentrated more on book illustration and has worked on historical subjects for the National Geographic Society of Washington DC. He has held several one-man exhibitions and is a member of the New York Society of Illustrators.*

1 *MAGAZINE:* BOY'S LIFE
DATE: 1973

2 *BOOK:* THE MAN WHO MADE
THE BEATLES
DATE: 1976

3 *MAGAZINE:* GOOD
HOUSEKEEPING
DATE: 1976

4 *MAGAZINE:* REDBOOK
DATE: 1976

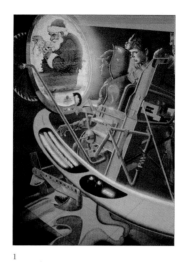

1

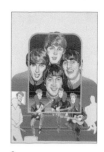

2

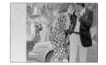

3

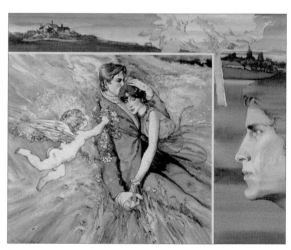

4

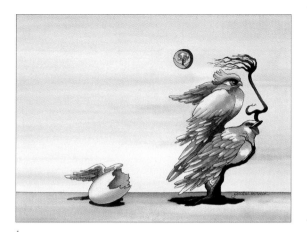

1

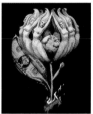

2

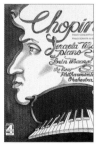

3

4

Born in New York. Trained
at the Pratt Institute and at
Hunter College. She worked
briefly as a textile designer,
then spent a year in Europe. On
her return to America in 1963,
she embarked on a career of
freelance illustration. Her style,
which she describes then as
being one of "anthropomorphic
double-images," was perfectly
suited to the psychedelic period
of the mid-to-late 1960s, and
after the publication of her
poster for the Electric Circus
she received many commissions
from magazines and advertising
clients. Using concentrated
watercolor, ink, and colored
pencils on watercolor paper,
she produced images that were
surreal, graphic, and intensely
colorful. She is now one of the
foremost watercolorists working
in America, and has exhibited
in New York, Germany, Japan,
and the UK. She published
Watercolor for Illustration
in 1986.

1 ADVERTISEMENT: "SWEDISH
TANNING PRODUCT"
DATE: 1970

2 MAGAZINE COVER: SUNDAY
MAGAZINE
DATE: 1971

3 RECORD ALBUM COVER:
CHOPIN
DATE: c. 1970

4 POSTER: "YEAR OF THE
WOMAN"
DATE: 1971

*Born in Leicester, UK. Studied
at Leicester College of Art
and then pursued a freelance
career in London, illustrating
album covers, greeting cards,
and Clement Freud's cookery
column in the Daily Telegraph.
After marriage and the birth
of his first child he returned
to Leicester and concentrated
on finely detailed crayon and
pencil drawings of animals. His
first book,* Ratsmagic *(1976),
was a great success and others
quickly followed, including*
Magic Circus, Mouse's Tale, *and
a collection of short stories,*
The Magic Inkstand, *written
by Heinrich Seidle. His one
adult book,* Flight of Dragons,
*written by Peter Dickenson,
was animated into a full-length
movie and shown on British and
American television.*

1–3 *BOOK:* RATSMAGIC *by
Wayne Anderson
DATE: 1976*

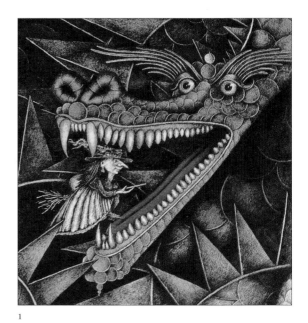

1

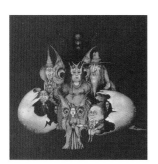

2

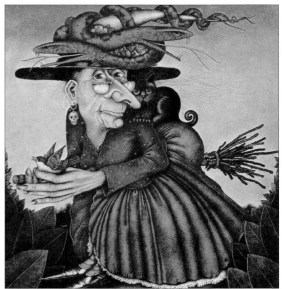

3

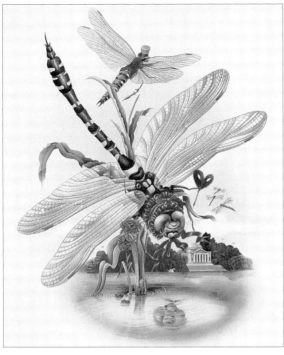

1

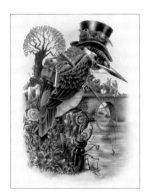

2

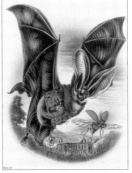

3

Born in Aylesbury, UK. He left Romford Technical College at 15 and drifted through a variety of jobs, including actor, insurance clerk, barrow boy, and stall holder in a London market. At the age of 20 he started to draw and took an evening class in graphic art. Success followed very quickly and soon his work was seen on book covers, album sleeves, posters, and in magazines such as Harper's, Nova, *and* The Sunday Times. *Within the world of music he was a celebrity artist and received many commissions from leading rock bands; his work appeared frequently in* Melody Maker. *In 1966 he became art director of Penguin Books and then set up his own studio in 1968. The following year he edited and contributed illustrations to both volumes of* The Beatles Illustrated Lyrics *(1969). To the psychedelic art of the 1960s Aldridge brought exquisite draftsmanship and the innovative use of the airbrush to control the subtle gradation of tone and color. And although his work was the epitome of the style and aesthetics of the time, it found a new audience when the decade was over. In 1974 he won the Children's Book of the Year Award for* The Butterfly Ball *(1973). He now works freelance in London and has designed animated movies.*

1–3 *BOOK:* THE BUTTERFLY BALL *by Alan Aldridge & William Plomer*
DATE: 1973

PAUL LEITH
(b. 1946)

*Born in South Shields, UK.
He studied commercial art
at Sunderland Art College
(1961–65) and attended the
London College of Printing
in 1969 before going on to
study illustration at the Royal
College of Art (1970–73). His
magazine clients include*
Vogue, The Sunday Times, The
Observer, Company, *and* She,
*and he has illustrated books
for Penguin, Futura, Octopus,
Pan/Picador, and Mitchell
Beazley. His advertising clients
include retailers Liberty, Next,
and The Body Shop, Royal
Bank of Scotland, Barclays
Bank, and the construction
company Costain. He exhibited
in the 1983, 1984 (when he won
first prize), and 1985 Benson
and Hedges Gold Awards
exhibitions. An admirer of the
Bauhaus and Russian art,
Leith favors a direct, no-
nonsense approach to his art.
He works mainly with stencils
and acrylic paint.*

---

1 TIME PASSING
*(Benson and Hedges Gold
Awards)*
BATE: 1984

---

2 RELEASING ENERGY
*(Benson and Hedges Gold
Awards)*
DATE: 1985

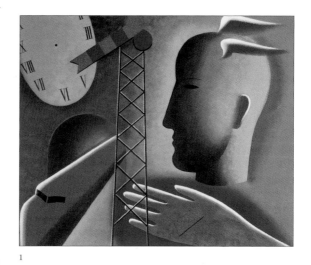

1

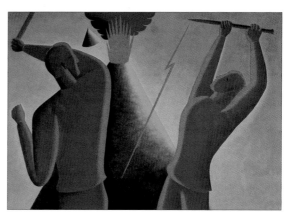

2

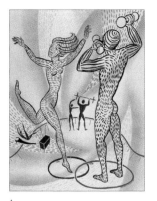

1

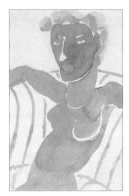

2

*Born in New York. Studied at
the Pratt Institute and the Pratt
Graphic Art Center in New
York, graduating in 1960. After a
brief spell as a textile designer,
she returned to her childhood
ambition to be an artist after
befriending Robert Weaver, who
gave her individual tuition
and the encouragement to
enter her work in the Society of
Illustrators show in 1960. Since
then she has received over 200
awards for excellence in fine
art and illustration. She has
illustrated album covers and
calendars and for numerous
magazines, including* Show,
New York Magazine, Audience,
Ms, Rolling Stone, The Boston
Globe, Newsweek, *and* Time. *She
has taken part in exhibitions
all over the world and her work
is represented at the Museum
of Modern Art in New York,
the Smithsonian Institution
in Washington DC, and Lund
Kunsthall Lund in Sweden.
She has taught at the School
of Visual Art, the Fashion
Institute of Technology, and
the Pratt Institute in New York.
Nessim employs many different
expressive media in her work,
including computer graphics.
She is worked on commissions
for lobby design in New York.*

1 *MAGAZINE:* V MAGAZINE
DATE: 1988

2 *PAINTING:* WOMAN SITTING
DATE: 1987

3 *PAINTING:* TEA LEAVES
DATE: 1989

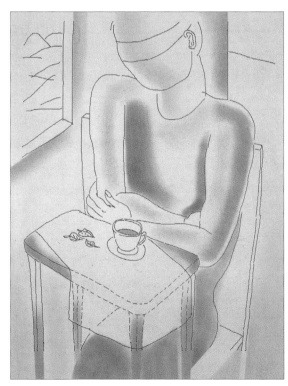

3

DAVID AND RENEE STREET
(b. 1957 and 1954)

Renee Gettier was born in Baltimore, USA and studied art at Towson State University before transferring to Maryland Institute, College of Fine Art. After graduating she worked as an illustrator's assistant for a year before turning freelance and starting Streetworks Studio with David Street. At various times her work has been selected as among the best of the year by Graphis, Print Magazine, *The* Illustrators Club, *and the Art Directors Club of Metropolitan Washington. Her clients include* The Washington Post, Psychology Today, 321 Contact, *McDonalds, and CBS Records. David Street was born in Washington, USA.*

He studied architecture at Virginia Polytechnic and State University before transferring to Maryland Institute, College of Fine Art. After starting work as a graphic designer he joined Renee as a freelance illustrator. His clients include The Boston Globe *and* National Wildlife Magazine. *He became President of the Illustrators Club of Washington in 1987.*

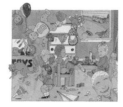

1

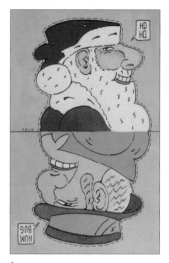

3

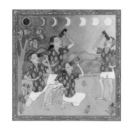

2

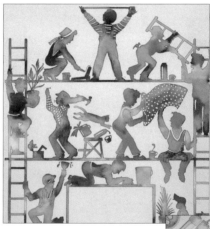

4

1 *CHILDREN'S NEWSPAPER:* PENNY WHISTLE PRESS *DATE:* 1988

2 *MAGAZINE:* SCIENCE '86 *DATE:* 1986

3 *NEWSPAPER:* THE WASHINGTON POST *DATE:* 1985

4 *CHRISTMAS CARD DATE:* 1987

5 *NEWSPAPER:* THE BALTIMORE SUN *DATE:* 1988

5

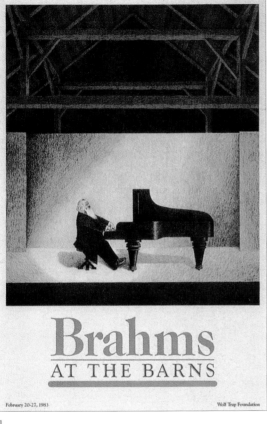

1

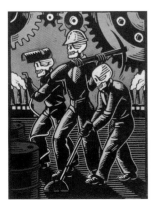

2

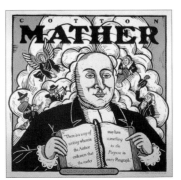

3

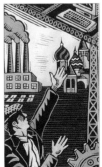

4

BILL NELSON
(b. 1946)

Born in Richmond, Virginia, USA. Graduated from the Richmond Professional Institute in 1970 with a BFA in Communication Art and Design and began work as a newspaper illustrator on The Richmond Mercury before setting up his own studio. His work, which has been described as "quiet elegance in colored pencil," has appeared in Newsweek, New Times, The Washington Post Magazine, and Time Life records. He has won two gold medals from the Art Directors Club of New York and two silver medals from the Society of Illustrators, which in 1983 sponsored a traveling exhibition of his work to Europe and Japan. He has lectured at a number of art schools throughout the USA and taught at the Virginia Commonwealth University's School of the Arts for two years.

1. *BOOK:* FINISHING THE HAT. TRENCH COAT
DATE: 1986

2 *RECORD ALBUM COVER:* MAHLER'S SYMPHONY FOR CHILDREN
DATE: 1988

3 AIN'T MISBEHAVIN
(*unpublished*)
DATE: 1988

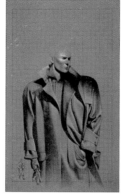

1

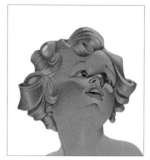

2

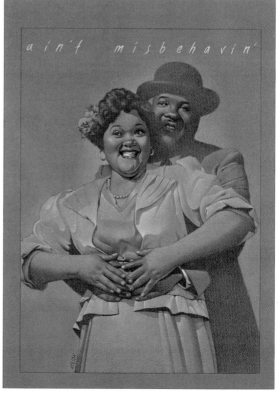

3

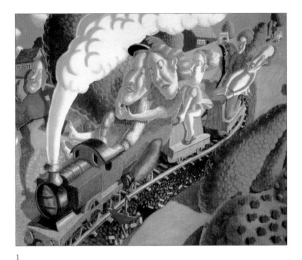

1

Born in Hampshire, UK. Studied
graphic design at Leicester
Polytechnic, specializing
in illustration. He has won
several Benson and Hedges
Gold Awards prizes, including
second prizes in 1983 and
1984 and first prize in 1986,
and was highly commended in
1987. He also won first prize in
the 1986 Reader's Digest Young
Illustrators Awards. His clients
include Cosmopolitan and The
Listener magazines, Penguin
Books, the Royal Academy of
Arts, BBC World Service, and a
number of advertising clients.
He has taken part in several
group exhibitions and his work
is on permanent show at the
Portal Gallery in London and
the David Adamson Gallery in
Washington DC. Adams prefers
to work in chalk pastel for
its good tonal quality, strong
colors, and speed, and cites his
influence as British naive art
and the work of Stanley Spencer.

1 THE JOURNEY
(non-commissioned)
DATE: 1987

2 THE FLORIST
(non-commissioned)
DATE: 1989

3 THE SHELL HOUSE AND
SUN FISH
(non-commissioned)
DATE: 1989

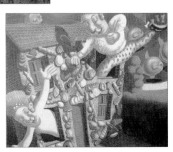

2

3

DAVE CALVER
(b. 1954)

Born in Rochester, New York. He graduated from Rhode Island School of Design in 1976 and immediately established himself as a freelance illustrator. His first commissions were from GQ, Psychology Today, *and* New York *magazine. Initially influenced by George Grosz and the movies of Fritz Lang, he works in colored pencil and wryly observes that it is the elegance of his style that led to his popularity with the publishers of murder mystery fiction. As well as illustrating book jackets he contributes regularly to* Vogue *and* Vanity Fair *and has worked for such advertising clients as Mobil, TWA, and United Airlines.*

1 *BOOK JACKET:* SEDUCTION BY LIGHT
DATE: 1988

2 *MAGAZINE:* PLAYBOY
DATE: 1986

3 *POSTER: "21ST ANNUAL COMPETITION, SOCIETY OF PUBLICATION DESIGNERS"*
DATE: 1986

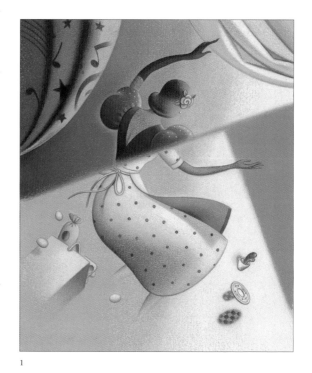

1

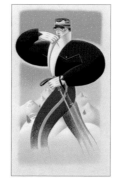

2

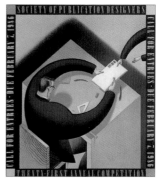

3

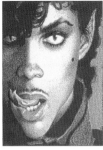

1

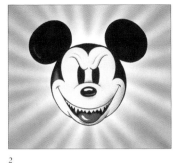

2

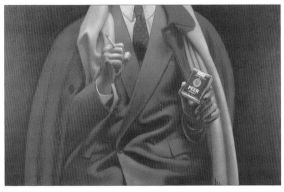

3

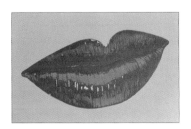

4

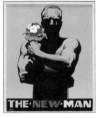

5

Born in London. Trained at Hornsey College of Art and has worked as a freelance illustrator since 1973. It is difficult to characterise his work, as he is not only prolific but extraordinarily versatile and has on many occasions been commissioned to parody the work of other artists, an example being his drawing for Heineken beer in the style of John Gilroy's poster for Guinness. His work has regularly appeared in the Design and Art Direction Annual, European Illustration, *Association of Illustrators exhibitions, and* The One Show Annual *(New York). He has exhibited at several art galleries, including the Pompidou Centre in Paris, and has held a one-man show in Hamburg, Germany entitled "Art for Commerce." His advertising and editorial clients include* The Sunday Times *and* Marie Claire *magazines, Guinness, Heineken, Walt Disney, and Handmade Films.*

1 *MAGAZINE:* THE SUNDAY TIMES
DATE: 1987

2 *MAGAZINE:* THE LISTENER
DATE: 1984

3 *ADVERTISEMENT:*
(unpublished)
DATE: 1986

4 *MAGAZINE:* MARIE FRANCE
DATE: 1983

5 *MAGAZINE:* THE LISTENER
DATE: 1986

Roger Law (see also page 233) and Peter Fluck met in 1957 as students at Cambridge School of Art, UK, where they co-art directed the Cambridge University magazine Granta *and were inspired by the example of their tutor Paul Hogarth, "a man doing something he really liked and making a living." After graduating in 1963, Fluck worked as a freelance cartoonist for numerous magazines, including* New Society, New Statesman, The Economist, *and the* Radio Times, *as well as designing costumes for the Royal Ballet. In 1975 the Luck and Flaw partnership was formed and produced caricature models for photography for several magazines and newspapers, illustrated Dickens'* A Christmas Carol *(1979) and Stevenson's* Treasure Island *(1986), and designed a range of ceramic caricature tableware. The* Spitting Image *TV series, a satirical show starring cruelly accurate caricature puppets, of politicians, celebrities and members of the royal family, became an instant success in 1984 and led to numerous spin-offs, including books, pop songs, and advertising commissions.*

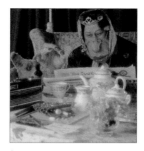

1

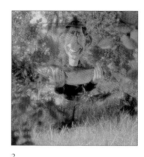

2

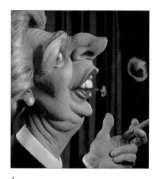

3

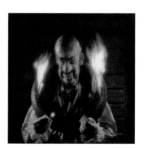

4

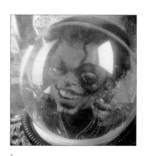

5

6

1–6 *TV SERIES:* SPITTING IMAGE

1 THE QUEEN *(1984)*

2 PRINCE CHARLES *(1984)*

3 FRANK BRUNO *(1985)*

4 MARGARET THATCHER *(1984)*

5 P W BOTHA *(1986)*

6 MICHAEL JACKSON *(1984)*

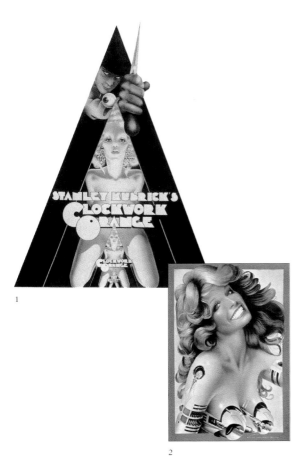

1

2

3

Born in Huddersfield, UK. Trained at Huddersfield School of Art and the Royal College of Art. While still a student he received his first commissions, in 1965, from The Sunday Times and Vogue magazines and in 1967 he was represented in an exhibition of five illustrators at the Time-Life Gallery. Since then he has designed a number of movie posters, including "A Clockwork Orange," "Full Metal Jacket," and "Mars Attacks" and worked on the 1973 Pirelli Calendar with Allen Jones. Castle has become one of the definitive artists of the hyper-realistic airbrush style. He has exhibited in San Francisco and at the Thumb Gallery and Francis Kyle Gallery in London. His magazine clients include Elle, Marie Claire, Stern, Jasmin, Playboy, and Time. His advertising clients include Heineken, Fiat, Ford Air Canada, and Volkswagen. He has produced two books: Airflow (1980) and Airshow (1989), and more recently has designed album covers for the band Pulp.

1 MOVIE POSTER: "A CLOCKWORK ORANGE"
DATE: 1971

2 POSTCARD: TRULY TRIONIC
DATE: 1978

3 PATRICK LIDSEY AIRFORCE
(private commission)
DATE: 1983

GUY BILLOUT
(b. 1941)

Born in Decize, France. Studied at the Ecole des Arts Appliqués in Beaune, Burgundy. In 1969 he moved to New York, where he joined an evening art class run by Milton Glaser. This led to his entire portfolio being reprinted in New York Magazine, of which Glaser was then editor. The idea for his first children's book, Bus Number 24 (1972), a picture story without words, came from a story by Heinrich Hoffman which he came across in an old German book. Since then he has produced several books for children and adults, four of which were chosen by The New York Times for their list of ten best illustrated children's books. He has also illustrated for Atlantic, New Republic, Time, Vogue, Playboy, and Rolling Stone magazines. Billout has received three gold and two silver medals from the Society of Illustrators, was selected as Illustrator of the Year for the All-Star Creative Team in Adweek Creativity (1986), and won first prize in an international contest to design a poster for the World Fair of 1992 in Seville, Spain. His intriguing, meticulously airbrushed images are influenced by Japanese woodblocks and by the flat tones of Hergé, creator of the Tintin comic strip.

1 MAGAZINE: ATLANTIC
MONTHLY
DATE: 1986

2 MAGAZINE: ATLANTIC
MONTHLY
DATE: 1988

3 MAGAZINE: ATLANTIC
MONTHLY
DATE: 1987

4 MAGAZINE: CORPORATE
MAGAZINE
DATE: 1987

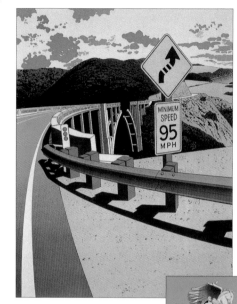

1

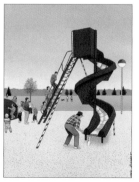

2

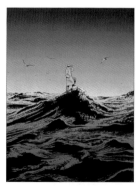

3

4

*Born in Rochdale, UK. Trained
at Rochdale School of Art, Saint
Martin's and the Royal College of
Art. After graduating he taught
at Cambridge School of Art and
over the next ten years divided
his time between teaching
and freelance illustration for
various publications, including
the Radio Times, for whom he
worked mostly in black-and-
white. He also undertook private
commissions and illustrated
a letter-heading for the
playwright Tom Stoppard, who
owns several of his paintings.
His early work in colored
pencils shows the influence
of David Hockney, but his
mature paintings are instantly
recognizable as being in his
own highly individual style.
He illustrated several books,
including Glynn Boyd Harte's
Venice (1988), and exhibited
at the Thumb and Francis Kyle
galleries and the Albemarle
Gallery in London.*

1 FOOD STILL LIFE
DATE: NOT KNOWN

2 *PROMOTIONAL BROCHURE:*
FONTANA BOOKS
DATE: 1983

3 *SELF-PROMOTIONAL
POSTER
DATE: 1985*

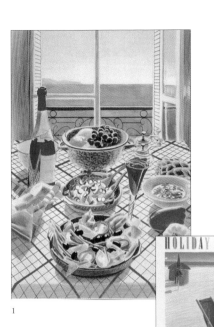

1

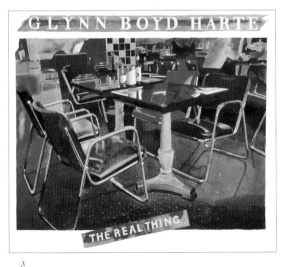

2

3

ANDRZEJ DUDZINSKI
(b. 1945)

Born in Sopot, Poland. Initially studied architecture at Gdansk Polytechnic but transferred after two years to the State College of Art, where he studied interior design and printmaking. He then studied poster design and painting at the Academy of Fine Art. He moved to New York in 1977. Since then his work has appeared in various magazines and newspapers in Europe and the USA, including The Boston Globe, The New York Times, Newsweek, Playboy, Rolling Stone, Vogue, Vanity Fair, Time, Elle, Tatler, *and* The Daily News. *He has exhibited at the National Arts Club in New York, the Dubois Gallery in Pennsylvania, the Atrium in Connecticut, and at the National Theatre in London. He taught at Parsons School of Design in New York and was visiting professor at the School of Visual Arts and New Media in Warsaw.*

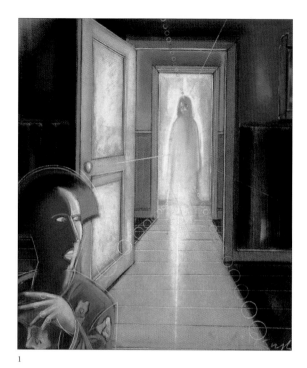

1

1 *MAGAZINE:* THE DAILY NEWS
DATE: 1986

2 *POSTER: "SPECTATOR, XIII"*
DATE: 1983

3 *POSTER*
DATE: 1986

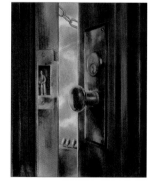

2

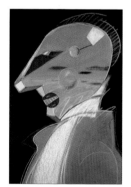

3

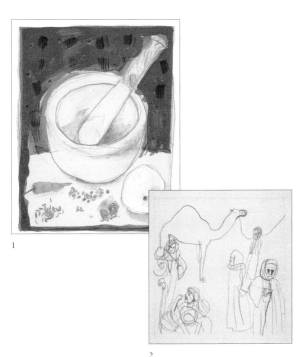

1

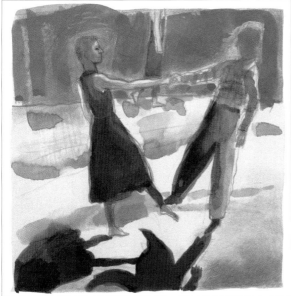

2

Born in London. Studied at Cambridge School of Art and the Royal College of Art. Her first illustrations were for The Sunday Times. *Since then she has worked for Habitat stores, Walker Books, and a number of advertising clients and contributed to* The Spectator *and* A La Carte. *She has recently designed a series of posters for the Seibu department store in Japan. She won the Lloyds Printmakers Prize in 1981, and in 1985 her work was represented in a British Council exhibition entitled "From Caxton to Chlöe."*

1 *MAGAZINE:* THE SUNDAY TIMES
DATE: 1981

2 *BOOK:* SPECTATOR BOOK OF TRAVEL WRITING
DATE: 1988

3 *MAGAZINE:* OBSERVER
DATE: 1985

3

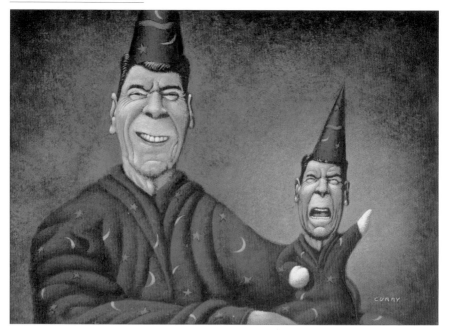

1

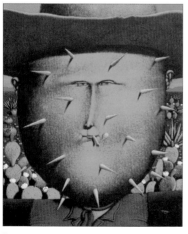

2

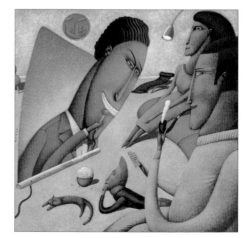

3

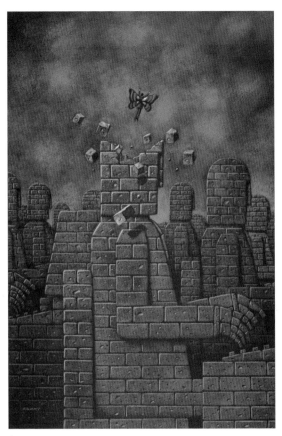

4

*Born in Texas, USA. Studied at
North Texas State University in
Denton, where he majored in
advertising art in 1968. After a
short period in an advertising
agency in Dallas, he was drafted
by the U.S. Army and stationed
in Germany, where he developed
an interest in the fine arts. On
his return to the USA he studied
painting and drawing at East
Texas State University and
became a commercial artist
in 1972. After a brief spell
working as art director at the
University of Texas he became a
freelance illustrator. As well as
being commissioned by various
advertising agencies, his work
appeared in such publications
as* Texas Monthly, Houston
City, *and* D Magazine. *In 1979
he co-founded the design and
illustration group Sagebrush
Studio and formed Curry and
Associates with two partners
in 1983.*

1 *MAGAZINE:* ATLANTIC
MONTHLY
DATE: 1986

2 *MAGAZINE:* TEXAS MONTHLY
DATE: 1985

3 *MAGAZINE:* VIDEO
MAGAZINE
DATE: 1986

4 *ILLUSTRATION FOR
ADVANCED GRAPHIC SYSTEMS
CO.
DATE:* 1987

CHRIS FOSS
(b. 1946)

Born in Devon, UK. As a child he loved to build models of steam engines and had a fascination for color, speed, and technology. While studying architecture at Cambridge University, he had a science-fiction comic strip published in Penthouse *magazine. In 1970 one of his paintings appeared in* Nova, *and this led to other commissions, most notably for Arthur C Clarke's* Coming of the Space Age. *The following three years saw Foss establish himself as one of the most prolific and sought after science fiction illustrators, with Isaac Asimov personally requesting that Foss should illustrate his* Foundation Series *(1973). Foss produces his highly detailed and colorful paintings in airbrush, and his revolutionary view of technology and transport in the future has influenced the entire genre. He has also worked on three movies, Richard Donner's* Superman *(1978) and Ridley Scott's* Alien *(1979), as well as Jodorowski's never-completed version of* Dune.

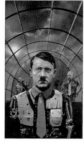
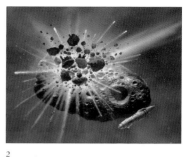

1   2

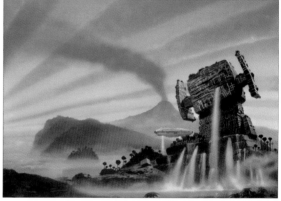

3

1 BOOK: WE CAN BUILD YOU
by Philip K Dick
DATE: 1986

2 BOOK: ASTEROID COLLISION
DATE: 1987

3 BOOK: STAR KING by Jack
Vance
DATE: 1988

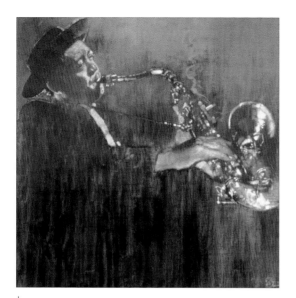

1

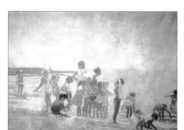

2

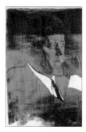

3

BERNIE FUCHS
(b. 1933)

Born in O'Fallon, Illinois, USA. Studied at the Washington University School of Fine Arts in St. Louis, Missouri. He began his career in 1957 in Detroit, Michigan working on automobile accounts. Later he moved to New York, where he illustrated for The Saturday Evening Post, The New Yorker, and Sports Illustrated, among others. His exquisite illustrations, which show the influence of the French Impressionists, ensured his early success as both an illustrator and a painter. At the age of only 30 he was named Artist of the Year by the Artists Guild of New York and in 1975 he was the youngest artist ever to be elected to the Illustrators Hall of Fame. Since then he has won the Hamilton King Award and many gold and silver medals from the Society of Illustrators. He has been commissioned to paint the portraits of several U.S. presidents, including Kennedy and Reagan. He has exhibited his work in New York, Chicago, Atlanta, New Orleans, England, Russia, and Japan. In 1991 he was named Sports Artist of the Year by the American Sport, Art, and Museum Archives and he has also designed a series of postage stamps on folk musicians.

1 RECORD ALBUM COVER:
TIME LIFE RECORDS
DATE: 1980

2 POSTER: "THE BIRTH
DEFECTS FOUNDATION"
DATE: 1988

3 MAGAZINE: TV GUIDE
DATE: NOT KNOWN

ROBERT GROSSMAN
(b. 1940)

Born in New York. He was encouraged to draw as a child and attended Saturday morning art classes at the Museum of Modern Art in New York. He studied art at Yale under Joseph Alber and contributed illustrations to the college magazine, The Yale Record. *He also edited a magazine called* Yew Norker *– a spoof on* New Yorker *magazine – which, after he graduated in 1961, led to his first job as a cartoon editor. Since becoming a freelance illustrator and cartoonist in 1965 he has illustrated for a number of magazines, including* Time, Newsweek, Esquire, *and* Forbes. *He has also designed the publicity poster for the movie* Airplane, *taught at Syracuse University in New York, and illustrated for a number of advertising clients.*

1 *MAGAZINE:* THE NEW REPUBLIC
DATE: 1988

2 *MAGAZINE:* FORBES
DATE: 1988

3 *MAGAZINE:* FORBES
DATE: 1988

4 *NEWSPAPER:* PENNSYLVANIA GAZETTE
DATE: 1988

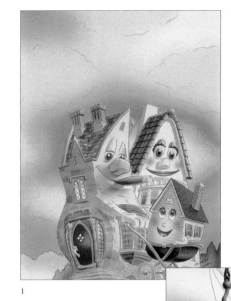

1

2

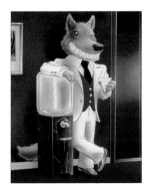

3

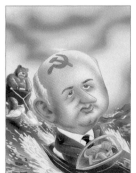

4

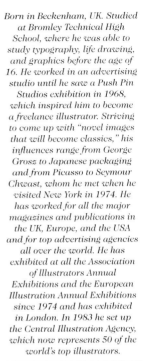

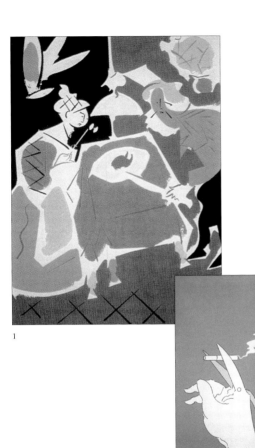

1

2

Born in Beckenham, UK. Studied at Bromley Technical High School, where he was able to study typography, life drawing, and graphics before the age of 16. He worked in an advertising studio until he saw a Push Pin Studios exhibition in 1968, which inspired him to become a freelance illustrator. Striving to come up with "novel images that will become classics," his influences range from George Grosz to Japanese packaging and from Picasso to Seymour Chwast, whom he met when he visited New York in 1974. He has worked for all the major magazines and publications in the UK, Europe, and the USA and for top advertising agencies all over the world. He has exhibited at all the Association of Illustrators Annual Exhibitions and the European Illustration Annual Exhibitions since 1974 and has exhibited in London. In 1983 he set up the Central Illustration Agency, which now represents 50 of the world's top illustrators.

1 *GERMAN MAGAZINE:* MANNERVOGUE *DATE: 1988*

2 *BOOK:* QUIT SMOKING *by Dr Miriam Stoppard DATE: 1981*

3 *PERSONAL CHRISTMAS CARD DATE: 1988*

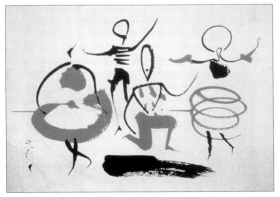

3

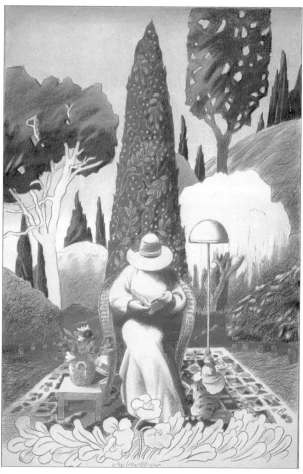

1

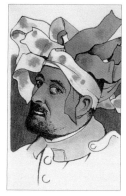

2

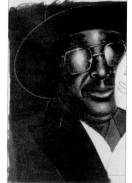

3

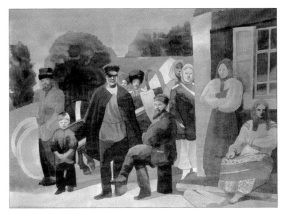

4

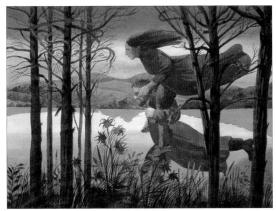

5

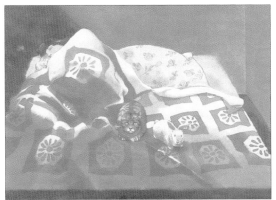

6

Born in New York. Attended the High School of Music and Art, then took evening classes at the Art Students League. At the Cooper Union Art School he won a scholarship in 1952 to study etching in Bologna, Italy with Giorgio Morandi. With Seymour Chwast, Ed Sorel, and Reynold Ruffins, he co-founded the Push Pin Studios in 1953 and Push Pin Graphic in 1957, and in 1968 he founded New York Magazine. He was also responsible for the redesign of Paris Match, Cue, Village Voice, New West, L'Express, L'Europeo, Jardin de Modes, and Esquire magazines. His books illustrated include The Milton Glaser Poster Book (1977), Asimov's The Illustrated Don Juan (1972), If Apples Had Teeth (1960) with Shirley Glaser, and Rimes de la Mère Oie (1971) with Seymour Chwast and Barry Zaid. In 1974 he designed a huge mural for the New Federal Office Building New York in, and in 1975 he designed the observation deck of the twin towers of the World Trade Center. Glaser's distinctive work, influenced by Islamic and Indian painting and Japanese woodcuts, has won him many awards, including a gold medal from the Society of Illustrators.

1 POSTER
DATE: 1986

2 BOOK: THE COLLECTED WORKS OF APOLLINAIRE
DATE: 1983

3 RECORD ALBUM COVER: ALBERT KING
DATE: 1976

4, 5 END PAPER ILLUSTRATION FOR BOOK ON GOGOL
DATE: 1987

6 PAINTING: SHIRLEY, ANNIE AND MR HOFFMAN
DATE: 1985

WALTER GURBO
(b. 1947)

*Born in New York. After
graduating from the Art
Students League and the Pratt
Institute, he taught at a New
York public school, painting in
his spare time. Recognizing that
his paintings lent themselves
well to magazine illustration, a
friend took a selection of them
to* Esquire, *and this led to his
first commission. Since then
his illustrations have appeared
in most of the major American
publications, including* Village
Voice, The New York Times,
Esquire, *and* Playboy. *Citing
the diverse influences of Robert
Crumb, William Blake, Max
Beckmann, and René Magritte,
he describes his work as a
combination of surrealism and
expressionism. Essentially a
painter, he has exhibited in
New York and Florida and has
worked on constructions made
with acrylic paints
and cardboard.*

1 *MAGAZINE:* VILLAGE VOICE
DATE: 1987

2. *MAGAZINE:* VILLAGE VOICE
DATE: 1989

3. *MAGAZINE,* VILLAGE VOICE
DATE: 1989

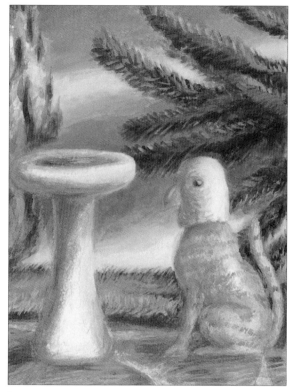

1

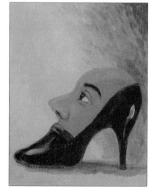

2

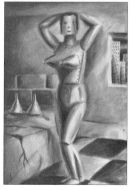

3

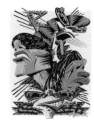
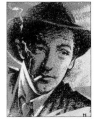

1   2   3

Born in London. Studied at the Central School of Art and Crafts, where he was influenced by his tutor Bob Gill. After graduating in 1973 he moved to Los Angeles and set himself up as a freelance illustrator. He has worked prolifically ever since and his brightly colored, intensely graphic illustrations have appeared in all the major American publications, including Time, The New Yorker, Playboy, Esquire, Vanity Fair, and Rolling Stone. *He cites the soul singer Otis Redding as a major influence on his work and has taught at the Art Center in Los Angeles and the Parsons School of Design.*

1 *MAGAZINE:* CHIC
DATE: 1976

2 *MAGAZINE:* NEW YORK
MAGAZINE
DATE: 1975

3. *MAGAZINE:* LA STYLE
DATE: 1987

4 MICKEY MONDRIAN
(uncommissioned)
DATE: 1976

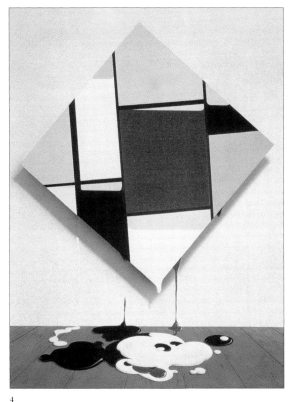

4

MARZENA KAWALEROWICZ
(b. 1952)

Born in Krakow, Poland. Educated at the academies of fine arts in Krakow and Warsaw, graduating in 1976. Since then she has held a number of one-woman shows in Poland, Paris, Italy, the USA, and Japan. Her magazine clients include Playboy, Gallery, Graphis, Elle, *and* Penthouse Letters *(USA),* Gunnars *and* Mode Avantgarde *(France),* City Life *(Germany),* Asahigraph *and* Illustration *(Japan), and* Projekt, Szutka, ITD, *and* Fantastyka *(Poland).*

1 *MAGAZINE:* FANTASTYKA
DATE: 1988

2 *MAGAZINE:* CITY LIFE
DATE: 1988

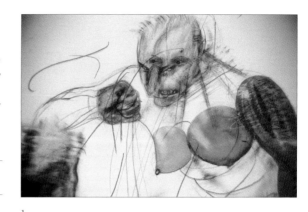

1

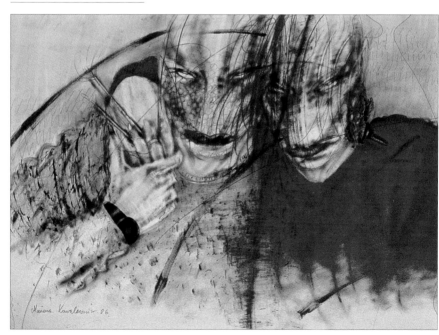

2

*Born in Marshalltown, Iowa,
USA. Trained at Binding School
of Art, Sarasota, then went
on to work as a staff artist for
public television, an assistant
advertising director, a graphic
designer, and an editorial
illustrator. Since 1978 she
has concentrated on freelance
illustration, and her elegantly
balanced compositions, subtle
colors, and great sense of action
and movement have made
her particularly popular with
sports and news publications
such as* Golf, Sports Illustrated,
U.S. News, *and* World Report.
*Her work has also appeared
in books, including* The Long
March *by Harrison Salisbury
(1984), andon record covers,
posters, and TV. She has won
numerous awards, including
the New York Society of
Illustrators Award of Merit in
1984; the Award of Excellence,
Communication Arts,* New
York *in 1985; and the 66th Art
Directors Annual DESI Award.
She has illustrated* Vilma
Martinez, *a learning book for
Spanish students.*

1 *MAGAZINE:* SPORTS
ILLUSTRATED
DATE: 1987

2 SWAN *(unpublished)*
DATE:: c. 1987

3 SHADE OF THE BEACH
(unpublished)
DATE: 1988

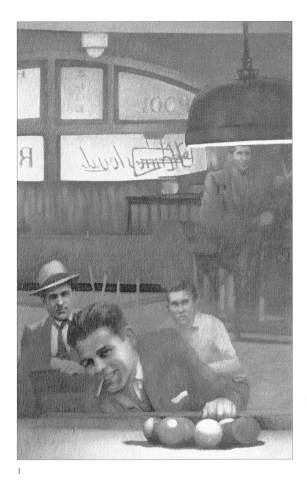

1

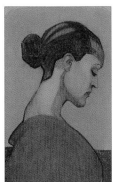

2

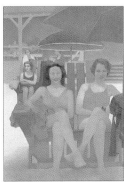

3

LIONEL KOECHLIN
(b. 1948)

Born in Paris. Trained at the Ecole Nationale Superieure des Métiers d'Art in the studio of general decoration, specializing in mural art and poster and theater design for children. From the mid-1970s he has had work published in numerous magazines, including Marie Claire, Rock and Folk, La Recherche, *and* Femme Pratique. *He has also illustrated a number of books, including his own* Le Rouge, Le Jaune, *and* Le Bleu *(all 1984) and Jan Van Aal's depiction of the advertising industry in France,* Au Clair de la Pub *(1986). His advertising clients include KP, Hewlett Packard, Ward Air, and Mobil Oil. His influences, which include the writings of Georges Simenon and the music of Louis Armstrong, are broad and constantly changing, as is the style and content of his work. He has had exhibitions in both Belgium and France.*

1 *BOOK:* ADVENTURES OF JOSEPH AND MIMI *by Anne-Marie Chapouton*
DATE: 1988

2 *LIMITED EDITION PRINT*
DATE: 1987

3 *MAGAZINE COVER:* THE NEW YORKER *(unpublished)*
DATE: 1982

4 *UNPUBLISHED*
DATE: 1979

5 *PUBLICITY POSTER*
DATE: 1987

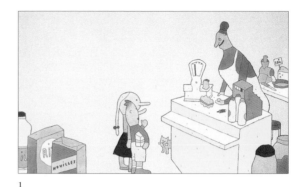

1

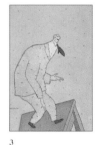

2

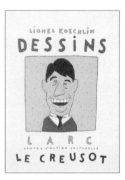

3

4

5

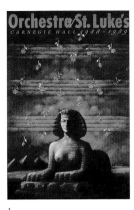

1

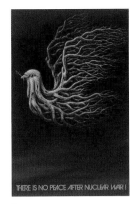

2

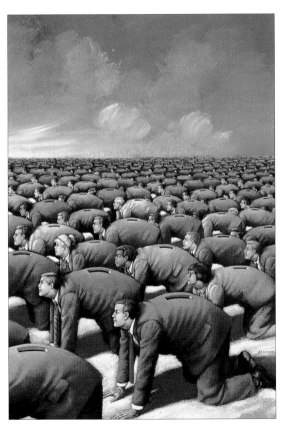

3

Born in Poland. He graduated
from the architectural
department of Warsaw
Polytechnical School with
a distinction in 1969, since
when he has achieved
international acclaim. His
illustrations have appeared
in Graphis (Switzerland),
Novum (Germany), and Idea
(Japan) magazines and in the
American publications Time,
Newsweek, The New York Times,
and Business Week. He has
also illustrated for a number of
advertising clients. He cites his
influences as "everybody," from
Saul Steinberg to Milton Glaser,
Marshall Arisman, and Brad
Holland, and characterizes his
work as "poetic surrealism." He
has won innumerable awards
for excellence in illustration
and design, including two silver
medals and one gold medal from
the Society of Illustrators, and
is represented at the Museum of
Modern Art (Poster Collection),
at the Carnegie Foundation in
New York, and at the Poster
Museum in Warsaw, Poland.
He lives in New York, where,
as well as being a freelance
illustrator, designer, and
painter, he teaches at the School
of Visual Arts.

1 PUBLICITY POSTER:
"CARNEGIE HALL CONCERT"
DATE: 1988

2 POSTER: "DOVE OF PEACE,
HIROSHIMA ANNIVERSARY"
DATE: 1985

3 BOOK JACKET: THE FOOL
AND HIS MONEY
DATE: 1988

ROBERT PARKER
(b. 1927)

Born in Norfolk, Virginia, USA.
Studied at the Art Institute of
Chicago and the Skowhegan
School of Painting and Sculpture
in Maine, where he was a
pupil of Jack Levine and Henry
Varnum Poor. His intention
was to be a fine artist and he
exhibited in 1952 at Atelier 17
in New York. Successful one-
man shows followed and his
work has been acquired by
the Museum of Modern Art, the
Metropolitan Museum of Art,
and the Whitney Museum. His
career as an illustrator began
when a series of watercolors,
painted for his son, was
published in Esquire magazine.
This inspired commissions
from several other magazines,
including The Lamp, Playboy,
Sports Illustrated, and Fortune,
which sent him on several major
reportage assignments around
the world. He also worked in
the movie industry, producing
the canvases for Kirk Douglas's
portrayal of Van Gogh in Lust for
Life, and his watercolors have
been used in movies to illustrate
the poetry of Wilfred Owen and
Keith Douglas. He has taught
at the Pratt Institute, Parsons
School of Design, and the Rhode
Island School of Design.

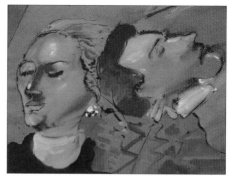

1

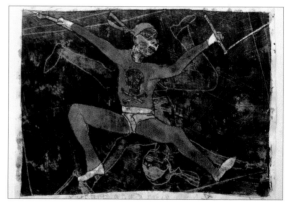

2

1 A DOUBLE PORTRAIT
DATE: 1986

2 A SCENE FROM GUNGA DIN
DATE: 1987

3 YOU STEPPED OUT OF A
DREAM
DATE: 1987

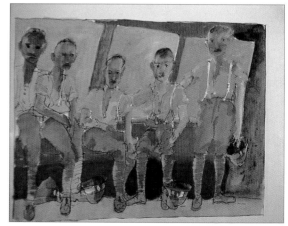

3

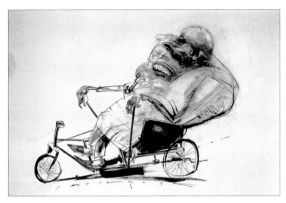

1

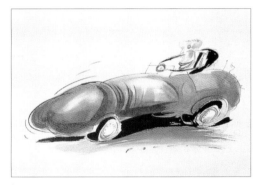

2

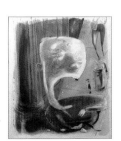

3

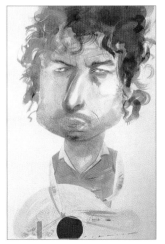

4

Born in Cheshire, UK and educated at Manchester Polytechnic and the Royal College of Art. As well as a number of one-man shows, he has exhibited in every European Illustration *Annual Exhibition and Association of Illustrators Annual Exhibition since 1975. He is represented in public collections throughout the UK, including the Victoria and Albert Museum and the Arts Council of Great Britain in London. He has illustrated for magazines such as* Rolling Stone *and* Men Only, *and designed the* Lear *poster for the National Theatre in London. He also does a large amount of design and advertising work, for clients such as Coopers and Lybrand, BP, and Saatchis. Books illustrated include* The Miracles of Christ *(1976),* Couples *(1979),* The Pepper Press Book of Catastrophes *(1981), and* Cartoon King Lear *(1984). He also designed* Tales of Terror *(1997), a series of postage stamps for the Royal Mail.*

1 *POSTER*
DATE: 1984

2 *MAGAZINE:* MEN ONLY
DATE: 1985

3 DRUNK ON THE BOWERY
DATE: 1987

4 *MAGAZINE:* ROLLING STONE
DATE: 1985

Born in Jamestown, New York.
On graduating in advertising
art from the Pratt Institute in
New York in 1960, he received the
Ida Gaskill Grant to travel and
study in Europe. After military
service he worked as a graphic
designer for General Motors,
taking figure-drawing classes in
the evenings. He then became an
illustrator. He has had one-man
shows in America, Europe, and
Japan and his paintings are
in the permanent collections of
the Brooklyn Museum and the
National Museum of American
Art. He has won awards from
the Society of Illustrators, the
American Institute of Graphic
Arts, the Society of Publication
Designers, and American
Illustration. His clients include
The New York Times, The
Nation, Mother Jones, Time, and
Penthouse magazines. Books
illustrated include Fitcher's
Bird (1983) and Frozen Images,
a book of illustrations on the
theme of violence. He also
created The Last Tribe, a series
of paintings, sculpture, and
video on the theme of the atomic
bomb and the future of mankind.
His influences include Andre
François, Velázquez, Goya,
primitive art, and the British
painter Francis Bacon, whose
influence is particularly evident
in violent and expressive images
reflecting his concerns for the
human condition.

1 *MAGAZINE:* THE NEW YORK
TIMES
DATE: 1986

2 *MAGAZINE:* TIME
DATE: 1987

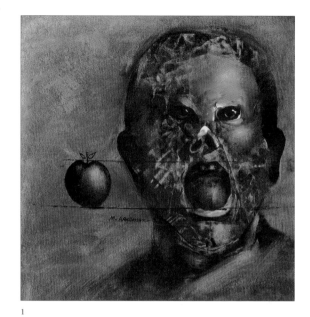

1

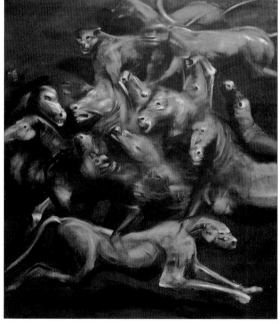

2

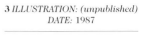

3 *ILLUSTRATION: (unpublished)*
DATE: 1987

4 *ILLUSTRATION: (unpublished)*
DATE: 1987

5 *MAGAZINE:* OMNI
DATE: 1986

6 *MAGAZINE:* OMNI
DATE: 1985

1

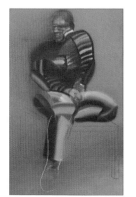

2

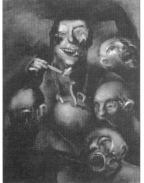

3

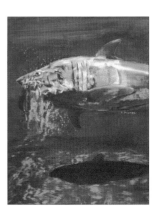

4

PAUL SAMPLE
(b. 1947)

*Born in Leeds, UK. Studied at
Bradford Art College and the
Central School of Art in London.
Since graduating in 1968 he
has become well known for
his humorous illustrations,
particularly those for the
Smirnoff Vodka and Listerine
mouthwash advertising
campaigns, and cites among
his influences Dudley D Watkin,
H M Bateman, Heath Robinson,
and George Morrow. He has
illustrated for newspapers,*
including the Daily Mirror, The
Sunday Times, *and* Observer,
and magazines, including
Penthouse, Management Today,
Men Only, Bella, *and* Campaign.
*Additionally he has designed
book jackets for the novels
of Compton McKenzie, Tom
Sharpe, and Flann O'Brien and
did a monthly strip cartoon,
"Ogri," for* Bike *magazine. He
works mainly in pen and ink
and watercolor wash.*

1 *ADVERTISEMENT:*
"SMIRNOFF VODKA"
DATE: 1984

2 *MAGAZINE:* ARCHITECT'S
JOURNAL
DATE: 1987

3 *BOOK JACKET:* THE THIRD
POLICEMAN *by Flann O'Brien*
DATE: 1987

4 *BOOK JACKET:* VINTAGE
STUFF *by Tom Sharpe*
DATE: 1983

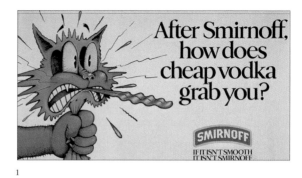

1

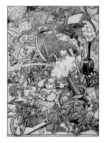

3

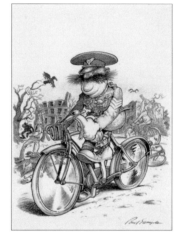

2

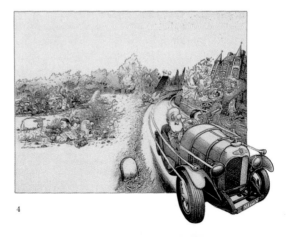

4

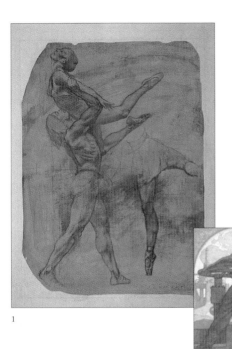

1

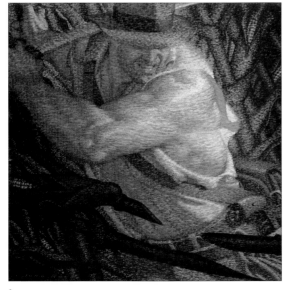

2

JOHN RUSH
(b. 1948)

Born in Indianapolis, Indiana, USA. Worked as an industrial designer and city planner for several years before studying illustration at Art Center College. Since then he has worked as an illustrator and painter. He has lived and worked in New York, Los Angeles, and Chicago and carried out assignments for a number of book and magazine publishers and advertising clients. He has won a gold medal from The Society of Illustrators and awards from the Society of Publication Designers and the Chicago Artists' Guild.

1 *ILLUSTRATION:* AMERICAN SOCIETY OF WOMEN ACCOUNTANTS
DATE: 1989

2 *ILLUSTRATION:* HUGHES UNITED PETROLEUM
DATE: 1988

3 STUDY OF AN ARM
(unpublished)
DATE: 1987

3

LANE SMITH
(b. 1959)

Born in California, USA. He graduated from the Art Center College of Design in Pasadena, California in 1983 and moved to New York the following year to take up freelance illustration. His work is regularly included in American Illustration and he has won a silver medal from the Society of Illustrators. In 1987 his Hallowe'en ABC (written by Eve Merriam) was picked as one of the ten best books of the year by The New York Times and the best book of the year by the School Library Journal. He has also published a wordless picture book called Flying Jake (Macmillan, 1988). His magazine clients include New York and Rolling Stone.

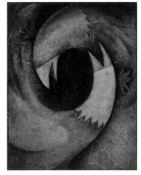

1

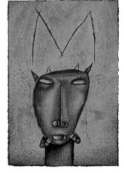

2

1 MAGAZINE: QUALITY REVIEW
DATE: 1987

2 BOOK: HALLOWE'EN ABC by Eve Merriam
DATE: 1987

3 MAGAZINE: CAR STEREO REVIEW
DATE: 1987

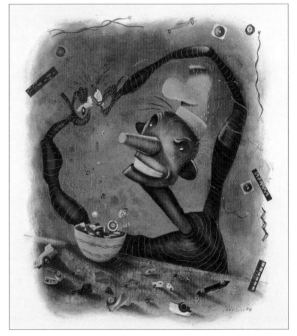

3

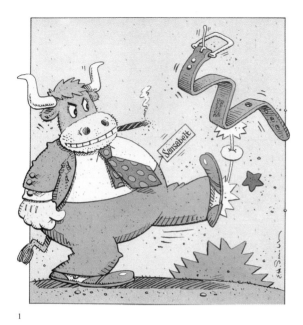

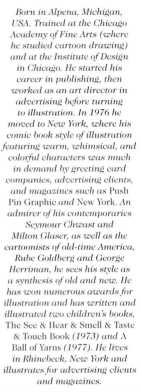

1

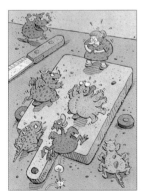

2

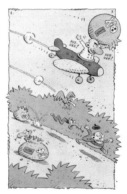

3

Born in Alpena, Michigan, USA. Trained at the Chicago Academy of Fine Arts (where he studied cartoon drawing) and at the Institute of Design in Chicago. He started his career in publishing, then worked as an art director in advertising before turning to illustration. In 1976 he moved to New York, where his comic book style of illustration featuring warm, whimsical, and colorful characters was much in demand by greeting card companies, advertising clients, and magazines such as Push Pin Graphic *and* New York. *An admirer of his contemporaries Seymour Chwast and Milton Glaser, as well as the cartoonists of old-time America, Rube Goldberg and George Herriman, he sees his style as a synthesis of old and new. He has won numerous awards for illustration and has written and illustrated two children's books,* The See & Hear & Smell & Taste & Touch Book *(1973) and* A Ball of Yarns *(1977). He lives in Rhinebeck, New York and illustrates for advertising clients and magazines.*

1 *NEWSPAPER:* DALLAS TIMES
HERALD
DATE: 1986

2 *MAGAZINE:* MEDICAL SELF
CARE
DATE: 1988

3 *MAGAZINE:* TIME
DATE: 1987

Born in New York. Studied at the High School of Music and Art and Cooper Union School of Art, where he met Seymour Chwast and Milton Glaser (with whom he formed the Push Pin Studios in 1953). In 1957 he left Push Pin to concentrate on a career as a freelance illustrator, and drawn more and more to political satire, published his first cartoon book, How to be President, *in 1960. His other books include* Making the World Safe for Democracy *(1972) and* Moon Missing *(1962). His regular contributions to* Village Voice *between 1974 and 1977 were eventually published as* Superpen *(1978). He has worked for a number of publications, including* New York Magazine, Harper's, Esquire, *and* The New York Times. *In 1981 he won the George Polk Award for his satirical drawings and in 1993 received the National Cartoonist Society Advertising and Illustration Award.*

1 POSTER: "THE GRADUATE SCHOOL OF MANAGEMENT AND URBAN PROFESSIONS"
DATE: 1986

2 *MAGAZINE:* GQ
DATE: 1988

3 *MAGAZINE:* ATLANTIC MONTHLY
DATE: 1986

4 *BOOK JACKET:* THINKING TUNA FISH, TALKING DEATH: ESSAYS ON THE PORNOGRAPHY OF POWER *by Robert Scheer*
DATE: 1988

5 *MAGAZINE:* AMERICAN HERITAGE
DATE: 1982

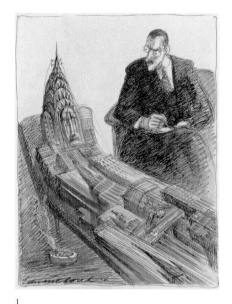

1

2

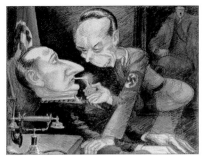

3

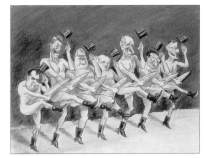

4

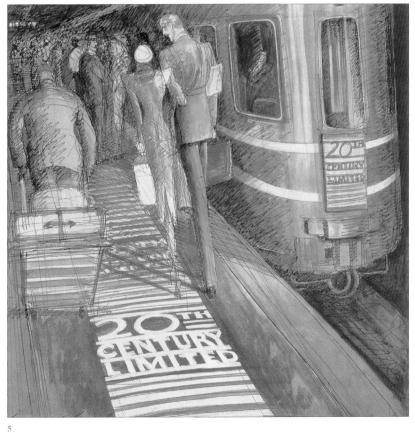

5

BUSH HOLLYHEAD
(b. 1949)

*Born in Northumberland, UK.
Trained at Newcastle-upon-
Tyne College of Art and Hornsey
College of Art, London. He joined
Nicholas Thirkell Associates
(a subdivision of Macmillan
Publishing Ltd.) in 1970 before
forming NTA Studios with
three partners in 1973. He
has illustrated for publishing
editorial, advertising, and
design groups in 13 countries.
His publishing clients include*
Radio Times, Time Out, The
Sunday Times, Design, *and*
Observer *magazines. His
advertising clients include
Schweppes, Cadbury's, Knorr,
the Greater London Council,
and the Milk Marketing Board.
He has exhibited regularly
in London, Paris, New York,
Minneapolis, and Amsterdam
and has won a number of
awards, including a Design and
Art Direction Annual silver in
the UK and a Grammy Award
nomination in the US. He enjoys
composing images in which
the elements are cohesive and
yet retain a sense of rhythm
and movement.*

1 *BOOK:* THE CREATIVE
HANDBOOK DIARY
DATE: 1981

2 *CALENDAR DESIGN*
DATE: 1982

3 *MAGAZINE:* THE LISTENER
DATE: 1984

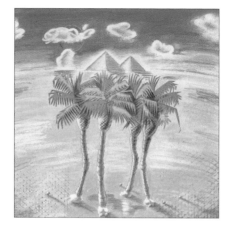

1

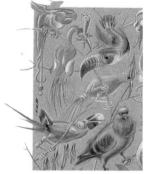

2

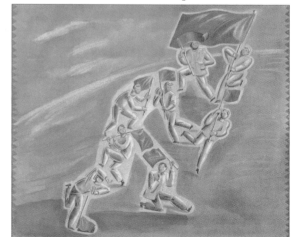

3

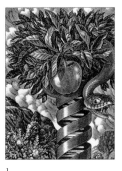

1

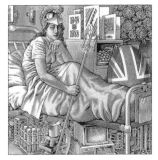

2

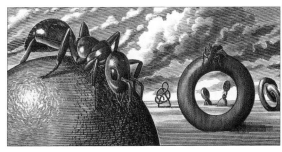

1

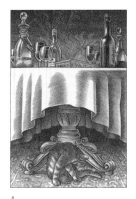

4

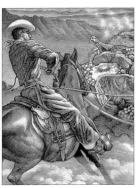

5

*Born in Horden, Co. Durham,
UK. Studied illustration at
Bristol and then taught art
part-time at a south London
comprehensive school. In 1973,
after he decided to abandon
teaching and become a freelance
illustrator, he presented a
commissioned drawing to
New Society magazine, only
to be told that their letterpress
printer couldn't reproduce
his delicate half-tones. It was
this disappointment that
led him to experiment with
scraperboard, a technique
that he uses exclusively today.
He has worked for many of
the major publications in
London, including The Times,
Time Out, Radio Times, New
Society, and the New Scientist,
and in America he contributes
regularly to Esquire, illustrating
such diverse subjects as
outdoor pursuits, personality
profiles, the gossip columns,
and the sports clinic. He has
advertising clients both in the
UK and the USA and illustrated
Harry Harrison's West of Eden
trilogy in 1988. As might be
expected of an artist working on
scraperboard, his influences are
predominantly 19th century and
he cites Cruickshank and Doré
as particular inspirations.*

1 *MAGAZINE:* NEW SCIENTIST
DATE: 1987

2 *MAGAZINE:* NEW SCIENTIST
DATE: 1988

3 *MAGAZINE:* NEW SCIENTIST
DATE: 1986

4 *CATALOG:* WINE SOCIETY
DATE: 1987

5 *MAGAZINE:* ESQUIRE
DATE: 1988

HELEN OXENBURY
(b. 1938)

Born in Ipswich, UK. Studied at Ipswich School of Art and the Central School of Art in London, specializing in theater design. After graduating she worked in theater, movies, and television. She began illustrating children's books when expecting her first child. In 1967 The Number of Things *was published and immediately established her as a major picture book artist. In 1970 she won the Kate Greenaway Medal for her illustrations for Lear's* Quangle Wangle's Hat *and* The Dragon of an Ordinary Family. *Since then her simple and observant watercolors have illustrated many internationally acclaimed children's books, including the* First Picture Books *(1983) and the* Pippo *series.*

1 *BOOK:* DANCING CLASS *by Helen Oxenbury*
DATE: 1983

2 *BOOK:* THE CHECK-UP *by Helen Oxenbury*
DATE: 1983

3 *BOOK:* TICKLE TICKLE *by Helen Oxenbury*
DATE: 1987

4 *BOOK:* WE'RE GOING ON A BEAR HUNT *by Helen Oxenbury and Michael Rosen*
DATE: 1989

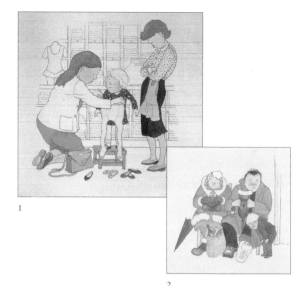

1

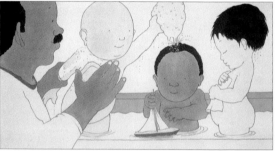

2

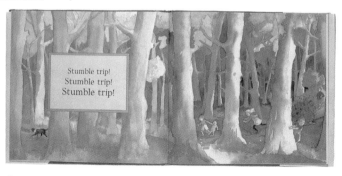

3

Stumble trip!
Stumble trip!
Stumble trip!

4

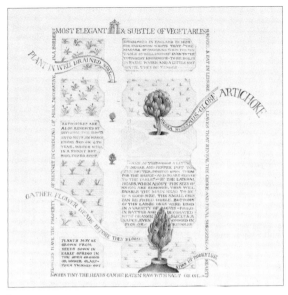

1

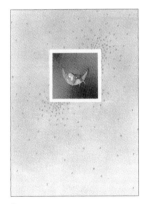

2

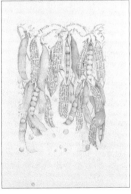

3

Born in Brighton, UK. Trained at Goldsmith's and St. Martin's schools of art. Midda is much admired for her very fine, delicate, and beautifully colored illustrations and the wonderful sense of humor which is evident in all her work. Her first book, In and Out of the Garden *(1982), in which the hand lettering is an integral part of the image, won her the Francis Williams V&A National Book League Award for Best Descriptive Illustration in 1982. She has also illustrated for* Harpers & Queen, The Sunday Times, *and* Cosmopolitan *magazines and* The Guardian *and* The New York Times *newspapers. She also designs a line of products (from food packaging and babywear to bed linen and china) under her own name for the Mitsukoshi department store in Japan. She has exhibited at the Cartoon, Langton, Thumb, and Chris Beetles galleries in London.*

1, 3 *BOOK:* IN AND OUT OF THE GARDEN *by Sara Midda*
DATE: 1982

2 *CHRISTMAS CARD*
DATE: 1984

DAN FERN
(b. 1945)

*Born in Eastbourne, UK.
Studied graphics at Manchester
College of Art and illustration
at the Royal College of Art in
London. As well as for various
advertising agencies, he has
illustrated for* The Sunday
Times, Radio Times, New
Scientist, *and* Penguin, Pan,
and Time-Life *books;* Arista,
Chrysalis, *and A&M records;
and Conran Design, Pentagram,
Thames Television, the Royal
Court Theatre, the BBC, and
the Joint Stock Theatre Group.
He was a member of the jury
of the Francis Williams Award
for Book Illustration in 1982
and has himself won both gold
and silver D&AD awards. He
is a regular juror on the D&AD
Annual, for which he also runs
workshops. He became Head
of Illustration at the Royal
College of Art in 1986 and was
appointed the first Professor of
Illustration at the Royal College
in 1989. Fern is a designer as
well as an illustrator, and his
interest in stamps and printed
ephemera is reflected in the
letter and number forms which
are often incorporated in
his work. He works mainly
with paper and collage, and
also has an interest in
computer-generated design
and illustration.*

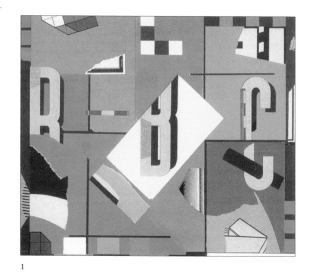

1

1 *WINNER'S CERTIFICATE:* BBC
DESIGN AWARDS
DATE: 1987

2 *POSTER: "LONDON
REGIONAL TRANSPORT"*
DATE: 1988

3 *COVER:* ART DIRECTORS
CLUB OF HOLLAND ANNUAL
DATE: 1986

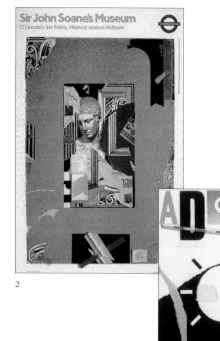

2

3

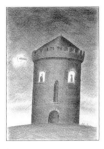 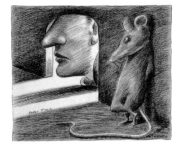

1   2

Born in Manchester, UK. He studied English Literature at Cambridge University and after graduating in 1967 worked mainly in theater, doing illustrations as a sideline. In the early 1970s he became a full-time illustrator, since when he has won a number of design and illustration awards. He has worked in advertising in Britain, Germany, Holland, the U.S., Sweden, Denmark, and Singapore. His magazine clients include The Sunday Times, Observer, New York, Esquire, Gentlemen's Quarterly, *and* Vogue. *In 1978 he made an animated movie,* The Beard. *Citing Saul Steinberg as among his influences, he is an entirely self-taught artist. His images have an element of the surreal and he enjoys juxtaposing disparate elements as a way of inviting viewers to make their own interpretations of the work.*

1 *POSTER: "ABERYSTWYTH ARTS CENTRE"*
DATE: 1988

2 *MAGAZINE COVER:* THE LISTENER
DATE: 1987

3 *MAGAZINE COVER:* NEW SCIENTIST
DATE: 1987

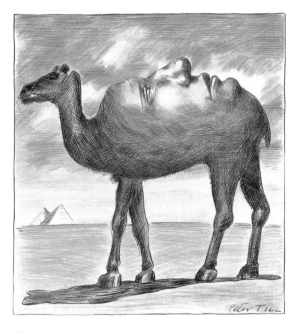

3

JIM BURNS
(b. 1948)

Born in Cardiff, Wales. In 1966 he joined the Royal Air Force as a trainee pilot but left in 1968 to study at Newport School of Art, then at St. Martin's School of Art in London, from where he received a diploma in art and design. He has painted numerous book and paperback covers for Sphere, Corgi Tandem, Quartet, Coronet, Methuen, and Fontana Books. In 1980 he assisted Ridley Scott on designs for the movie "Blade Runner." He has also illustrated a series of novels by Robert Silverberg for Bantam Books and a collection of short stories entitled Eye (1985) by Frank Herbert. Burns specializes in historical romances and science fiction in gouache, acrylic, watercolor, and oil. A collection of his work featuring one hundred color illustrations was published by Dragon's World in 1986. His work fetched a high price at Sothebys and the major Washington gallery, Worlds of Wonder.

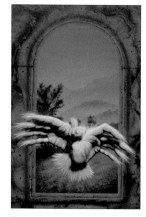

1

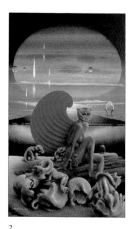

2

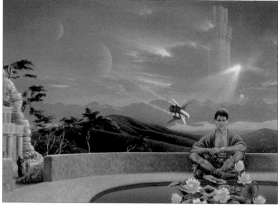

3

1 *BOOK:* OTHER EDENS
DATE: 1987

2 *BOOK:* THE CONGLOMEROID
COCKTAIL PARTY *by Robert
Silverberg*
DATE: 1985

3 *BOOK:* THE CHANTRY GUILD
by Gordon R Dickson
DATE: 1988

4 FRONTIER CROSSINGS
DATE: 1987

5 *BOOK:* FREEWAY FIGHTER *by
Ian Livingstone*
DATE: 1984

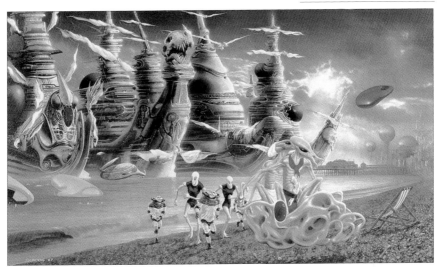

4

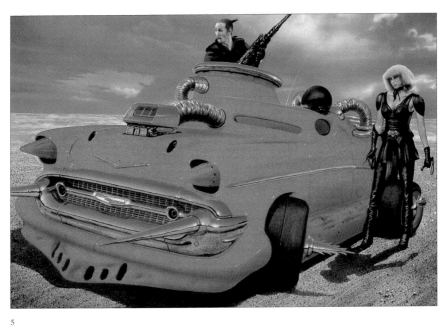

5

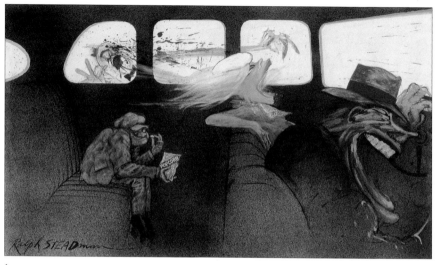

1

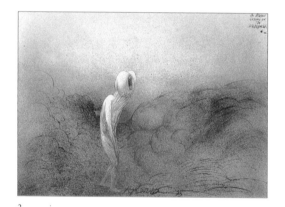

2

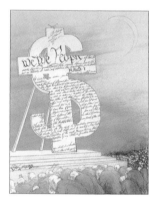

3

1 *BOOK:* FEAR AND LOATHING IN LAS VEGAS *by Hunter S Thompson*
DATE: 1971

2 *BOOK:* SCAR STRANGLED BANGER *by Ralph Steadman*
DATE: 1987

3 *FRONTISPIECE:* SCAR STRANGLED BANGER *by Ralph Steadman*
DATE: 1987

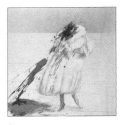

4

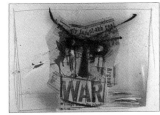

5

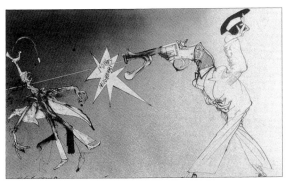

6

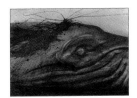

7

*Born in Cheshire, UK. Studied
part-time at the London
College of Printing and took
the Percy V Bradshaw Press
Arts School course. He drew
political cartoons for* Private
Eye *when it first appeared in
1961 and at about the same
time discovered George Grosz
and John Heartfield, whose
powerful and caustic statements
against the Establishment were
a stimulus to his own work.
The author Hunter S Thompson
was another major influence.
Their collaboration culminated
in Steadman being voted
Illustrator of the Year by the
American Institute of Graphic
Arts in 1979. His extraordinary
range has ensured him equal
acclaim for his children's
illustrations, and his version
of* Alice in Wonderland *(1967)
won the Francis Williams
Book Illustration Award in
1973. Steadman has worked
on advertising campaigns and
illustrated Will Self's column in*
The Independent *newspaper.*

4 *MAGAZINE:* SATURDAY
NIGHT
DATE: 1978

5 *COLLAGE / MIXED MEDIA:*
FALKLANDS WAR
DATE: 1982

6 *MAGAZINE:* ROLLING STONE
DATE: 1980

7 *MAGAZINE:* PENTHOUSE
DATE: 1979

8 *BOOK:* ALICE IN
WONDERLAND *by Lewis Carroll*
DATE: 1967

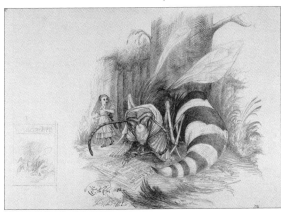

8

RAYMOND BRIGGS
(b. 1934)

Born in London. Studied at Wimbledon School of Art and the Slade School. He has written and illustrated several children's books and in 1964 his Fee Fi Fo Fum *was runner-up for the Kate Greenaway Medal, an award he won in 1966 with the publication of* The Mother Goose Treasury *and again in 1973 with* Father Christmas. *He works in a variety of media – pencil, crayons, gouache, watercolor and line – to produce richly colorful drawings which are often presented in the format of a strip cartoon. Two of his books have been made into movies.*

The Snowman *(1978), the wistful story of a child's dream told entirely in pictures, was adapted by Briggs for television in 1982 and* When the Wind Blows *(1982), a despairing adult story of life after the nuclear holocaust, was made into a full-length animated feature. He continued to produce work for children, with the* Unlucky Wally *series and* The Bear, *and his graphic novel* Ethel and Ernest *won Best Illustrated Book in the 1998 British Book Awards.*

1 *BOOK:* THE SNOWMAN *by Raymond Briggs*
DATE: 1978

2 *BOOK:* FATHER CHRISTMAS *by Raymond Briggs*
DATE: 1973

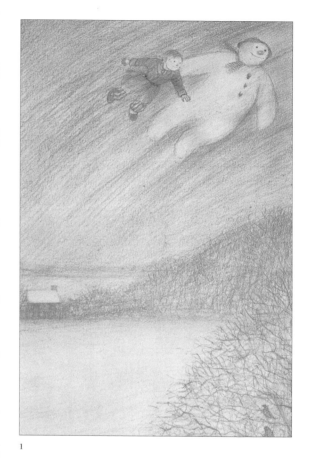

1

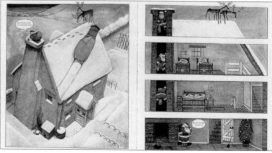

2

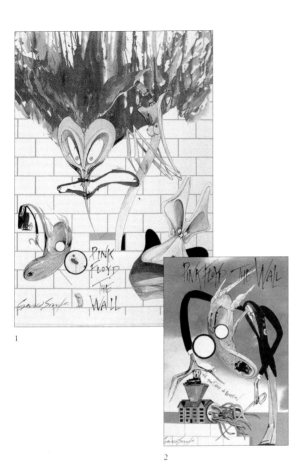

1

2

Born in London. After leaving school he worked for his uncle, a commercial artist, took evening classes in figure drawing at Saint Martin's School of Art, and attended drawing classes at the Victoria & Albert Museum. In 1960 he started drawing for Punch, The Evening Standard, *and* The Daily Sketch, *and in 1964 was sent by* The Sunday Times *magazine to cover the Goldwater-Johnson election in the USA. He worked there intermittently for two years, producing several covers for* Time *magazine and working as a reportage artist. In 1966 he undertook similar projects for the* Daily Mail *and* The Sunday Times *in London. His cartoons use an exquisite sense of line to cruelly caricature political and public figures, but his satirical eye has not confined its vision to the printed page. He has had an exhibition of his papier-mâché models at the National Portrait Gallery, has designed for the theater and opera, and made animated movies for the BBC and Alan Parker's feature* Pink Floyd: The Wall. *In recent years he has directed award-winning documentaries for television and comedies for Channel 4. In 2006 he was named Cartoonist of the Year at the British Press Awards.*

1–2 *PUBLICITY POSTER: "PINK FLOYD: THE WALL"*
DATE: 1980

3 *COSTUME DESIGN:* ORPHEUS IN THE UNDERWORLD
DATE: 1983

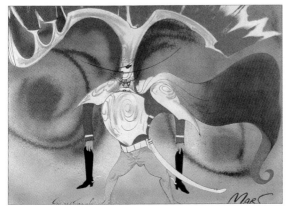

3

PIERRE LE TAN
(b. 1950)

Born in Paris. Studied briefly at L'Ecole des Arts Decoratifs in Paris before pursuing a career as a freelance illustrator. By the age of 18 he had already sold two covers to The New Yorker *magazine, and over the next few years his work appeared predominantly in such American publications as* The New York Times, Harper's Bazaar, *and* Atlantic. *He illustrated the books of American author* John Train *and in 1977 started to write and illustrate children's stories, including* The Afternoon Cat *(1977) and* A Trip to the North Pole *(1988). The striking simplicity of his style has proved popular with advertising agencies and he has illustrated campaigns for Glenfiddich whiskey in the USA, Manpower Services in the UK, and Gallery Lafayette in Paris. Although he professes no great love of traveling he had a column in Condé Nast's* The Traveller, *in which he visited and illustrated various locations around the world. He still lives and works in Paris, where he is taking fewer commissions and concentrating on his own adult writing. He wrote and illustrated* Rencontres d'une Vie *in 1986 and* Paris de ma jeunesse *in 1988.*

1 *MAGAZINE:* THE NEW YORKER
DATE: 1987

2 *MAGAZINE:* THE NEW YORKER
DATE: 1980

3 *BOOK:* RENCONTRES D'UNE VIE *by Pierre Le Tan*
DATE: 1986

4 *EXHIBITION INVITATION*
DATE: 1980

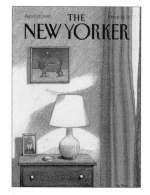

1

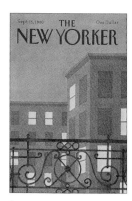

2

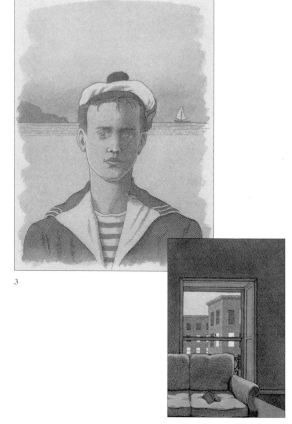

3

4

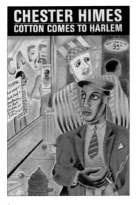

1

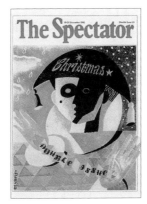

2

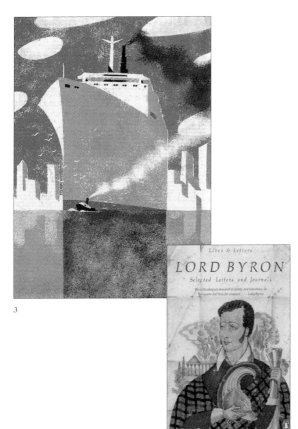

3

4

Born in London. While still at school he won a National Portrait Gallery competition, his entry was a London Underground poster publicizing the gallery. He studied at Chelsea School of Art under Susan Einzig, whom he cites as a major influence and who introduced him to the illustrators of the 1940s and 1950s, "the golden age of illustration." While still a student he received his first major commission, designing greeting cards for Jan Pienkowski's company Gallery Five in 1973. While studying at the Royal College of Art he illustrated for a number of publishers and magazines, including Tatler *and* Vogue *(where he had been a contributing editor on the permanent staff since 1989).*

He has taught at Hornsey, Wolverhampton and Berkshire art colleges and wrote a regular column, Modern Types, *for the* Observer *newspaper throughout 1987. Describing himself as "a commercial artist rather than an illustrator," he has designed costumes and sets for video and theater, and also paints portraits and murals. He illustrates in a range of styles, making a specialty of affectionate pastiche.*

1 *BOOK:* COTTON COMES TO
HARLEM *by Chester Himes*
DATE: 1984

2 *MAGAZINE:* THE SPECTATOR
DATE: 1982

3 *MAGAZINE:* TATLER
DATE: 1982

4 *BOOK:* LORD BYRON:
SELECTED LETTERS AND
JOURNALS
DATE: 1984

MICHAEL FOREMAN
(b. 1938)

*Born in Suffolk, UK. Trained
at the Royal College of Art,
where he won a scholarship
to the USA in 1963. He was
art director on* Playboy, King,
and Ambit *magazines and
has made animated movies
in Scandinavia and for the
BBC in the UK. He has written
and illustrated 14 books for
children, including* War and Peas
(1974), Panda and his Voyage of
Discovery *(1977),* Panda and the
Odd Lion *(1979), and* War Boy
(1989). He has also illustrated
The Saga of Erik the Viking
(1983) and Nicobobinus *(1986)
by Terry Jones,* Tales for the
Telling *(1986) by Edna O'Brien,
and Rudyard Kipling's* Just So
stories *(1987). His expressive
and sensitive watercolor
illustrations have won him
several awards, including the
Silver Eagle prize at the Festival
International du Livre, France
(1972), first prize in the Francis
Williams Book Illustrations
Award (1972 and 1977), the
Graphics Prize at Bologna
(1982), and the Kurt Maschler
Award (1982). He
won the Nestle Smarties Book
Prize in 1993 for* After the
War Was Over, *which he wrote
and illustrated.*

1–2 *BOOK:* THE SAGA OF ERIK
THE VIKING *by Terry Jones*
DATE: 1983

3 *BOOK:* WAR BOY: A SUFFOLK
CHILDHOOD *by Michael
Foreman*
DATE: 1989

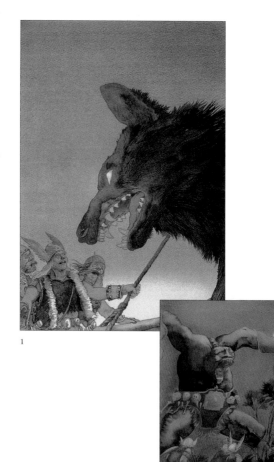

1

2

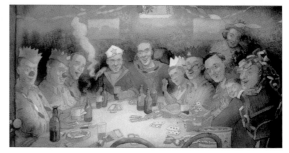

3

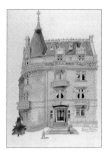

1

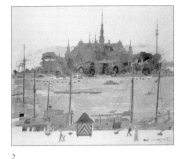

2

3

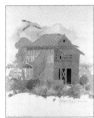

4

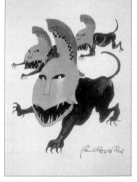

5

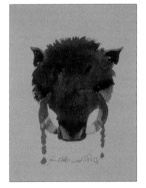

6

*Born in Kendal, UK. Studied
at Manchester College of Art
and Saint Martin's. In 1946–48
he was a staff illustrator for
Shell, after which he began his
life as artist-traveler. Hogarth
was prolific during the 1950s,
illustrating* Jane Eyre *(1954),*
The Adventures of Sherlock
Holmes *(1958),* The Gold of the
Snow Goose *(1958), and* King
Solomon's Mines *(1958), as
well as writing and illustrating*
Looking at China *(1956) and*
People Like Us *(1958). During
the 1960s he made a name
for himself on the pages of*
Fortune *and* Sports Illustrated
*and also collaborated with
Brendan Behan on books about
Ireland and New York. His
illustrations for Robert Graves'*
Poems *gained him a Francis
Williams Illustration Award for
best illustration in 1983. His
best-known works are those
based on his own extensive
travels, and his classic survey,*
Artist as Reporter, *received the
Yorkshire Post Award as the best
art book of 1986. He illustrated
many covers for Penguin Books,
including all of Graham Greene's
novels since 1962, and provided
illustrations for John Betjeman's*
In Praise of Churches *(1996).*

1 *BOOK:* WALKING TOURS
OF OLD WASHINGTON AND
ALEXANDRIA *by Paul Hogarth*
DATE: 1985

2–4 *BOOK:* GRAHAM GREENE
COUNTRY *by Paul Hogarth*
DATE: 1986

5 *BOOK:* NEW PENGUIN
SHAKESPEARE: TROILUS AND
CRESSIDA
DATE: 1989

6 *BOOK:* NEW PENGUIN
SHAKESPEARE: VENUS
AND ADONIS
DATE: 1989

*Born in New York. Studied
graphic design at the Cooper
Union School in New York,
where he met Milton Glaser,
Reynold Puffins, and Ed Sorel,
with whom he co-founded the
celebrated Push Pin Studios
in 1953. After graduating
he worked for* The New York
Times *and* Esquire, House
and Garden, *and* The Boston
Globe *magazines. In 1953 he
privately published* A Book of
Battles, *and in 1985 produced
his own retrospective volume,*
Seymour Chwast: The Left
Handed Designer. *In 1982 he and
Alan Peckolick formed Pushpin
Lubalin Peckolick. Clients have
included leading corporations,
advertising agencies, and
publishing companies in the
USA and abroad. He has won
numerous design awards,
including the St. Gauden's
medal from Cooper Union, and
was elected to the Art Directors
Club of Fame. He cites Ben
Shahn as a major influence on
his work, and the immediacy
and directness of his style
has become synonymous with
the "Push Pin style," which
has had enormous influence
internationally.*

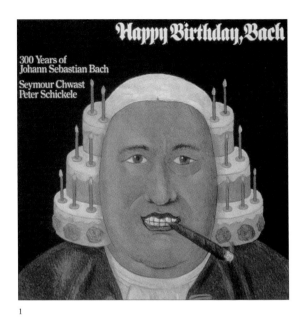

1

1,4 *BOOK:* HAPPY BIRTHDAY
BACH *by Seymour Chwast &
Peter Schickele
DATE:* 1986

2 *BOOK:* SAM'S BAR *edited by
Steven Heiter
DATE:* 1987

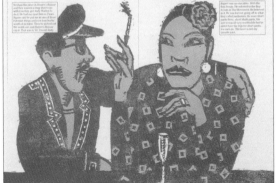

2

3 *THEATER POSTER
DATE:* 1986

5 *POSTER: "FORBES
MAGAZINE"
DATE:* 1967

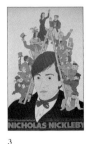

3

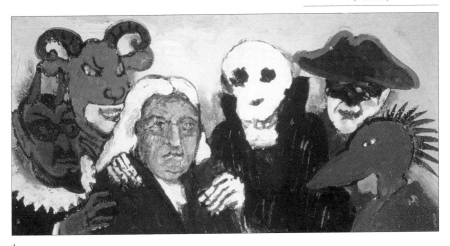

4

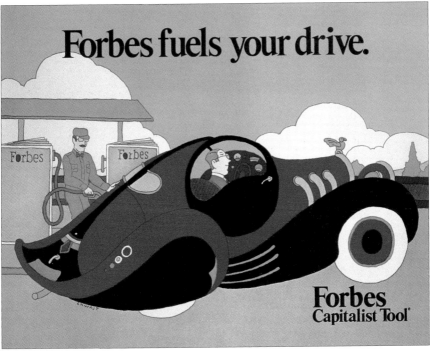

5

BRAD HOLLAND
(b. 1943)

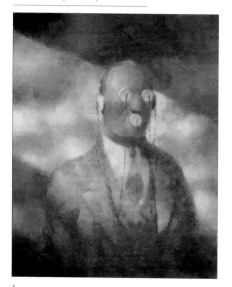

1

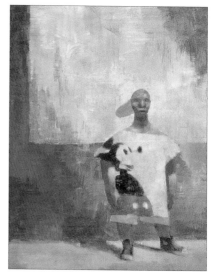

2

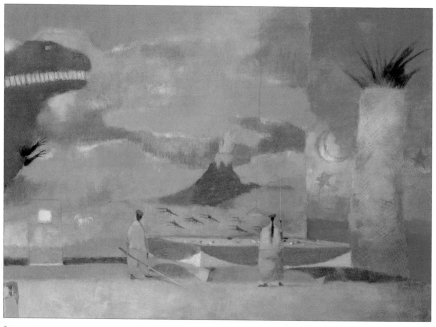

3

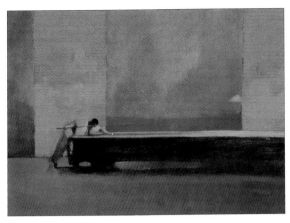

4

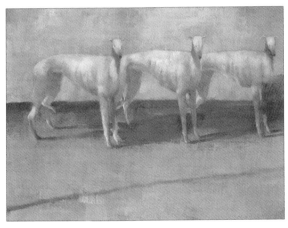

5

Born in Fremont, Ohio, USA. At 17 he left home and moved to Chicago, where he worked for a short time as a tattoo artist, then as a "short-order" artist. In Kansas City in 1964 he formed Asylum Press to print "eccentric projects with friends." In 1967 Holland moved to New York City and contributed to various underground magazines. In 1971 he became one of the founding artists of the Op-Ed page of The New York Times. *He also designed postage stamps for the U.S. government, executed a mural for the United Nations Building in New York, contributed to* Playboy, Time *and* Newsweek, *and wrote a book* Human Scandals (1977). *As well as displaying an exquisite technique with both pen and brush, Holland's illustrations invariably contain powerful images, often achieved with the incongruous yet revealing juxtaposition of symbols. His work has won gold medals from the Art Directors' Club of New York, the Society of Illustrators, and the Society of Publication Designers.*

1 DETAILS AT ELEVEN
(unpublished)
DATE: 1987

2 *MAGAZINE:* FRANKFURTER
ALLGEMEINE, MICKEY MOUSE
ON SIXTH AVENUE
DATE: 1987

3 *MAGAZINE:* FRANKFURTER
ALLGEMEINE, THE DINOSAUR
LOUNGE
DATE: 1988

4 *MAGAZINE:* FRANKFURTER
ALLGEMEINE, BLUE
POOLROOM
DATE: 1988

5 *MAGAZINE:* FRANKFURTER
ALLGEMEINE, THREE
GREYHOUNDS
DATE: 1987